Camaro
AND
Firebird

GM's Power Twins

D1457241

Published by

Krause Publications, a division of F+W Media, Inc.
700 East State Street • Iola, WI 54990-0001
715-445-2214 • 888-457-2873
www.krausebooks.com

To order books or other products call toll-free 1-800-258-0929
or visit us online at www.krausebooks.com or www.Shop.Collect.com

Library of Congress Control Number: 2010931152

ISBN-13: 978-1-4402-1550-6
ISBN-10: 1-4402-1550-2

Designed by Sharon Bartsch
Edited by Brian Earnest

Printed in the United States of America

CONTENTS

ROOM FOR TWO

It's been a bittersweet past couple years for lovers of General Motors' legendary F-body siblings — the Chevrolet Camaro and Pontiac Firebird. Connoisseurs of both nameplates went into mourning when The General discontinued both nameplates following the 2002 model year, and it would be seven long years before Camaro nation could celebrate again with the release of the awesome 2010 model.

Alas, the news was tainted a bit with the realization that the Camaro would have to go it alone in the future. In April of 2009, it was announced that Pontiac would go the way of the woolly mammoth — and countless other car brands — and be discontinued by the end of 2010.

Perhaps the Firebird/Trans Am will resurface again at some point under one of the other GM banners and the Camaro and 'Bird will ride together again. But even if that doesn't happen, auto enthusiasts have a long, glorious run to look back on. For 36 years, the two pony/muscle cars thrilled car enthusiasts with their similar ability to match style and performance in a variety of packages that most car buffs could actually afford.

In these pages, we salute both the Camaro and Firebird — two of the coolest rides ever to roll off American auto assembly lines, and two that live on together in the hearts of millions of fans.

THE 1967 Z/28 WAS A FAVORITE OF RACING ENTHUSIASTS.

1967

The original 1967 Camaro was introduced to the public on Sept. 26, 1966, as Chevrolet's belated answer to Ford's enormously popular Mustang. "Camaro is band-box new by Chevrolet and a freshly styled example of how fine an exciting road machine can look," said the first sales catalog for the new car, which described it as "a go as well as show machine."

It was the fourth totally new line of cars that Chevrolet had introduced since the Corvair first appeared late in 1959. Each of these cars — Corvair, Chevy II, Chevelle and Camaro — filled a different niche in Chevrolet's marketing scheme. While inspired by the "pony car" segment that the Mustang had carved out of the marketplace, the first Camaro was really promoted as more of a "Junior Corvette" that gave the family man with a hunkering for a real sports car the opportunity to buy one with four seats.

Chevrolet copywriters put major emphasis on the Camaro's "wide stance stability" and "big-car power" and explained how enthusiasts could personalize their Camaro Sport Coupe or convertible by adding extras and option packages. There was the base version with bucket seats and carpeting as standard equipment, the Rally Sport option with "hideaway" headlights and the SS 350 with its "bumblebee" stripes and powerful standard V-8. An optional 396-cid V-8 was released for the Super Sport after November 1966.

To these basic "building block" options the buyer could add a custom interior, a variety of engines and transmissions and accessories such as vinyl roofs and Rally wheels. Those who wanted to customize their Camaro even further could combine some extras to create such "model-options" as the now-highly-desirable RS/SS variant.

A TOTAL OF 602 Z/28S WERE MADE FOR 1967, ALL OF THEM WERE SPORT COUPES.

When all the possibilities were added up, Chevrolet reported the production of 154,698 Camaros in Lordstown, Ohio, 65,008 in Van Nuys, California. In its heyday — during the late 1970s — the Camaro would capture some 260,000 customers for smiling Chevrolet dealers.

CAMARO – SERIES 23/24 – SIX/V-8

The 1967 Camaro rode a 108-in. wheelbase and measured 185 in. stem to stern. Sport Coupe and convertible body styles were offered. It had a unitized body with a bolted-on front frame section to carry the engine, front suspension, steering and sheet metal components. Its overall appearance included a long hood and short rear deck with the popular "Coke bottle" shape dominating the design. Many options and options packages were available with some "model-options" that essentially turned the basic Camaro into several distinct models. Standard equipment included a satin silver horizontal bars grille with six vertical dividers, inset headlights and parking lights, twin-segment taillights with integral back-up lights on the inboard segment, all-vinyl front bucket seats, an all-vinyl rear bench seat, elegant new interior door styling with bright metal inserts, shielded door handles, a three-spoke steering wheel with circular "Camaro" horn button, a new gauge cluster with large round speedometer and fuel gauges and monitoring lights, standard cowl side vents and two adjustable vent-ports mounted on the instrument panel, an energy-absorbing steering column, seat belts with push-button buckles for all passenger positions, shoulder belts for the driver and right front passenger with push-button buckles and a convenient storage provision on Sport Coupe models, a 230-cid 140-hp Turbo-Thrift inline six-cylinder engine or a 327-cid 210-hp Turbo-Fire V-8 and a fully synchronized three-speed manual transmission with column-mounted gearshift. The convertible also had a manual convertible top, bright windshield moldings, a bright windshield header with convertible top latches, special sun visors, special inside rear quarter panels with built-in armrests, dual courtesy lights and a convertible top boot.

A CUSTOM INTERIOR COULD BE ORDERED IN SEVEN DIFFERENT COLORS.

THE 1967 CONVERTIBLE CAMARO WAS CHOSEN TO PACE THE INDY 500.

CAMARO RALLY SPORT – SERIES 23/24 + Z22 – V-6/V-8

"From hideaway headlights to unique taillights this Camaro says swinger from all angles," boasted the 1967 Camaro sales catalog in the section devoted to the Rally Sport model-option. The RPO Z22 Rally Sport package cost Chevrolet dealers $76 and retailed for $105.35. In addition to or in place of the standard equipment listed above for base Camaros, cars with the Rally Sport package also featured a vertical ornament with an "RS" emblem in the center of the grille, a similar emblem on the round gas filler cap at the center of the rear body panel, an "RS" emblem on the circular steering wheel horn button, a black-finished full-width lattice grille with electrically operated concealed headlights, lower body side moldings, a black accent below the body side moldings (with some body colors), color-keyed body accent stripes, sporty styling for the front parking and turning lights, sports-style back-up lights, a distinctive edged-in-black taillight treatment with two lamps in each taillight unit for driving, braking and turn signal direction, bright metal front wheel opening moldings, bright metal rear wheel opening moldings and a bright drip rail molding on Sport Coupes. The Rally Sport option could be added to any Camaro with any engine. The prices given immediately below are for base Camaros with the Rally Sport package added. To determine the cost of other model-options with Rally Sport equipment installed add the package price of $105.35 to the factory prices for the specific SS or Z/28 model.

CAMARO SS – SERIES 24 – V-8

"The go machine look outside tells everyone you've got the new 350 V-8 inside!" said Chevrolet about what was the hottest available option for its new Camaro – at least at the start of the year. The RPO Z27 SS 350 package cost Chevrolet dealers $152 and retailed for $210.65. In addition to or in place of all of the standard equipment listed above for base Camaros, the SS 350 package included a special hood with raised simulated air intakes, a big "SS 350" emblem for the center of the grille, a 350-cid 295-hp V-8, a color-keyed "bumblebee" type front accent band, "SS" identification inside the breaks on the bumblebee striping, "SS 350" identification on the round fuel filler cap at the center of the rear body panel, red stripe wide-oval tires on 14 x 6-in. wheels and the F41 suspension with stiffer shock absorbers and springs. After the beginning of the model year, two engine options based on the 396-cid "big-block" Turbo-Jet V-8 were offered. They included the L35 with 325 hp and the L78 with 375 hp. When either of these motors was added, the engine call-outs on the grille emblem and fuel cap emblem were deleted and the rear body panel carried flat black finish.

CAMARO Z/28 – SERIES 24 + Z/28 – V-8

The Z/28 package first appeared in December 1966. During the second half of 1967 a limited number of Camaros were built with the new option, which was available for Camaro Sport Coupes only. It was most sought after by enthusiasts with a serious interest in racing. In addition to or in place of the standard equipment listed above for the base Camaro, all Z/28s included a high-performance 302-cid small-block V-8 engine, a 2 1/4-in. diameter dual exhaust system, dual deep-tone mufflers, a heavy-duty suspension, special front coil springs, special Mono-Leaf rear springs, heavy-duty front and rear shock absorbers, 21.4:1 quick-ratio steering, 15 x 6-in. wheel rims, special 7.35 x 15 nylon white-stripe high-performance tires, a 3.73:1 rear axle ratio and paint stripes on the hood and rear deck lid. In the first year there were no Z/28 emblems on the exterior of the vehicle. Z/28s were also required to have the following extra-cost options: a close-ratio or heavy-duty close-ratio four-speed manual transmission and power front disc brakes or heavy-duty front disc brakes with metallic rear linings. Adding a positraction rear axle was recommended. The Z/28's 302-cid V-8 included a special camshaft, mechanical valve lifters, an aluminum "tuned inlet" manifold, a high-capacity oil pump, special oil pan baffling, a dual-belt fan drive, an external bypass water pump, a thermostatically controlled five-blade cooling fan, a chrome-plated air cleaner cover, chrome-plated rocker arm covers, a chrome-plated oil filler tube and a chrome-plated oil cap.

Jerry Healey photo

**CHEVROLET CONTINUED ITS COMMITMENT TO BUILDING A FAST,
SPORTY CAR WITH THE 1968 Z/28 SPORT COUPE.**

1968

Camaro No. 2 came along in 1968 and was little more than a slightly modified version of the first edition that gained a "big-block" 396-cid V-8 during the year. To spot a 1967 model you can look for vent windows. To spot a 1968 model you should look for no vent windows, plus the addition of front and rear side marker lights (required to conform with new federal safety regulations). There were engineering refinements that Chevrolet said were "designed to keep the '68 Camaro the finest car in its field."

Glamour was the strong point of the 1968 Rally Sport package and husky performance was the calling card of the Camaro SS option. The base Camaro engine was again a 230-cid inline six-cylinder, while the 327-cid small-block remained the base V-8. A 350-cid V-8 was standard in the Camaro SS, but the Turbo-Jet 396-cid V-8 was the hot ticket for the lead-footed set. Cars with this engine were treated to a black-finished rear body panel to set them off as something special.

CAMARO –
SERIES 23/24 – SIX/V-8

Standard equipment included a satin-silver horizontal bars grille with six vertical dividers, inset headlights and parking lights, twin-segment taillights with integral back-up lights on the inboard segment, new one-piece curved side windows, new rear side marker lights ahead of the rear bumper ends, new front side marker lights behind the front bumper ends, all-vinyl front bucket seats, an all-vinyl rear bench seat, new interior door styling with bright metal inserts, shielded door handles, a three-spoke steering wheel with circular "Camaro" horn button, a new gauge cluster with large, round speed-

**THE RALLY SPORT CONVERTIBLE, THIS ONE WITH A 327 V-8,
HAD HIDDEN HEADLIGHTS AND A FEW OTHER "CLASSY" FEATURES.**

ometer and fuel gauges and monitoring lights, a 230-cid 140-hp Turbo-Thrift inline six-cylinder engine or a 327-cid 210-hp Turbo-Fire V-8 and a fully synchronized three-speed manual transmission with column-mounted gearshift. The convertible also had a manual convertible top, bright windshield moldings, a bright windshield header with convertible top latches, special sun visors, special inside rear quarter panels with built-in armrests, dual courtesy lights and a convertible top boot.

CAMARO RALLY SPORT – SERIES 23/24 + Z22 – V-6/V-8

Chevrolet described cars equipped with the optional Rally Sport package as "a more glamorous version" of the Camaro. The RPO Z22 Rally Sport package cost Chevrolet dealers $81.35 and retailed for $105.35. In addition to or place of the standard equipment listed above for base Camaros, cars with the Rally Sport package also featured concealed headlights, a special full-width grille, small rectangular parking and directional signal lights mounted below the bumper instead of in the grille, an RS em-

blem on the center of the grille, small rectangular back-up lamps mounted below the rear bumper (both taillight segments had red lenses), an "RS" emblem on the round gas filler cap in the center of the rear body panel, bright lower body side moldings with black lower body finish under the molding, bright "Rally Sport" scripts on the upper front fenders behind the wheel openings, a bright roof drip molding on Sport Coupes and a bright belt line molding. The Rally Sport option could be added to any Camaro with any engine. The prices given immediately below are for base Camaros with the Rally Sport package added. To determine the cost of other model-options with Rally Sport equipment installed add the package price of $105.35 to the factory prices for the specific SS or Z/28 model.

CAMARO SS - SERIES 24 - V-8

Chevrolet boasted that the 1968 Camaro SS (Super Sport) was dedicated to the "fun crowd." The sales catalog said it was "a husky performer and looks it." Big engines, a beefed-up suspension and special equipment features made this model-option stand out. The prices of the RPO

Z27 SS package varied according to engine. With the L48 V-8 the dealer paid $152 and got $210.65 at retail. With the L35 engine the dealer cost was $190 and the retail price was $263.30. With the L34 V-8 the dealer cost was $266 and the retail price was $368.65. The L78 version of the SS wholesaled for $361 and retailed for $500.30. The L78/L89 version with aluminum cylinder heads retailed for $868.95 (dealer cost unknown).

CAMARO Z/28 – SERIES 24 + Z/28 – V-8

In 1968, the popularity of the Camaro Z/28 Special Performance package started to climb based on the car's first-year racing reputation. During the later part of the 1967 model year, only 602 Z/28s had been released and Chevrolet wasn't sure if it wanted to market the option strictly for racing or to the public. Output climbed to 7,199 cars in 1968, making it clear that a decision had been made. The Z/28 package was available for Camaro Sport Coupes only. It came in four different variations. In addition to, or in place of, the standard equipment listed above for the base Camaro, all Z/28s included a high-performance 302-cid small-block V-8 engine, a dual exhaust system, deep-tone mufflers, special front and rear suspensions, a heavy-duty radiator, a temperature-controlled de-clutching radiator fan, quick-ratio steering, 15 x 6-in. wheel rims, E70 x 15 special white-letter nylon tires, a 3.73:1 rear axle ratio, paint stripes on the hood and paint stripes on the rear deck lid. Z/28s were also required to have the following extra-cost options: a close-ratio four-speed manual transmission and power front disc brakes or heavy-duty front disc brakes with metallic rear linings. Adding a Positraction rear axle was recommended. The least expensive version of the Z/28 was the standard Z/281 option as described above. It cost dealers $288.80 and retailed for $400.25. Next came the Z/282 option with a plenum air intake. It cost Chevy dealers $345.80 and retailed for $479.25. The Z/283 version came with exhaust headers. It wholesaled for $562.40 and retailed for $779.40. Finally, there was the Z/284 version with both the plenum air intake and exhaust headers. This "ultimate" Z/28 had a dealer cost of $619.40 and retailed for $858.40.

Gene Stransky photo

A '68 RS/SS 396 WITH YELLOW AND BLACK EXTERIOR. THIS ONE HAS AN AUTOMATIC TRANSMISSION AND DELUXE INTERIOR PACKAGE.

Chip Myers photo

THE 1969 CAMARO WAS THE LAST OF THE FIRST-GENERATION CAMAROS AND IS A FAVORITE AMONG ENTHUSIASTS. THIS RS/SS IS A SHOW WINNER THAT BOASTS A 350-CID L48 ENGINE AND FOUR-SPEED TRANSMISSION.

1969

The SS 396 Camaro was big news for the go-fast set, but the 1969 model went one step further with big news for every class of buyer. It sported a heavy exterior facelift featuring muscular-looking new sheet metal.

The last of the first-generation Camaros is considered by many enthusiasts to be the most popular one. The concept behind the new design was to make the Camaro look more "aggressive." The new body provided a longer, lower and wider appearance and had sculpted body sides. The wheel wells were flattened with sculptured feature lines flowing off them toward the rear of the car and rear-slanting air slots ahead of the rear wheel. An RS/SS convertible with a 396-cid Turbo-Jet V-8 under its hood paced the 1969 Indy 500 and this time Chevrolet sold replicas of the pace car to the public starting on Feb. 4, 1969. Experts say 3,675 of these Z11 convertibles were made, along with

a few hundred hardtops with a rare Z10 Indy Sport Coupe package.

Chevrolet started promoting the Camaro as the "Hugger" this year and even had a Hugger Orange paint color for those who really wanted to catch attention on the street. The name, however, did not really stick and was rarely heard after 1970.

A new 307-cid base V-8 was added to the Camaro's engines list, as was an optional 250-cid straight six with 15 hp more than the standard inline six. Performance buffs could chose between the 350-cid and 396-cid V-8 offerings. Those who wanted to go even faster down a drag strip had the option of visiting a handful of dealerships across the country that would gladly stuff a 427-cid "Rat" motor into a Camaro for mucho bucks.

Chevy built 211,922 Camaros at Norwood in 1969, plus 31,163 more in Van Nuys.

Jerry Heasley photo

THE SS-396 WAS AVAILABLE WITH THREE DIFFERENT ENGINES, GENERATING BETWEEN 325 AND 375 HP.

CAMARO – SERIES 23/24 – SIX/V-8

At the front of standard Camaros was a grille with 13 slender vertical moldings and five horizontal moldings forming a grid surrounded by a bright molding. A badge with the Chevrolet bow-tie emblem was in the center. There were single round headlamps near both outer ends of the grille. The full-width bumper integrated with the body-color outer grille surround and there was a license plate holder in the center of the valance panel. Round parking lights were positioned on either side of the license plate. At the rear were wider taillight bezels with triple-segment lenses. Standard equipment included an Argent Silver radiator grille, a bow-tie radiator emblea 230-cid 145-hp Turbo-Thrift inline six-cylinder engine or a 327-cid 210-hp Turbo-Fire V-8 engine, a three-speed manual transmission and E78 x 14 two-ply (four-ply-rated) black sidewall tires. (Note: In January 1969 a 307-cid 200-hp Turbo-Fire V-8 replaced the 327-cid V-8 as the base V-8 engine).

CAMARO RALLY SPORT – SERIES 23/24 + Z22 – V-6/V-8

The RPO Z22 Rally Sport package initially cost Chevrolet dealers $101.65 and retailed for $131.65. In May, after automakers issued revised prices, the dealer cost of this option rose to $104.15, but the retail price remained unchanged. The Rally Sport package included a special grille that filled only the space between where the headlights normally appeared in full view, instead of going fully across the front of the car like the standard grille. The grille had an "RS" emblem in its center. The license plate was still mounted below the center of the full-width bumper and the round parking lamps flanked it. The headlights were actually there, but they were hidden behind triple segmented "doors" that flanked the grille. Chevrolet even included a "fail safe" system to open the headlight doors if the vacuum motor failed and headlight washers. The headlamp covers actually consisted of a body-color outer door with three horizontal openings in it and a chrome door that was slotted to allow light to shine through if it if it if the system wasn't operating. Other Rally Sport content included fender striping (except when the sport striping or Z/28 options were added), bright accents on the air vents ahead of the rear wheel opening, front and rear wheel opening moldings, black body sills (except on cars painted Dusk Blue, Fathom Green, Burnished Brown or Burgundy), "Rally Sport" fender nameplates, bright taillight accents, bright parking light accents, back-up lights below the rear bumper, an RS steering wheel emblem, black steering wheel accents and bright roof drip moldings on coupes.

CAMARO SS – SERIES 24 – V-8

The Camaro SS (Super Sport) was a performance-oriented option package that initially cost Chevrolet dealers $228.51 and retailed for $295.95 early in the 1969 model year. On May 1, 1969, there was an increase in Chevrolet pricing and the dealer cost of the Z27 package rose to $246.63, which increased the retail price to $311.75.

CAMARO INDY SPORT CONVERTIBLE (INDY 500 OFFICIAL PACE CAR REPLICA) – MODEL 12467 + Z11 – V-8

The first Camaro had served as Official Pace Car for the 1967 Indianapolis 500-Mile Race and Indianapolis Motor Speedway. That year, only a limited number of actual Indy 500 Pace Cars and "Official Cars" were made and these were not intended for sale to the public as new cars. In 1969, Chevrolet was invited to supply a Camaro Pace Car once again. By this time auto sales were in a slump and the company decided to get extra mileage out of the promotional effort by creating the RPO Z11 "Indy Sport Convertible" package. A confidential Chevrolet Passenger Car Product Bulletin issued on Feb. 4, 1969, described this option as "Midseason Change No. 13" and stated the following: "A new Regular Production Option (Z11) will be released to provide a modified Camaro SS/RS Convertible similar to the Indianapolis 500 Pace Car. The RPO Z11 is comprised of: Camaro SS/

Jerry Heasley photo

THE POWERFUL, AND SCARCE, ZL1 CAMAROS ARE AMONG THE GREAT AMERICAN MUSCLE CARS.

Rally Sport (Camaro SS RPO Z27 with Rally Sport equipment RPO Z22).

CAMARO INDY SPORT COUPE – MODEL 12437 + Z10 – V-8

Camaro club enthusiasts have documented that a Pace Car Sport Coupe was offered as a promotional model by the Chevrolet Southwest Sales Zone and sold in a number of states, including Arizona, Oklahoma, Texas and Wisconsin. The package was coded as RPO Z10 and was for the Camaro coupe with RS/SS equipment. These were similar to the Z11 convertible on the outside, but had some interior differences such as black (standard, custom or houndstooth) and ivory (standard and houndstooth) interior choices, in addition to orange houndstooth. They also came with the optional woodgrained steering wheel, ComforTilt steering wheel, a vinyl top and other options. It is believed that the Norwood factory built 200 to 300 of these cars.

CAMARO Z/28 – SERIES 24 + Z/28 – V-8

In 1969, the popularity of the Camaro Z/28 achieved a three-year high with production climbing from 602 in 1967 to 7,199 in 1968 to 20,302 in 1969. To a large degree, the boom in interest was generated by the 1969 Z/28s that Roger Penske's racing team campaigned in the Sports Car Club of America's Trans-Am series. Penzke's dark blue and yellow Camaros appeared in Sunoco gasoline advertisements, as well as in promotions for Sears Die-Hard batteries. The Z/28 package was available for Camaro Sport Coupes with power disc brakes and a four-speed manual transmission. A Positraction rear axle (as an extra-cost option) was recommended to go with the package. In addition to or in place of that model's standard equipment, the Z/28 featured a special 302-cid V-8, a dual exhaust system with deep-tone mufflers, a special front suspension, a special rear suspension, rear bumper guards, a heavy-duty radiator, a temperature-controlled de-clutching fan, quick-ratio steering, 15 x 7-in. Rally wheel rims, special E70-15 white-letter tires, a 3.73:1 ratio rear axle and special Rally stripes on the hood and rear deck lid.

Jerry Heasley photo

AN SS-396 CONVERTIBLE (LEFT) WAS CHOSEN AS THE INDY PACE CAR AND MARKETED TO THE PUBLIC. AN SS-350 WAS ALSO PRODUCED (RIGHT).

Jerry Heasley photo

IN ONE MAGAZINE TEST, THE 1970 Z/28 OUTPERFORMED THE MUSTANG.

1970

An all-new second-generation Camaro arrived later than usual in the 1970 model year. The announcement day for the new Camaro was Feb. 26, 1970. Luckily, it was a hit! The revamped Camaro had a smooth European sports car image and came only as a coupe. The sleek long hood-short deck fastback body was longer, lower and wider than the first-generation Camaro.

Driver safety was enhanced by the use of side-guard door beams, while the performance-options list gained a 350-cid 360-hp LT1 engine for the Z/28 model, which had formerly relied on a hot "302." More importantly, the gorgeous new body would survive for 12 long model years, ultimately bringing the Camaro to one of its high points in both popularity and profitability.

CAMARO - SERIES 23/24 - SIX/V-8

Standard equipment included seat belts with push-button buckles for all passenger positions, shoulder belts with push-button buckles for the driver and front passenger, two front seat head restraints, an energy-absorbing steering column, passenger-guard door locks with forward-mounted lock buttons, safety door latches and hinges, folding seat back latches, an energy-absorbing instrument panel and front seat back tops, contoured roof rails, a thick-laminate windshield, padded sun visors, safety armrests, a safety steering wheel, side-guard beam door structures, a cargo-guard luggage compartment, side markers with reflectors (front side marker lights flash with directional signals), parking lights that illuminate with the headlights,

Tim Mellem photo

THE 1970 (OR 1970 1/2) Z28 WITH THE 360-HP LT1 ENGINE LIVED UP TO CHEVROLET'S VISION FOR A TRUE SPORTS CAR.

a four-way hazard warning flasher, back-up lights, a lane-change feature in the directional signal control, a windshield defroster, windshield washers, dual-speed windshield wipers, a vinyl-edged wide-view inside day/night mirror with shatter resilient glass, a left-hand outside rearview mirror, a dual master cylinder brake system with a warning light, E78-14 bias-belted ply tires, and a 250-cid 155-hp inline six-cylinder engine or a 307-cid 200-hp V-8 and a three-speed manual transmission with floor shift.

CAMARO RALLY SPORT - SERIES 23/24 + Z22 – SIX/V-8

The RPO Z22 Rally Sport package was a factory option designed to make the Camaro a bit flashier and more luxurious. The 1970 version retailed for $168.55. It was available separately for the base Sport Coupe or it could also be combined with the SS or Z/28 packages. In addition to all of this, the Rally Sport package added the Style Trim group, roadlight-styled parking lights mounted adjacent to the headlights, left and right front bumpers (replacing the standard full-width bumper), a color-matched resilient grille frame, Hide-A-Way windshield wipers, RS identification and more. Shown below are the prices for base Camaro Sport Coupes with the Rally Sport option.

CAMARO SS - SERIES 24 - V-8

The Camaro SS, or Super Sport, was a real muscle car for the streets. The RPO Z27 SS package was a factory option that retailed for $289.65 in 1970. It was available for V-8-powered Camaros with four-speed or Turbo-Hydra-Matic transmission. In addition to all the RS options, the SS option package added the 300-hp Turbo-Fire 350 V-8, a black-finished grille with a bright outline and SS identification, a remote-control left-hand outside sport type rearview mirror, power disc brakes, special hood insulation, dual exhaust outlets, Hide-A-Way windshield wipers, 14 x 7-in. wheels, F70 x 14 wide-oval white-letter bias-belted tires and special SS ornamentation on fenders, steering wheel and front grille. A 350-hp (L34) and a 375-hp (L89) "396 Turbo-Jet" V-8 were optional for cars with the SS package. Both engines available with the package came with a bright air cleaner cover. On Camaro SS models with the bigger engine the buyer got a heavy-duty Sport suspension with front and rear stabilizer bars and special shock absorbers.

CAMARO Z/28 - SERIES 24 + Z/28 – V-8

The Camaro Z/28 grew out of Chevrolet's desire to field a car in the popular Sports Car Club of America Trans-Am racing series. SCCA

Jerry Heasley photo

THE SS OPTION ADDED THE 300-HP TURBO-FIRE 350 V-8, A BLACK-FINISHED GRILLE WITH A BRIGHT OUTLINE AND SS IDENTIFICATION. THERE WERE TWO OTHER AVAILABLE SS ENGINES FOR 1970 — A 350-HP V-8 AND 375-HP V-8 - MAKING THE CAMARO SS ONE OF THE MOST MUSCULAR CARS AROUND.

rules put maximum displacement restrictions of 305 cid on the so-called sedan racers. The rules were changed in 1970 and, as a result, the Z/28's high-performance small-block V-8 was increased from 302-cid to 350-cid. However, it was a very special 350-cid engine that was virtually identical to the LT1 Corvette engine. The major difference was that the Camaro had a more restrictive exhaust system that robbed away about 10 hp and gave the engine a 360-hp rating. In addition, the Z/28 option added a heavy-duty radiator, a black-painted grille, a Z/28 grille emblem, Z/28 front fender emblems, a Z/28 rear deck lid emblem, rear bumper guards, the F41 performance suspension, heavy-duty front and rear springs, 15 x 7-in. wheels, bright lug nuts, special center wheel caps, wheel trim rings, hood insulation, F60 x 15 white-letter bias-belted tires, a rear deck lid spoiler and special paint stripes on the hood and rear deck lid. A second spoiler option was approved by the SCCA later in the year. It was a three-piece model.

THE CAMARO RS CAME WITH EITHER A 250-CID INLINE SIX-CYLINDER OR 307-CID V-8.

Jerry Heasley photo

CHEVROLET ROLLED OUT 4,862 NEW Z/28S FOR 1971.

1971

Chevrolet added high-back bucket seats (pirated from its sub-compact Vega) in 1971 and a new steering wheel with a cushioned hub. There were few other basic changes. In mid-1971, the Camaro front end was changed to accept "big Chevrolet" steering parts. The steering knuckles were switched to nodular iron castings, rather than forgings, and the tread was widened accordingly.

There were also new nameplates and new paint colors. A new type of thinner windshield glass was used. Technical changes were more important, as the engines were modified to operate on low-lead or lead-free gasoline blends. This meant lower compression ratios and horsepower ratings. GM also switched from net to gross horsepower ratings.

This was a great year for Chevrolet sales in general, but the Camaro didn't bask in the glory of Chevrolet Motor Division's first 3 million-unit year and its production dropped by more than 50 percent due to a lengthy strike in the fall of 1970. Also, the government and insurance companies were making life very hard for muscle car fans.

CAMARO - SERIES 23/24 - SIX/V-8

Standard equipment included seat belts with push-button buckles for all passenger positions, shoulder belts with push-button buckles for the driver and front passenger, two front seat head restraints, an energy-absorbing steering column, passenger-guard door locks with forward-mounted lock buttons, safety door latches and hinges, folding seat back latches, an energy-absorbing instrument panel and front seat back tops, contoured roof rails, a thick-laminate windshield, padded sun visors, safety armrests, a safety-cushioned steering wheel, side-guard beam door structures, a cargo-guard luggage compartment, side markers with reflectors (front side marker lights flash with directional signals), parking lights that illuminate with the

Daniel B. Lyons photo

THE 1971 CAMARO SPORT COUPE COULD BE PURCHASED WITH EITHER A STANDARD INLINE SIX OR 307-CID V-8, OR AN OPTIONAL 350-CID V-8 LIKE THIS CAR HAS.

headlights, a four-way hazard warning flasher, back-up lights, a lane-change feature in the directional signal control, a 250-cid 155-hp (110 SAE net horsepower) inline six-cylinder engine or a 307-cid 200-hp (140 SAE net horsepower) V-8 and a three-speed manual transmission with floor shift.

CAMARO RALLY SPORT - SERIES 23/24 + Z22 – SIX/V-8

The RPO Z22 Rally Sport package was a factory option that cost Chevrolet dealers $141.65 and retailed for $179.05. Standard equipment included a 250-cid 155-hp (110 SAE net horsepower) inline six-cylinder engine or a 307-cid 200-hp (140 SAE net horsepower) V-8 and a three-speed manual transmission with floor shift.

CAMARO SS - SERIES 24 - V-8

The RPO Z27 Super Sport or SS package

was a factory option that cost Chevrolet dealers $248.34 and retailed for $313.90. It was available for V-8-powered Camaros with four-speed or Turbo-Hydra-Matic transmission. Standard equipment included most items standard on the base Sport Coupe such as seat belts with push-button buckles for all passenger positions, shoulder belts with push-button buckles for the driver and front passenger, two front seat head restraints. The SS option added the 270-hp (210 SAE net horsepower) Turbo-Fire 350 V-8, a black-finished grille, a remote-control left-hand outside rearview mirror, power brakes, special hood insulation, dual exhausts, Hide-A-Way windshield wipers, 14 x 7-in. wheels, F70 x 14 wide-oval white-letter bias-belted tires and special SS ornamentation. A 300-hp (260 SAE net horsepower) "396 Turbo-Jet" V-8 was optional for cars with the SS package. Both engines available with the package came with chrome dress-up parts. On Camaro SS models with the

Daniel B. Lyons photo

THE Z/28 WAS ACTUALLY A PRODUCT OF THE RPO Z/28
SPECIAL PERFORMANCE PACKAGE. IT WAS A FACTORY OPTION
THAT COST CHEVROLET DEALERS $622.41 AND RETAILED FOR $786.75.

bigger engine the buyer got a heavy-duty Sport suspension with front and rear stabilizer bars and special shock absorbers.

CAMARO Z/28 - SERIES 24 + Z/28 – V-8

The RPO Z/28 Special Performance package was a factory option that cost Chevrolet dealers $622.41 and retailed for $786.75. It was available for V-8-powered Camaros with a four-speed manual or Turbo-Hydra-Matic transmission. In addition, the Z/28 came with an exclu-sive Turbo-Fire 350 V-8, bright engine accents, finned aluminum valve covers, a left-hand re-mote-controlled sport style outside rearview mirror, special instrumentation, power brakes, a 3.73:1 positraction rear axle (4.10:1 optional), a heavy-duty radiator, dual exhausts, a black-fin-ished grille, Z/28 emblems on the front fender, rear bumper guards, a Sport suspension, heavy-duty front and rear springs. The four-speed manual or Turbo-Hydra-Matic transmission was required at extra cost. Air conditioning, wheel covers and Rally wheels were not available.

Daniel B. Lyons photo

A STRIKE-MARRED PRODUCTION SCHEDULE WAS ONE REASON WHY FEW CHANGES CAME TO THE Z/28 (OR THE REST OF THE CAMARO LINE) FOR 1972.

1972

The 1972 run was horrible for Camaro production, which slid to 68,651 units. For many years, this was the low point in the nameplate's popularity, although there would be worse years later on. Three-point safety belts were one new feature, but there were few changes overall.

GM didn't have the time or money to think about product changes because of outside factors. First, there was a massive strike by the United Auto Workers Union that shut down the Camaro factory in Ohio for 117 days. By the time the labor dispute was settled, cars left sitting on the assembly line could not be finished and sold. New government safety and emissions standards had come into law during the strike period and it was impossible to modify the half-built cars to meet the new regulations. More than 1,000 F-Cars were simply scrapped.

This situation left a bad taste in the mouths of GM brass, who contemplated killing off both cars and being done with the problem. Luckily, a group of passionate enthusiasts who worked within the corporation lobbied for keeping the Camaro and Firebird. In the end, this faction won the battle and engineers devised a cheaper way to satisfy the government standards. The Camaro and its Pontiac cousin were saved.

The 1972 Camaro was promoted as "the closest thing to a Vette yet." It was almost identical in general appearance to the 1971 model, but had a slightly coarser grille mesh.

CAMARO - SERIES 23/24 - SIX/V-8

Standard equipment for the base Camaro Sport Coupe included front disc/rear drum brakes, E78-14 black sidewall tires, a 250-cid 110-hp inline six-cylinder engine and a three-speed manual transmission with a floor shifter. The base V-8 was an overhead-valve 307-cid two-barrel.

Chuck Dunlap photo

THERE WERE ONLY 68,651 CAMAROS BUILT FOR 1972,
WHICH MAKES AN ALL-ORIGINAL Z/28 LIKE THIS ONE A NICE PRIZE.

CAMARO RALLY SPORT - SERIES 23/24 + Z22 – SIX/V-8

The RPO Z22 Rally Sport package was a factory option that cost Chevrolet dealers $92.04 and retailed for $118. Standard equipment included most items standard on the base Sport Coupe, including a 250-cid 110-hp inline six-cylinder engine and a three-speed manual transmission with a floor shifter. The base V-8 was a 307-cid two-barrel. In addition, the Rally Sport option added a special black-finished grille with Argent Silver accents, a special rubber-tipped vertical grille center bar, a smaller grille grid pattern (identical to the 1971 Rally Sport grille), parking lights with bright accents mounted on the grille panel between the headlights, independent right- and left-hand front bumpers replacing the standard full-width bumper, a license plate bracket, a dent-resistant body-color hard rubber grille frame, Rally Sport emblems on the sides of the fenders and Hide-A-Way concealed windshield wipers. The RS package could be added to six-cylinder or V-8 Camaros as shown immediately below. It could also be combined with the SS package by adding $118 to the SS prices shown further below.

CAMARO SS - SERIES 24 - V-8

The RPO Z27 Super Sport or SS package was a factory option that cost Chevrolet dealers $237.90 and retailed for $306.35. It was available for V-8-powered Camaros with four-speed or Turbo-Hydra-Matic transmission. Standard equipment included most items standard on the base Sport Coupe. In addition, the SS option added the 200-hp Turbo-Fire 350 V-8, Hide-A-Way windshield wipers, a black-finished grille, a remote-control left-hand outside rearview mirror, front and rear spoilers, power brakes, special hood insulation, dual exhausts, 14 x 7-in. wheels, F70-14 wide-oval white-letter bias-belted tires and SS fender emblems. A 240-hp "396 Turbo-Jet" (actually 402-cid) V-8 was optional for cars with the SS package. Both engines available with the package came with chrome dress-up parts, heavy-duty engine mounts and a heavy-duty starter. On Camaro SS models with the bigger engine the rear body

Daniel B. Lyons photo

THE Z/28 PACKAGE COST $597.48 FOR 1972.

panel was finished in black and the buyer got a heavy-duty Sport suspension with front and rear stabilizer bars and special shock absorbers. The 240-hp engine was not available for cars being registered in the State of California. Both SS engines required a four-speed manual or Turbo-Turbo-Hydra-Matic transmission attachment.

CAMARO Z/28 - SERIES 24 + Z/28 – V-8

The RPO Z/28 Special Performance package was a factory option that cost Chevrolet dealers $597.48 and retailed for $769.15. It was available for V-8-powered Camaros in two versions. The Z28/YF8 version included black striping and the Z28/ZR8 version included white striping. Standard equipment included most items standard on the base Sport Coupe. In addition, the Z/28 came with an exclusive 255-hp Turbo-Fire 350 V-8, finned aluminum rocker covers, bright engine accents, dual sport style outside rearview mirrors (left-hand remote-control), special instrumentation, power brakes, a 3.73:1 positraction rear axle, dual exhausts, a black-finished grille, Z/28 emblems, rear bumper guards,

a Sport suspension with heavy-duty springs and front and rear stabilizer bars, heavy-duty engine mounts, a heavy-duty starter, a heavy-duty radiator, 15 x 7-in. wheels with bright lug nuts, special wheel center caps, wheel trim rings, F60-15/B bias-belted white-letter tires, special paint stripes on the hood and rear deck lid. A four-speed manual or Turbo-Hydra-Matic transmission was required at extra cost and air conditioning, wheel covers or Rally wheels were not available. It was possible to order a Z/28 in 1972 and delete the hood and deck lid stripes.

HISTORICAL FOOTNOTES

Model-year production included 4,821 six-cylinder Camaros and 63,830 Camaro V-8s for a total of 68,651 units all made at the Norwood factory (which also built 29,951 Firebirds and 2,852 Novas). The totals included 3,698 units built for export. Of the 68,651 Camaros, 82.7 percent had automatic transmissionA road test in the August 1972 issue of *Motor Trend* involved a Z/28 with the 350-cid 255-hp V-8, four-speed manual transmission and 3.73:1 rear axle. The car did 0 to 30 mph in 3.1 sec. 0 to 60 mph in 7.7 sec. and the quarter mile in 15.2 seconds.

Jerry Heasley photo

DESPITE AN OIL EMBARGO IN THE MIDDLE EAST, CHEVROLET STILL PRODUCED 96,752 CAMAROS FOR 1973, INCLUDING 11,574 Z/28S.

1973

The resurrected Camaro entered 1973 as a coupe only — the last of the so-called "steel bumper" cars. A new Type LT "luxury touring" version was added to the product mix and it was truly a separate 1S87 model, whereas the RS and Z/28 were considered to be options for the base 1Q87 model. The SS package was dropped entirely.

The Type LT Camaro was aimed at female buyers and later took the Berlinetta name to move even further in that direction. It featured such add-ons as rocker panel accent moldings, Rally wheels and windshield wipers that parked out of view under the cowl panel. With the right engine options, the Type LT could still be made into quite a "macho" performance machine rivaling the old SS. In fact, RS, SS or Z/28 equipment could be added to the Type LT.

Chevy's other hot-running Camaro — the

Z/28 — got a new Rochester four-barrel carburetor as a performance upgrade, but the aluminum intake model used on previous Zs was replaced with a cast-iron type. Chevy also replaced the neat Z/28 emblems on the rear body panel with foil-type stickers, although the metal emblems were still used on the sides of the front fenders.

Calendar-year sales of Camaros didn't exactly zoom in 1973, although they started heading in the right direction once again and peaked at 108,381 units. That was more than double the 45,330 sales in calendar 1972. Model-year production climbed to 96,751 cars.

CAMARO - SERIES 1FQ - SIX/V-8

The last of the steel-bumper Camaros was

the 1973. It continued using the body introduced in 1970 and added rubber-faced vertical guards to the standard, full-across bumper to satisfy new government frontal impact standards. Other changes included a conventional automatic transmission shifter replacing the "can-crusher" style and new options like power windows. Base Camaro engines were the 250-cid inline six or the 307-cid V-8. Standard equipment for the base Camaro Sport Coupe included seat belts, two built-in front-seat head restraints, steel-belted radial tires, posh wall-to-wall deep-twist carpeting, recessed headlights and parking lights, Camaro emblems, a Delcotron generator with built-in solid state regulator, corrosion-fighting inner fender liners, a four-spoke sport steering wheel, an independent front suspension with coil springs, minor-impact-cushioning front and rear bumper systems, contoured full-foam Strato-bucket front seats, rear leaf springs, self-adjusting front disc brakes with audible wear indicators, drum-type rear brake, a coolant recovery system, tight all-welded unit-body construction, front ball joints with wear indicators, self-cleaning rocker panels, a 18-gal. gas tank, a power ventilation system, a perforated acoustical headliner, double-panel construction doors and hood and deck lid, a Delco Energizer sealed side-terminal battery and a floor-mounted three-speed manual transmission.

CAMARO TYPE LT - SERIES1FS - V-8

The Camaro Type LT or luxury touring model was seen for the first time in 1973 and filled a gap in the model lineup left by the elimination of the SS package. It was a separate model, rather than an option package, and had a distinct model number 1FS87 instead of the 1FQ87 used for other Camaros. In addition to the features that were standard on the base Camaro Sport Coupe, the Type LT included special trim, special LT identification (on the front, the roof rear quarter and the rear end panel), Hide-A-Way windshield wipers, dual sport style outside rearview mirrors (left-hand remote-con-

trolled), rocker panel accents, 14 x 7-in. Rally wheels with caps and trim rings, variable-ratio power steering, a sport steering wheel, deluxe seat trim, woodgrained trim on the doors and instrument panel, extra sound insulation, a glove compartment lamp and special instrumentation (including a tachometer, an ammeter, a temperature gauge and an electric clock). The front bucket seats in the Type LT were of a full-foam, molded design with a choice of two upholstery options. A mixed-tone cloth-and-vinyl selection was available in black and white, black and blue or green and black. Also available was all-vinyl trim in neutral or black. Color-keyed deep-twist carpeting protected the floor. Red or blue accent carpeting was optional. The standard engine in the Type LT Camaro was the Turbo-Fire 350-cid V-8 with a two-barrel carburetor.

CAMARO RALLY SPORT - SERIES 1FQ OR 1FS WITH Z22 - SIX/V-8

All 1973 Camaro Sport Coupes and Type LT coupes could be equipped with the Rally Sport package. It included a special black-finished grille with silver accents, a resilient grille surround, split bumpers (one on each side with no bumper across the grille) and Hide-A-Way windshield wipers. The front parking lights were repositioned from the normal location under the bumper to a space between the headlights and grille.

CAMARO Z/28 - SERIES 1FQ - V-8

In 1973, the Camaro Z/28 special performance package was a $598 option for the base Camaro Sport Coupe or a $502 option for the Camaro Type LT coupe. In addition to or in place of the base model's standard equipment listed above, the Z/28 package included bright engine accents, finned aluminum valve covers, a heavy-duty radiator, dual exhausts, a black-finished grille, Z/28 emblems, a sport suspension, heavy-duty front and rear springs, 15 x 7-in. wheels, special center caps and trim rings, hood

Thomas Glatch Productions photo

THIS 1973 Z/28 FEATURED THE MIDNIGHT BLUE METALLIC EXTERIOR WITH BLACK INTERIOR. IT FEATURES THE 350-CID AUTOMATIC AND STILL HAS THE ORIGINAL TIRES. Z/28S COULD HAVE A SPLIT BUMPER AND FINER-MESH GRILLE, ALONG WITH THE CIRCULAR TURN SIGNALS, IF THE Z/28 PACKAGE WAS ORDERED ON A CAR WITH THE RS PACKAGE.

insulation, F60 x 15/B white-letter, a rear deck lid spoiler and special paint stripes on the hood and rear deck lid. The 1973 Z/28 engine had hydraulic valve lifters, which lowered horsepower to 245, but permitted the addition of air conditioning at extra cost. A Rochester four-barrel carburetor and a cast-iron intake manifold were used instead of a Holley carb and aluminum intake manifold.

HISTORICAL FOOTNOTES

In 1973, F.J. McDonald was general manager of Chevrolet Motor Division. The 1973 Camaro went into production the week ending Sept. 1, 1972, and was introduced to the public 20 days later. Total Chevrolet sales climbed to 2,281,517 cars and 14.9 percent of those vehicles were sports models like the Camaro. In fact, the most dramatic gain in production over 1973

totals was realized by the Camaro due to the fact that its 1972 output had been curtailed by the strike at the Norwood, Ohio, assembly plant. The strike inspired GM to stop building Novas at Norwood, so the factory built only Camaros and Firebirds during 1973. Another factor that actually helped Camaro sales in 1973 was the Arab oil embargo coupled with cuts in domestic gasoline production. Industry trade journals of the era reported that model year production in the United States included 3,614 six-cylinder Camaros and 93,138 V-8s for a total of 96,752 units. Other sources say one less (96,751). *Car and Driver* (September 1973) tested a Camaro Z/28 with the wide-ratio four-speed transmission and a 3.42:1 axle. The car did 0 to 60 mph in 6.7 sec. and the quarter mile in 15.2 sec. at 94.6 mph.

**THE 1974 CAMARO Z/28 SPORT COUPE RAN A
15.2-SECOND QUARTER MILE IN ONE MAGAZINE TEST.**

1974

Bigger changes came along for 1974, when the Camaro received new styling fore and aft. The revised nose and tail incorporated stronger, impact-absorbing aluminum-faced bumpers that were designed to keep Uncle Sam happy. Although the bumpers themselves were lighter in weight, the overall bumper system added performance-robbing pounds to the F-Cars and also made them 7 in. longer.

There was a body-color fascia above the front bumper. At the rear, new taillights that replaced the trademark round units of 1970-1973 were more rectangular and notched into the body sides

Power selections were reduced in number to keep the industry watchdogs happy, and while Camaro engines actually gained cubic inches and horsepower, they did not make the cars appreciably faster. A 350-cid 145-hp engine re-

placed the "307" as the base V-8, while the L48 engine had 10 more horsepower than it did in 1973. The Z/28 used the same V-8 as the year before and gained a breakerless HEI ignition system during the model run. Radial tires were introduced, along with front brake pad sensors. A seat belt interlock system that forced front-seat passengers to buckle up before the car could be operated was a very unpopular new safety feature.

CAMARO - SERIES 1FQ - SIX/V-8

Standard equipment for the base Camaro Sport Coupe included steel-belted radial tires, posh wall-to-wall cut-pile carpeting, recessed headlights and parking lights, Camaro emblems, a Delcotron generator with built-in solid state regulator, corrosion-fighting inner fender

THIS 1974 CAMARO LT FEATURES A 350-CID VI WITH QUADRA-JET FOUR-BARREL CARBURETOR, DUAL EXHAUST, AUTOMATIC TRANSMISSION AND RALLY WHEELS.

liners, a four-spoke sport steering wheel, an independent front suspension with coil springs, minor-impact-cushioning front and rear bumper systems, contoured full-foam Strato-bucket front seats, rear leaf springs, self-adjusting front disc brakes with audible wear indicators, drum-type rear brake, a coolant recovery system, tight all-welded unit body construction, Saginaw variable-ratio power steering (on cars with a V-8 engine), front ball joints with wear indicators, self-cleaning rocker panels, a 21-gal. gas tank, a power ventilation system a perforated acoustical headliner, a standard 250-cid inline six-cylinder engine and a floor-mounted three-speed manual transmission.

CAMARO TYPE LT - SERIES 1FS - V-8

The Camaro Type LT was the luxury touring model for 1974. Its upscale image was enhanced through the use of additional sound-deadening materials, woodgrained interior trim, knit vinyl or cord-ridge fabric upholstery, a color-coordinated instrument panel and a color-coordinated steering wheel and column. The 307-cid base V-8 of 1973 was dropped and a 350-cid V-8 with a two-barrel carburetor was standard. This was the L65 engine in all states except California. In California, the LM1 350-cid V-8 was standard, but cost $49 extra.

The Type LT Camaro came standard with an especially well-trimmed interior with LT bucket seats having distinctive deep-contour seat backs, dressed-up door panels with map pockets and door pulls, a special instrument panel with a clock and a tachometer, sport mirrors on both sides (left-hand remote controlled), Rally wheels with center caps, bright wheel trim rings, Type LT nameplates on the sides and back, a base 350-cid two-barrel V-8 and a floor-mounted three-speed manual transmission.

CAMARO Z/28 - SERIES 1FQ - V-8

Technically the Camaro Z/28 was an option for the base Camaro Sport Coupe or the Camaro Type LT coupe in 1974. It was available throughout the United States. Major elements of the Z/28 package included special trim and badges, engine and drive train upgrades and suspension and tire upgrades. The package added $572 to the price of the Sport Coupe and $502 to the price of the Type LT coupe.

HISTORICAL FOOTNOTES

A total of 130,446 new Camaros were registered in the U.S. during calendar year 1974. *Car and Driver* (September 1973) tested a 1974 Camaro Z/28 with the wide-ratio four-speed transmission and a 3.42:1 axle. The car did 0 to 60 mph in 6.7 sec. and covered the quarter mile in 15.2 sec. at 94.6 mph.

THE 1975 CAMARO TYPE LT SPORT COUPE CARRIED A BASE PRICE OF $4,070 AND WAS BILLED AS A MORE UPSCALE CAMARO.

1975

Chevy temporarily killed the Z/28 starting in 1975. Some say that this was due to the fact that a catalytic converter was required this year and Camaro lovers at the division felt they could not build a true performance car with a converter-clogged exhaust system. Others say it was simply a bad marketing decision — bad because Pontiac stuck with the Trans Am and it sold great. The Z-car would return in mid-1977.

The ninth annual edition of the Camaro continued with a good-looking design dominated by a low profile, a wide stance and a sloping rear deck. The '75 models also got a new wrap-around rear window to reduce a blind spot that had troubled many drivers. A new Rally Sport option with multi-color paint schemes and bold stripes bowed in the middle of the season. There was also a rare factory interior selection that was the only leather upholstery option offered for first- or second-generation Camaros.

A breakerless HEI ignition system was stan-dard on all 1975 Camaros as were radial tires. You could get air conditioning in a six-cylinder Camaro this year and power door locks were a new option.

CAMARO - SERIES 1FQ - SIX/V-8

Standard equipment for the base Camaro Sport Coupe included an anti-theft steering column lock, a catalytic converter, a fuel tank nozzle restrictor, a High Energy Ignition (HEI) system, a carburetor air intake extension (to bring in cooler outside air), steel-belted radial tires, a 21-gal. gas tank, a power ventilation system, a perforated acoustical headliner, a standard 250-cid inline six-cylinder engine, a floor-mounted three-speed manual transmission and a 2.73:1 or 3.08:1 rear axle (depending on engine).

CAMARO RALLY SPORT - SERIES 1FQ/Z85 - SIX/V-8

Big news for Camaro lovers in 1975 was the

THE 1975 CAMARO WAS NOT LACKING IN AMMENITIES. BUYERS COULD PICK FROM AN OPTION LIST THAT INCLUDED POWER WINDOWS AND DOOR LOCKS, HIDDEN WINDSHIELD WIPERS, AND LEATHER UPHOLSTERY.

return of the Rally Sport as an option package. Designated the Z85 package, it was available for the base Sport Coupe at $238. The Rally Sport features included a flat black hood, a flat black forward roof section, a flat black grille, a flat black rear end panel, tri-color trim stripes, Rally wheels, dual sport mirrors and assorted decals. Front and rear spoilers that looked great with this package were available at extra cost.

CAMARO TYPE LT - SERIES 1FS - V-8

. Chevrolet literature described the Type LT (Luxury Touring) Camaro as "a step up" car that represented "everything the Sport Coupe is, plus an interesting mix of tasteful touches outside and in." The Type LT Camaro came standard with an especially well-trimmed interior with standard plaid knit-cloth seat and door trim (knit vinyl was also available as well as, for a short time, genuine leather), LT bucket seats with distinctive deep-contour seat backs, dressed-up door panels with map pockets and door pulls, a special instrument panel insert with simulated bird's-eye maple accents, a clock, a tachometer, added sound deadeners and insulation, sport mirrors on both sides (left-hand remote controlled), variable-ratio power steering, a color-keyed steering wheel with an LT emblem on the hub, Rally wheels with center caps, bright wheel trim rings, bright parking light trim, bright vertical bars on the parking lights, a lighted glove box, Hide-A-Way windshield wipers, Type LT nameplates on the sides and back, a base 350-cid two-barrel V-8 and a floor-mounted three-speed manual transmission.

CAMARO TYPE LT RALLY SPORT - SERIES 1FS/Z85 - SIX/V-8

The return of the Rally Sport was also good news for Camaro Type LT buyers. They could get it on the V-8-only Type LT for $165. The lower price was explained by the fact that the Type LT model already had some of the ingredients, such as Rally wheels. Except for the base engine, this version of the Z85 package was identical to the version offered for the Sport Coupe and included the same content such as a flat black hood, a flat black forward roof section, a flat black grille, a flat black rear end panel, tri-color trim stripes, Rally wheels, dual sport mirrors and assorted decals.

HISTORICAL FOOTNOTES

Camaro sales for model year 1975 came to 135,102 units. Camaro sales for calendar year 1975 came to 145,029. A total of 138,679 new Camaros were registered in the U.S. during calendar year 1975.

THE 1976 CAMARO TYPE LT SPORT COUPE GOT A NEW 305-CID V-8 AND HAD A FEW INTERIOR AMENITIES DESIGNED TO MAKE IT A "LUXURY TOURING" VEHICLE.

1976

Chevrolet really had little motivation to change anything on the Camaro for 1976, since production of 182,959 cars — the highest total since 1969 — was realized. In fact, production of Camaros at the Van Nuys, California, factory had to be resumed in August of 1975 just to keep up with demand.

The base Sport Coupe looked similar to the 1975 version. The crosshatch grille was made up of thin bars that peaked forward at the center. The grille was surrounded by a bright molding with rounded upper corners. Round, deeply recessed parking lamps sat between the grille and the recessed round headlamps. Front fenders held small side marker lenses. Taillights with bright moldings wrapped around the body sides, tapering to a point. Small vertical back-up lights were in the taillight housings. Rectangular emblems sat on the hood and deck. The body styling incorporated a long hood and short deck appearance with a swept-back roofline.

There were only three engine options for 1976 models, including a new 305-cid 140-hp V-8. The LM1 350-cid V-8 gained 10 hp, while the base inline six was unchanged. Power brakes were now standard and cruise control was now optional. The vinyl top option was revised to in-

corporate a canopy look with a painted rear band. The Type LT had a new bright aluminum rear body panel and simulated leather dashboard.

CAMARO - SERIES 1FQ - SIX/V-8

Standard equipment for the Camaro Sport Coupe included new narrow bright rocker panel moldings, a padded vinyl-covered four-spoke steering wheel with a crest, a left-hand outside rearview mirror, a wide-tread suspension, front disc brakes, finned rear drum brakes, variable-ratio power steering, contoured full-foam Strato-bucket front bucket seats, bucket-styled full-foam rear seats, standard all-vinyl seat trim, bright bumpers with protective black rubber strips, right top and side windshield moldings, bright side window moldings, bright full rear window moldings, Magic-Mirror acrylic finish, a built-in heater-defroster system, flow-through power ventilation, wall-to-wall cut-pile carpeting, double-panel steel construction (in the roof, doors, hood and deck lid), protective inner fenders, self-cleaning rocker panels, a front stabilizer bar, a coil spring front suspension, a leaf spring rear suspension and 14 x 6 in. wheels, FR78-14 steel-belted radial ply black sidewall tires. As be-

*NOT MUCH NEW WAS ADDED TO THE 1976 CAMARO SPORT COUPE,
WHICH COULD STILL BE HAD NEW WITH A V-8 FOR LESS THAN $4,000.*

fore, the 250-cid inline six was the base engine. A new 305-cid small-block V-8 engine replaced the 350-cid V-8 as the standard V-8.

CAMARO RALLY SPORT - SERIES 1FQ/Z85 - SIX/V-8

A Rally Sport package was available. In addition to the standard Sport Coupe equipment, the Rally Sport package included Low Gloss Black finish on the forward section of the roof, the hood, the radiator grille, the header panel, the headlight bezels, the upper fenders, the rocker panels and the rear panel. Rally wheels were standard. Tri-color striping separated the black-accented areas from the basic body color. The package also included bright headlamp trim, "Rally Sport" decals on the rear deck lid, "Rally Sport" front fender decals and Argent Silver paint accents. Rally Sport Camaros came in a limited range of base colors, including Antique White, Silver, Light Blue Metallic, Firethorn Metallic and Bright Yellow. The package was $260 for the base Camaro Sport Coupe.

CAMARO TYPE LT - SERIES 1FS - V-8

The Type LT (Luxury Touring) Camaro also looked similar to the 1975 version. Every Type LT Camaro had a "Type LT" nameplate on the right side of the bright rear end panel and a brushed aluminum appliqué across the full width of the rear end panel. Type LT seat trim now used vertical stitching for both cloth and vinyl upholstery. The Type LT Camaro offered three Dover knit cloth-and-vinyl interiors in black, dark blue and dark firethorn as well as all-vinyl interiors in black, white or light buckskin. The Type LT interiors also had special bucket seats with deep-contour seat backs and built-in padded armrests. Hide-A-Way windshield wipers, sport-style outside rearview mirrors (left-hand remote-controlled) and 14 x 7 in. Rally wheels were also standard. Inside the LT was a tachometer, a clock, a voltmeter and a temperature gauge, plus a color-keyed steering wheel, a glove compartment light and simulated leather instrument panel trim. The new 305-cid V-8 was standard in the Type LT.

THE STYLISH 1976 CAMARO RALLY SPORT HAD A FLASHY PAINT SCHEME THAT INCLUDED TRI-COLOR STRIPING, AND A BLACK FINISH ON THE HOOD, ROOF, FRONT END AND ROCKER PANELS.

CAMARO TYPE LT RALLY SPORT - SERIES 1FS/Z85 - V-8

The Rally Sport model-option package included Low Gloss Black finish on the forward section of the roof, the hood, the radiator grille, the header panel, the headlight bezels, the upper fenders, the rocker panels and the rear panel. Rally wheels were standard. Tri-color striping separated the black-accented areas from the basic body color. The package also included bright headlamp trim, "Rally Sport" decals on the rear deck lid, "Rally Sport" front fender decals and Argent Silver paint accents. Rally Sport Camaros came in a limited range of base colors, including Antique White, Silver, Light Blue Metallic, Firethorn Metallic and Bright Yellow. The package could be ordered for the Camaro Type LT. This combination added the special contents of the Rally Sport package to the special contents of the Type LT equipment list (described above). Since the Type LT model already included shared features such as Rally Wheels, the Rally Sport package cost a little less when added to a Type LT. The suggested retail price was $173.

HISTORICAL FOOTNOTES

Chevrolet realized a hefty comeback in sales this year and so did the Camaro. Model-year production of 1976 Camaros is reported by most sources as 182,959. The engine breakouts reported in one industry trade journal reflected a further swing towards six-cylinder models, with production of 38,047 such cars being recorded. This source showed that model-year production of Camaro V-8s also rose to a total of 144,912 units. Camaro sales for model year 1976 came to 163,653 units. Camaro sales for calendar year 1976 came to 172,846 for a 2 percent market share. A total of 166,689 new Camaros were registered in the U.S. during calendar year 1976.

LIKE THE SPORT COUPE AND RALLY SPORT, THE 1977 TYPE LT CAMARO COULD BE HAD WITH A STRAIGHT SIX, 305-CID V-8, OR 350-CID V-8.

1977

Does excitement sell automobiles? It must, if the 1977 Camaro model year is any example. In the middle of the year, Chevrolet brought back the Z28 (the / was dropped starting this year) to stir up enthusiasts and production zoomed to 218,853 units.

The new version of the "Z" was merchandised as a separate model, although it was factory coded as an option for the base Camaro. Its 185-hp V-8 was less muscular than past editions, but the badges, stripes, and decals made it look exciting and a heavy-duty suspension setup made for some heart-racing road manners.

The Camaro changed little for 1977. When the new models were introduced in the fall the lineup included the standard Camaro Sport Coupe and the upscale Camaro Type LT (or Luxury Touring edition). The familiar 250-cid inline six-cylinder engine was the standard power plant for 1977 Camaros. Options included a 305-cid V-8 and a 350-cid V-8. Transmission choices ranged from a standard three-speed manual gearbox, to four-speed manual gearbox to a Turbo-Hydra-Matic transmission. The standard axle ratio for both V-8s with automatic changed from 2.73:1 to 2.56:1 to help boost fuel economy. The four-speed transmission shift pattern was revised and reverse gear was now engaged by a rearward (toward the driver) lifting motion, rather than forward as before. A new refillable carbon-dioxide canister replaced the disposable freon-filled unit used to inflate the Stowaway spare tire. Intermittent windshield wipers joined the Camaro's option list and all models had Hide-A-Way windshield wipers.

CAMARO SPORT COUPE - SERIES 1FQ - SIX/V-8

Standard equipment for the Camaro Sport Coupe included a wide-tread suspension, front disc brakes, finned rear drum brakes, variable-ratio power steering, a soft-rim vinyl-covered four-spoke sport steering wheel, contoured full-foam front bucket seats, bucket-styled full-foam rear seats, standard all-vinyl seat trim, wrap-around taillights with bright moldings, bright bumpers with protective black rubber strips, bright lower body moldings, bright top and side windshield moldings, bright side window moldings, bright full rear window moldings, Magic-Mirror acrylic finish, a built-in heater-defroster system, flow-through power ventilation, wall-to-wall cut-pile carpeting, double-panel steel construction (in the roof, doors, hood and deck lid), protective inner fenders, self-cleaning rocker panels, a front stabilizer bar, a coil spring front suspension, a leaf spring rear suspension and FR78-14 steel-belted radial ply black side-wall tires.

CAMARO RALLY SPORT - SERIES 1FQ/Z85 - SIX/V-8

The Rally Sport package was actually an option that added $281 to the price of the base Sport Coupe, but many Camaro fans viewed it as a separate model. Some call this a "model-option." The Rally Sport package added a dramatic appearance to the Camaro Sport Coupe or Camaro Type LT coupe. It featured special contrasting paint areas with the buyer's choice of Low Gloss Black or new-for-1977 Gray Metallic, Dark Blue Metallic or Buckskin Metallic finish on the forward top surfaces of the body as well as the rear end panel and standard dual sport mirrors. The grille and lower body area were also finished in Low Gloss Black and a distinctive tri-color striping package separated the contrasting color from the body color in appropriate areas. The Rally Sport package also included bright-edged headlight bezels, Rally wheels and Rally Sport decals on the deck lid and front fenders. Exterior colors available with the Rally Sport package were limited.

CAMARO TYPE LT - SERIES 1FS - SIX/V-8

The Camaro Type LT was the Luxury Touring model. Every Type LT coupe had dual sport mirrors (left-hand remote-controlled), dual horns, Rally wheels with bright center caps and trim rings, special instrumentation (including a tachometer, voltmeter, temperature gauge and electric clock), the interior décor Quiet Sound group (including simulated leather trim on the instrument cluster, additional instrument lighting, additional body sound insulation and a one-piece hood insulator), bright radiator grille outline moldings, a black-finished accent panel under a bright lower body molding, a brushed-aluminum trim panel between the taillights (with bright upper and lower moldings), a bright trim ring with a vertical center bar on the parking lights, a "Type LT" nameplate behind the side window, a "Type LT" nameplate on the rear trim panel, special Type LT front bucket seats with deep-contoured backs and a special color-coordinated interior trim treatment.

CAMARO TYPE LT RALLY SPORT - SERIES 1FS/Z85 - SIX/V-8

The Rally Sport model-option package could also be ordered for the Camaro Type LT. This combination added the special contents of the Rally Sport package to the special contents of the Type LT equipment list, as described above. Since the Type LT model already included shared features such as Rally Wheels, the Rally Sport package cost a little less when added to a Type LT. The suggested retail price was $186.

CAMARO Z28 - SERIES 1FQ - V-8

After being away from the lineup for two years, the high-performance Camaro Z28 returned as a 1977 1/2 model. It made its debut at the Chicago Auto Show. The Camaro Z28 rode on special GR70-15 white-lettered wide-profile

THE Z28 RETURNED AFTER A TWO-YEAR ABSENCE IN 1977, BOASTING A 350-CID V-8 AND BORG-WARNER FOUR-SPEED TRANSMISSION.

steel-belted radial tires that were mounted on color-keyed 15 x 7-in. mag-style wheels. Under the hood was a special 350-cid V-8 that had an identifying decal. It was linked to a Borg-Warner four-speed manual transmission and 3.73:1 rear axle. Turbo-Hydra-Matic transmission was required in California. The chassis held front and rear stabilizer bars, special spring rates and quicker steering. This new Camaro Z28 also had body-color bumpers, body-color spoilers, body-color mirrors, body-color wheels, a black-out grille, a blacked-out rear-end panel, black-finished rocker panels, black moldings, black headlamp bezels, black taillight bezels, a Stowaway spare tire and "open" exhausts with dual resonators. Rounding out the Z28's appearance were stripes on the rocker panels and wheel housings, special emblems and a Z28 badge on the driver's side of the grille. The Z28

came only in seven body colors with bumpers to match. The special "Z28" identification was available in four tri-color variations.

HISTORICAL FOOTNOTES

Camaro sales climbed. Model-year production of 218,853 Camaros included 31,389 six-cylinder models and 187,464 Camaro V-8s. This model-year production at Van Nuys was higher than production at Norwood. Industry trade journals reported that the California plant built 153,671 Camaros and the Ohio factory built 65,183 Camaros. (In addition, all 155,736 Firebirds made in 1977 were built at Norwood.) Of the Camaros built, 89.8 percent had automatic transmission, 6.2 percent had a four-speed manual transmission, 6.6 percent had a standard V-8, 79.1 percent had an optional V-8 and 14.3 percent had a six-cylinder engine,

THE Z28 ADDED A NEW POINTED HOOD PANEL AIR SCOOP WITH A BLACK THROAT AND FUNCTIONAL SLANTED FRONT FENDER AIR LOUVERS.

1978

The 1978 Camaros continued the second generation, but got a heavy facelift to make them look more up to date. Though unchanged in basic design, the 1978 Camaro managed a fresh look with a new body-colored soft nose section and rear bumper. The new design used the same cellular urethane as the Corvette to replace the former aluminum face bar and spring bumper system. The Camaro grille was similar to the 1977 grille, but had fewer horizontal bars, larger openings (10 rows across) and a deeper repeated lower section below the narrow bumper. At the rear of the car were wedge-shaped wraparound taillights with amber-colored inboard directional signal lamps and clear back-up lamp lenses. This became a new Camaro trademark, replacing the characteristic round taillights of the early '70s.

Model-options were expanded to Sport Coupe, Rally Sport, Type LT, Type LT Rally Sport and Z28 using about the same power teams as in 1977.

A new option, that was actually introduced in late 1977, was a hatch roof with removable glass panels that soon became popularly known as the "T-top." The 305-cid V-8 got a new aluminum intake manifold and a 350-cid V-8 with a four-barrel carburetor and dual exhausts was used in the Z28. There were also suspension improvements designed to increase front-end rigidity and reduce rear axle hop.

CAMARO SPORT COUPE - SERIES 1FQ - SIX/V-8

The standard Camaro engine was a 250-cid inline six rated at 110 hp and linked to a three-speed manual transmission. Options included 305- and 350-cid V-8s. A four-speed manual gearbox was standard with both V-8s. Camaros sold in California came only with automatic transmissions. Car buyers in so-called high-altitude counties were limited to the 350-cid V-8 and automatic transmission. The six-cylinder engine had improved exhaust system isolation this year. An aluminum intake manifold helped cut the 305-cid V-8's weight by 35 lbs. Chassis improvements included front frame reinforcements. The brake-pressure differential switch was now made of nylon. Axle ratios for all Camaros were lowered in an attempt to boost gas mileage.

CAMARO RALLY SPORT - SERIES 1FQ/Z85 - SIX/V-8

The Camaro Rally Sport became a model

THE 1978 CAMARO RALLY SPORT FEATURED PAINT SCHEMES THAT USED BLACK AROUND THE HOOD, ROOF AND NOSE.

this year rather than an option. It featured new paint striping. Rally Sport Coupe models had a bold contrasting paint scheme. The forward roof section, hood surface and front header (to below the grille opening) were black metallic. Tri-color striping separated those black surfaces from the basic body color. Rally Sport decals were on front fenders and rear deck lid. Engines were the same as on the base Camaro.

CAMARO TYPE LT - SERIES 1FS - SIX/V-8

The Camaro Type LT (Luxury Touring) model included special identification and trim, concealed windshield wipers, dual sport mirrors, Rally wheels with caps and trim rings, a sport steering wheel, deluxe interior trim, wood-grain accents, a glove compartment lamp, added sound insulation and special instrumentation.

CAMARO TYPE LT RALLY SPORT - SERIES 1FS - SIX/V-8

Like the standard Type LT, the Type LT Rally Sport Coupe also had the bold Rally Sport paint scheme with contrasting colors. The forward roof section, hood surface and front header (to below the grille opening) were done in metallic black paint. Tri-color striping separated those black surfaces from the basic body color. Rally

Sport decals were seen on the front fenders and rear deck lid.

CAMARO Z28 - SERIES 1F - SIX/V-8

The high-performance Camaro Z28 added a new pointed hood panel air scoop with a black throat, functional slanted front fender air louvers, a body-color rear deck lid spoiler, modified body striping and a simulated string-wrapped steering wheel. The base Z28 power plant was the 350-cid V-8 with four-barrel carburetor and dual exhaust outlets, which put out 185 hp. Z28s also had a 3.42:1 or 3.73:1 rear axle ratio, a special handling suspension and GR70-15/B white-letter tires. Suspension revisions this year increased the Z28's front-end rigidity and limited transverse movement of the rear axle. A Z28 decal was placed below the air louvers.

HISTORICAL FOOTNOTES

Model-year production of 272,631 Camaros included 36,982 six-cylinder models and 235,649 Camaro V-8s. Of the Camaros built, 87.9 percent had automatic transmission, 9.7 percent had a four-speed manual transmission, 20.1 percent had a standard V-8, 66.3 percent had an optional V-8, and 13.6 percent had a six-cylinder engine.

THE BERLINETTA TOOK THE PLACE OF THE TYPE LT IN 1979.

1979

The new Camaro Berlinetta Sport Coupe with pin striping, a bright grille and black rocker panels replaced the Type LT in 1979. All Camaros got a new instrument panel and anti-theft steering column. The performance Z28 had a new blackout grille, flared front wheel openings and a three-piece front air dam that wrapped around the sides. New options included a CB radio, a cassette player and an AM/FM stereo with a built-in clock.

The base inline six had a lower axle ratio to raise gas mileage. Both 305 and 350-cid V-8s were available. The Z28 came with a standard 350-cid four-barrel V-8, a four-speed transmission and body-color front and rear spoilers. This would be the last year of the second-generation Camaro's production boom. Chevy built 152,657 cars in California and 129,925 in Ohio.

It was a great year for business, as the 1979 models proved to be the best-selling Camaros in history. In addition, an important change in sales patterns was realized this season when the Z28

became the second best-selling Camaro models. With the Z-car's higher price, that added up to more profits for Chevrolet.

CAMARO SPORT COUPE - SERIES 1FQ - SIX/V-8

Standard equipment for the base Sport Coupe included power steering, a Delco Freedom battery, a front stabilizer bar, concealed two-speed windshield wipers, carpeting, a heater and defroster, front bucket seats, a center dome light, a four-spoke sport steering wheel, a day/night mirror and FR78 x 14 steel-belted radial tires. The base 250-cid (4.1-liter) inline six had a lower axle ratio this year to increase its gas mileage. Optional V-8s included 305- and 350-cid engines. Only 2,438 Camaros were produced with a performance axle ratio, while 33,584 had optional removable glass roof panels, which most people called "T-tops." New audio options included Citizen's Band (CB) radio, cassette player or clock built into an AM/FM

THE 1979 CAMARO LINEUP INCLUDED THE Z28, RALLY SPORT, BERLINETTA AND BASE SPORT COUPE.

stereo. Mast and windshield type radio antennas were available.

CAMARO RALLY SPORT - SERIES 1FQ/Z85 - SIX/V-8

Standard equipment for the 1979 Camaro Rally Sport Coupe included power steering, a Delco Freedom battery, a front stabilizer bar, concealed two-speed windshield wipers, carpeting, a heater and defroster, front bucket seats, a center dome light, a four-spoke sport steering wheel, a day/night mirror, FR78-14 steel-belted radial tires, a rear deck lid spoiler, a sport suspension, black-finished rocker panels, a black grille, black headlamp bezels, bright reveal moldings, sport mirrors, color-keyed Rally wheels and a bold two-tone paint scheme. Engine options were the same as those for the base model.

CAMARO BERLINETTA - SERIES 1FS - SIX/V-8

A new Camaro Berlinetta model took the place of the Type LT. The Berlinetta was promoted as the "new way to take your pulse." It had body pin striping, a bright grille and black-finished rocker panels.

CAMARO Z28 - SERIES 1FQ - V-8

The high-performance Camaro Z28 had new flared front wheel openings as well as a three-piece front air dam that wrapped around the sides and up into wheel openings. The Z28 also had a blacked-out front end with a center grille emblem. Its identifying decal was moved from the front fender to the door. A rear spoiler was standard equipment, but 81 cars were produced without this item. The Z28 came with a special 350-cid 175-hp (170-hp in California) four-barrel V-8, a four-speed close-ratio manual gearbox, a bolt-on simulated hood air scoop with a black "throat," black windshield moldings, black back window moldings, two-tone front fender striping, front fender flares, an air dam, door panels, a rear deck lid panel, front fender air louvers, body-color spoilers (front and rear), a black-out style grille, black headlamp bezels, black taillight bezels, a body-color back bumper, P225/70R15 steel-belted white-letter tires and 7-in. body-color wheels.

HISTORICAL FOOTNOTES

This was a year in which consumers experienced a mid-summer gasoline crisis and the Camaro, although in tune with the times, was not immune to such pressure. Its model-year sales declined from 247,437 in 1978 to 233,802 in 1979. Calendar-year sales wound up at 204,742 (a 2.5 percent share of industry).

Thomas Glatch Productions photo

THE 1979 Z28 HAD ITS IDENTIFYING DECAL MOVED FROM THE FRONT
FENDER TO THE DOOR. A REAR SPOILER WAS STANDARD EQUIPMENT.

Nancy Glueck photo

CHEVROLET SOLD MORE THAN 111,000 CAMARO SPORT COUPES FOR 1979.
THEY COULD BE HAD WITH A STRAIGHT SIX, 305-CID V-8,
OR A 350-CID V-8, LIKE THIS CAR HAS.

Daniel B. Lyons photo

THE Z28 CAME WITH WHITE-LETTER TIRES AND BODY-COLOR WHEELS FOR 1980.

1980

Camaro entered 1980 wearing a new grille with tighter crosshatch pattern and offering a revised engine selection. A lighter, more economical 3.8-liter (229-cid) V-6 rated at 115 hp replaced the old familiar 250-cid inline six as the standard power plant. Camaros sold in California also had a base 3.8-liter V-6, but it was Buick's 231-cid engine. There was also a new 4.4-liter (267-cid) V-8 option with a 120-hp rating, plus a 305-cid 155-hp V-8. Camaros with automatic transmission had a new torque converter clutch to eliminate slippage. The grille used on the standard Camaro Sport Coupe had an emblem in the center. Berlinettas had wire wheel covers as standard equipment.

Chevrolet billed the 1980 Z28 as "the maximum Camaro!" It had a new rear-facing functional hood scoop facing with an electrically activated flap that opened when the gas pedal was pounded on. Also available was the Rally Sport package with a rear spoiler, a sport suspension, black rocker panels, a black grille, black headlamp bezels, bright reveal moldings, sport mirrors and color-keyed Rally wheels.

Production tapered off to 152,005 units due to a second gas crisis in the Middle East combined with the start of a deep economic recession.

CAMARO SPORT COUPE - SERIES 1FP - V-6/V-8

Standard Camaro equipment included a V-6 engine, a three-speed manual transmission, P205/705R14 SBR tires, body-color front and rear bumper covers, bucket seats, a console, a day/night mirror and a cigarette lighter.

CAMARO RALLY SPORT - SERIES 1FP/Z85 - V-6/V-8

Rally Sport Camaros came with an all-black "thin-line" grille. Standard equipment included a V-6 engine, a three-speed manual transmission, P205/705R14 steel-belted radial tires, body-color front and rear bumper covers, bucket

Gene Stransky photo

**THE Z28 WAS BILLED AS "THE MAXIMUM CAMARO"
AND HAD A FUNCTIONAL REAR-FACING HOOD SCOOP.**

seats, a console, a day/night mirror, a cigarette lighter, a rear spoiler, a sport suspension, black-finished rocker panels, a black grille, black headlamp bezels, bright reveal moldings, sport mirrors and color-keyed Rally wheels. Rally Sport engine options included the new 4.4-liter (267-cid) V-8 and the 305-cid 155-hp V-8.

CAMARO BERLINETTA - SERIES 1FS - V-6/V-8

The 1980 Camaro Berlinetta carried a version of the new Rally Sport grille with bright finish and the emblem in the center. Berlinettas also had new standard wire wheel covers. Standard equipment included a V-6, a three-speed manual transmission, P205/705R14 white sidewall steel-belted radial tires, body-color front and rear bumper covers, front bucket seats, a console, a day/night mirror, a cigarette lighter, bright headlamp bezels, bright upper and lower grille moldings, bright windshield moldings, bright window reveal moldings, black-finished rocker panels, dual horns, an electric clock, special instrumentation, the quiet sound group, sport mirrors and wire wheel covers. Engine choices included the new 4.4-liter (267-cid) V-8

and the 305-cid 155-hp V-8.

CAMARO Z28 - SERIES 1FP - V-8

The 1980 Z28 grille had a pattern of horizontal bars with a large Z28 emblem in the upper corner. The high-performance Z28 model was billed as "the maximum Camaro." A new functional hood air-intake scoop faced to the rear and had an electrically activated flap that opened up when the driver stepped harder on the gas. A side fender port allowed hot engine air to exit and boosted acceleration at the same time. Also new to the Z28 were rear fender flares. Economy-conscious buyers could order their Z28 with a 165-hp version of the RPO LG4 305-cid V-8 that had a Rochester M4ME four-barrel carburetor and get a $50 credit off base price. The RPO LM1 350-cid that produced 190 hp was standard and available in Z28s only. The hot Camaro model also came with P225/70R15 white-letter tires, body-color 15 x 7-in. wheels, black headlamp bezels, body-color upper and lower grille moldings, black reveal moldings, sport mirrors, a body-color front spoiler, body-color front flares, a hood scoop decal, front fender louvers, a rear spoiler, a Sport suspension, power brakes and a four-speed manual transmission with floor-mounted gear shifter.

HISTORICAL FOOTNOTES

This year the rising popularity of small cars combined with an auto industry downturn put a pinch on Chevrolet's business. The Camaro suffered mightily as its model-year sales declined from 233,802 in 1979 to 152,005 in 1980. Calendar-year sales wound up at 116,824 (a 1.8 percent share of industry). Trade journals of the era listed model-year production of 152,005 Camaros in tables showing production by series and engine, by engine or by body style. However, the same sources listed production of a slightly higher 152,021 units when broken out by model year or by factory of origin.

The engine breakouts given in such sources were 51,104 six-cylinder Camaros and 100,901 Camaro V-8s, or 152,005 total cars. However, the trade journals recorded the Van Nuys, California, plant as building 84,178 Camaros (and 57,912 Firebirds) and the Norwood, Ohio, factory as building 67,303 Camaros (and 49,428 Firebirds). That means Camaro numbers by factory total 152,021. The figures used by most enthusiasts show production by each of the four Camaro model-options and total 152,005. Of the Camaros built, 87.3 percent had automatic transmission, 8.1 percent had a four-speed manual transmission, 66.4 percent had a V-8, and 33.6 percent had a six-cylinder engine. A total of 117,164 new Camaros were registered in the U.S. during calendar year 1980. That was down from 203,904 in 1979 and 251,983 in 1978.

Daniel B. Lyons photo

BLACK HEADLAMP BEZELS, AND BLACK UPPER AND LOWER GRILLE MOLDINGS WERE PROMINENT ON THE FRONT OF THE 1980 Z28.

FOR 1981, CHEVROLET BUILT ONLY 20,253 OF THE STYISH CAMARO Z28 SPORT COUPES.

1981

The Rally Sport left the Camaro lineup this year, leaving only the base Sport Coupe, Berlinetta and Z28 to represent the final year of the second-generation Camaro. Not much else changed, beyond the use of GM's new Computer Command Control engine management system on all models. Power brakes, a lightweight Freedom II battery, new low-drag front disc brakes and a stowaway spare tire became standard on all Camaros. Halogen headlamps were a new option.

Optional automatic transmissions added a lock-up torque converter clutch in third gear. The basic Camaro Sport Coupe had an Argent Silver grille that was split into upper and lower sections, plus wraparound taillights.

The base engine for the Sport Coupe and fancier Berlinetta remained a 229-cid V-6, while Z28s had a standard four-barrel 305-cid V-8 teamed with a new wide-ratio four-speed manual transmission. Z28 buyers could add a 350-cid V-8 at no charge, but only if they wanted an automatic transmission. In a reversal of recent buying habits, Chevrolet built only 20,253 Z28s compared to 62,614 Sport Coupes and 43,272 Berlinettas. America was on an economy binge again!

CAMARO - SERIES 1FP - V-6-/V-8

Base Camaro Sport Coupes used the 229-cid V-6 as standard equipment. It came linked to a three-speed manual transmission. Also featured were power steering, power brakes, P205/75R14 steel-belted radial tires, a front stabilizer bar, multi-leaf rear springs, concealed two-speed wipers, front bucket seats with a console, a dome light, a four-spoke sport steering wheel, a day/night mirror and body-colored bumpers. Halogen headlamps were a new option. Cloth or vinyl interiors came in beige, black, dark blue, camel, red or silver.

CAMARO BERLINETTA - SERIES 1FS - V-6-/V-8

The Berlinetta's Argent Silver grille had bright accent moldings. The upscale Camaro came with a standard Quiet Sound Group that included a layer of sound-absorbing materials inside the roof and a soft foam-backed headliner. Special paint and striping emphasized its "sculptured lines." Body stripes came in silver, black, blue, beige, gold or red. Berlinetta identification was seen on the grille header panel, on the side pillars and on the rear deck lid. The body sills were black as opposed to the bright-finished sills on the base Camaro Sport Coupe. The standard engine for the posh Berlinetta was the standard 3.8-liter V-6 (229 cid/115 hp in 49 states or 231 cid/110 hp in California) hooked to a three-speed manual transmission. Options included the 4.4-liter (267-cid) V-8 and the 5.0-liter (305-cid) V-8 with an automatic or four-speed manual transmission required in either case.

CAMARO Z28 - SERIES 1FP - V-6-/V-8

The Camaro Z28's distinctive grille was body-colored with horizontal bars. There was Z28 identification on the driver's side of the grille and a Z28 decal on the doors. Other Z28 features included black headlamp bezels, black taillight bezels, a black rear end panel, a black-finished license plate opening, black parking light bezels, black body sill moldings, black

Daniel B. Lyons photo

THE 1981 CAMARO Z28'S DISTINCTIVE GRILLE WAS BODY-COLORED WITH HORIZONTAL BARS.

window moldings, black windshield moldings, tri-tone striping on the rear spoiler, tri-tone striping on the lower body side, tri-tone striping ond the front air dam and tri-tone striping on the fender flares. The front and rear bumper covers were formed of body-color urethane plastic. The Z28's solenoid-activated hood air intake actually drew in cold air. So did its fender air scoops. Seven Z28 striping colors were available: silver, charcoal, blue, dark gold, gold, red and orange. The Z28's torque converter clutch was computer-controlled in both second and third gears. Standard equipment nationwide included a 5.0-liter (305-cid four-barrel V-8) and a new wide-ratio four-speed manual transmission (optional on other Camaros) with a 3.42:1 low-gear ratio that delivered both economy and low-end performance. Z28 buyers could also get a 5.7-liter (350-cid) V-8 at no extra charge, but only with automatic transmission, which added $61 to the price.

HISTORICAL FOOTNOTES

The 1981 Camaro line was introduced on Sept. 25, 1980. Robert D. Lund was general manager of Chevrolet Motor Division in 1980, but would pass the title on to Robert C. Stempel by 1982. Lund then joined the General Motors Sales and Marketing Staff. Chevrolet projected a sales increase for 1981, but failed to realize its goal. The Camaro's popularity deteriorated further, with model year sales sliding from 131,066 in 1980 to 109,707 in 1981. That was a 17.9 percent decline, which was attributed to the fact that the basic Camaro body was 11 years old and that its technology was out of step with modern times.

THE BACK END OF THE Z28 WAS MARKED BY BLACK BEZELS AND TRIM, AND TRI-COLOR STRIPING.

Scott Moyer photo

*ALL OF THE INDY PACE CAR REPLICAS SOLD TO THE PUBLIC HAD
SILVER BLUE METALLIC FINISH, INDY 500 LOGOS, RED-ACCENTED
SILVER ALUMINUM WHEELS AND GOODYEAR EAGLE GT WHITE-LETTER TIRES.*

1982

An all-new rear-wheel-drive Camaro with a lighter-weight fastback format arrived late in the 1982 model year. Chevy said it captured "the essence of the contemporary American performance expression."

The flush-mounted 62-degree windshield produced one of the lowest drag coefficient readings ever measured by GM. The new Camaro was 10 in. shorter and 470 lbs. lighter. Instead of a rear window, it had a new lift-up hatch back with a huge piece of curved glass. A hatch release lock was located behind the license plate. The fuel filler door was on the driver's side quarter panel.

A 151-cid inline four with electronic fuel injection was the base engine. Options included a 173-cid 102-hp EFI V-6 and a 305-cid 145-hp V-8 with a four-barrel carburetor. Z28 buyers could pay $450 for an optional 305-cid 165-hp Crossfire fuel-injected V-8.

The Camaro's interior space was similar to before, even though the outside was smaller. The all-new fastback body was nearly 10 in. shorter than that of the previous Camaro. It rode on a 7-in. shorter 101-in. wheelbase. Each model had its own styling features, including a specific front air dam and rear fascia. The Z28 front end had no upper grille opening, its "ground effects" hugged the ground and it rode on special five-spoke aluminum wheels.

The new body featured unit construction with bolt-on front sheet metal. The front suspension was of a modified MacPherson strut design with coil springs and a stabilizer bar. At the rear, coil springs replaced leaf springs and the suspension used longitudinal torque tubes, short control arms ahead of the solid axle and lateral track rods. Z28s added a link-type rear stabilizer bar.

There were Sport Coupe, Berlinetta and Z28 models. A Z28 paced the Indy 500 and 6,360 commemorative editions of the Z28 were sold on a one-per-dealer basis. They were silver and blue with Indy 500 logos, red-accented silver aluminum wheels and Goodyear Eagle GT white-letter tires.

CAMARO - SERIES 1F - FOUR/V-6/V-8

The standard engine for the base Sport Coupe model was a Pontiac-built 151-cid (2.5-liter) 90-hp "Iron Duke" four with electronic fuel injection. Optional engines included a variant of the Citation's 173-cid (2.8-liter) V-6 rated at 102 hp or a 305-cid V-8 with a four-barrel carburetor that produced 145 hp. A four-speed manual gearbox was standard in the base Camaro and the old three-speed manual transmission was gone for good. Four-wheel disc brakes were available with V-8-powered cars. Inside, a new center console held a glove box, a parking brake lever and controls for the heater, optional stereo radio and air conditioning. The instrument panel had a black finish to minimize reflections. Twin speedometer needles showed both miles and kilometers per hour. Interior space was similar to before, even though the car's outside dimensions had shrunk. The rear seat backrest folded down, turning the rear section into a cargo area that was accessible through the hatch. Each model had its own styling features, including specific front air dam and rear fascia. All Camaros had deeply recessed quad rectangular headlamps and tri-color wraparound taillights (not far removed from prior designs). The optional F41 Sport suspension added a link-type rear stabilizer bar. Standard equipment for the base Sport Coupe included the four-speed manual transmission, power brakes, power steering, a front stabilizer bar, dual black sport mirrors, a black

windshield molding, concealed windshield wipers, body-color wheels, hubcaps, P195/75R14 fiberglass-belted radial tires, reclining front bucket seats, and a day/night mirror.

CAMARO BERLINETTA - SERIES 1F - V-6/V-8

The concept behind the Berlinetta was to enhance the Camaro's appeal to female buyers. When it replaced the LT in 1979, it became the "luxury touring" version of the sporty Chevy. The new-for-1982 Berlinetta played the same role in the Camaro model lineup. In addition to the features that were standard on the base Sport Coupe, the Berlinetta added the V-6, P205/70R14 steel-belted radial tires, body pin striping, body-color sport mirrors, black lower-body accenting (with stripes) and gold-accented cast-aluminum spoked wheels.

CAMARO Z28 - SERIES 1F - V-8

The Camaro Z28 front end had no upper grille opening and its ground effects air dams reached nearly to the ground. It also had operating air inlets. Four-wheel disc brakes were available. For an extra $611, Z28 buyers could even order an optional Lear-Siegler "Conteur" seat with six adjustments (backrest bolster, thigh support, cushion bolster, lumbar and recliner). A six-way power seat was optional. Z28s rode on special 15-in. five-spoke aluminum wheels with gold or charcoal accents. The suspension added a link-type rear stabilizer bar. Other standard equipment included P215/65R15 white-letter tires, a rear stabilizer bar, a specially tuned suspension, dual mufflers and tailpipes, body-color sport mirrors, a front air dam, a ground effects rocker molding area and a rear deck spoiler. Twin air scoops adorned the special Z28 hood. A 305-cid (5.0-liter) V-8 was standard in the Camaro Z28. It could also have an optional Cross-Fire injected 305-cid V-8 rated at 165 hp. That version carried a Cross-Fire Injection decal below the Z28 badge just behind the front wheel housing.

CAMARO Z28 INDY PACE CAR - SERIES 1F - V-8

A total of 6,360 Indy 500 Commemorative Editions of the Z28 were built this year, marking the use of the new Camaro Z28 as the year's "Official Pace Car" for the Indy 500. All of the Indy Pace Car replicas sold to the public had Silver Blue Metallic finish, Indy 500 logos, red-accented silver aluminum wheels and Goodyear Eagle GT white-letter tires. The Indy Pace Car's blue cloth and silver vinyl interior included the Lear-Siegler Contour driver's seat, along with special instruments, a leather-wrapped steering wheel and an AM/FM radio.

HISTORICAL FOOTNOTES

The all-new Camaro was introduced on Jan. 14, 1982. In one illuminating survey that held portents of the future, Chevrolet discovered that nearly 37 percent of Camaros purchased in 1980 were bought by women. That was higher than any other Chevrolet passenger car and well above the industry average of 24.5 percent.

Twin slogans for the restyled Camaro also suggested what was to come as the decade unrolled. "Excess is out. Efficiency is in!" predicted the rising emphasis on fuel-efficiency and modest size. "Brute power is out. Precision is in!" seemed to toll the death knell for the big V-8, although it would stay around for some time yet. Robert C. Stempel was general manager of Chevrolet Motor Division in 1982. While Chevy's overall model-year sales declined by more than 300,000 vehicles, the redesigned Camaro's popularity rose. Model-year sales went from 109,707 in 1981 to 148,649 in 1982. Unfortunately, that was below the target number of 155,000 units. Part of the reason for missing the goal was that the Camaro was not introduced until Jan. 14, 1982, while other Chevy products bowed on Sept. 24, 1981. Calendar-year sales wound up at 182,848. Industry trade journals of the era show model-year production of 189,735 Camaros, which represented a 3.68 percent share of the industry total. Other sources show a slightly higher production total of 189,747.

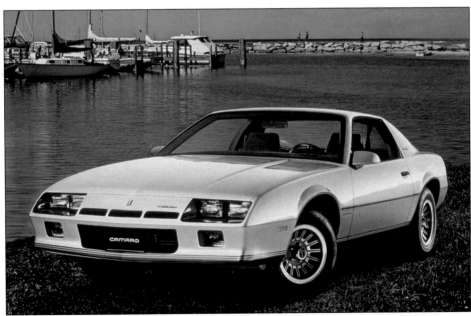

THE CAMARO RECEIVED A COMPLETE REDESIGN FOR 1982. THE CARS WERE SHORTER, LIGHTER, HAD A SLEEKER FRONT END, AND HATCH BACK. THIS BERLINETTA WAS STILL MARKETED AS A MORE STYLISH TOURING CAR.

AFTER A MAJOR FACELIFT IN 1982, THE 1983 CAMARO RECEIVED ONLY MINOR CHANGES.

1983

The Camaro's looks changed little following its 1982 restyling, but more power train combinations were available. Engine choices were essentially the same until a new 305-cid 190-hp H.O. V-8 with cam revisions and a four-barrel carburetor arrived late in the model year. A five-speed overdrive manual transmission was now optional for the base Sport Coupe and standard on other models. Also new was an available four-speed overdrive automatic with lockup torque converter.

Maroon was dropped from the body color list and brown replaced maroon as an interior choice, but color choices otherwise remained the same as before. Production, which had raced up to 189,747 in the third generation's first year, tapered back down (but only temporarily) to 154,381 units.

CAMARO - SERIES 1F - V-6/V-8

Camaros again had a rear glass hatch, reclining front bucket seats, and standard power steering. Joining the option list: a rear compartment cover to hide cargo. Optional mats now were carpeted instead of plain rubber. The standard equipment list included all GM safety, occupant protection, accident avoidance and anti-theft features plus dual black outside rearview mirrors, quad headlamps, a carpeted cargo floor with a storage well, a hinged stowage compartment in the front center console, a power ventilation system, reclining front bucket seats, side window defoggers, a front stabilizer bar, P195/75R-14 black sidewall tires, a power front disc/rear drum braking system with audible front wear sensors, fast-ratio power steering, a rear suspension with a torque arm to handle driving and braking forces and 14 x 6-in. body-color wheels with hubcaps.

CAMARO BERLINETTA - SERIES 1F - V-6/V-8

Berlinettas came standard with the 173-cid (2.8-liter) V-6. A five-speed overdrive manual transmission was also standard. Berlinetta equipment included an AM/FM stereo electronic-tuning radio, a digital clock, hood and sail panel emblems, a lockable fuel filler door, dual horns, a five-speed manual gearbox, a smooth-ride suspension, intermittent windshield wipers, custom vinyl reclining front bucket seats with adjustable head restraints, a front stabilizer bar and P205/70R-14 black sidewall tires, color-keyed sport mirrors, lower accent body paint with striping and 14 x 7-in. finned aluminum wheels with gold accents.

CAMARO Z28 - SERIES 1F - V-6/V-8

The standard Camaro V-8 was carbureted, but Z28s could have the Cross-Fire fuel-injected V-8. Camaros with this CFI engine had functional dual air intake hood scoops. Five-speed overdrive manual transmission was standard. New four-speed overdrive automatic (with lockup torque converter) was also available. A new high-output 305 V-8 engine with revised cam and four-barrel carburetor arrived late in the model year. It developed 190 hp. A total of 3,223 H.O. V-8s were installed in 1983 Camaros. Optional "Conteur" multi-adjustment driver's seats got matching passenger seats. Stereo radios offered electronic tuning. Z28 had new three-tone upholstery featuring multiple Camaro logos. The Z28 standard equipment list included all GM safety, occupant protection, accident avoidance and anti-theft features, plus dual body-color Sport outside rearview mirrors (left-hand remote controlled), a front air dam and ground effects rocker molding in silver or gold, quad headlamps, a rear deck lid spoiler, a carpeted cargo floor with a storage

well, a hinged stowage compartment in the front center console, a power ventilation system, reclining front bucket seats, side window defoggers, a 1.22-in. diameter front stabilizer bar, P215/65R-15 steel-belted radial-ply white letter tires, a power front disc/rear drum braking system with audible front wear sensors, fast-ratio power steering, a rear suspension with a torque arm to handle driving and braking forces and 15 x 7-in. five-spoke cast-aluminum wheels with gold, charcoal or silver accent color.

HISTORICAN FOOTNOTES

The nation's economic condition may have improved during 1983, but Chevrolet's status remained shaky. Model-year sales rose by only 6 percent. Robert C. Stempel, Chevrolet's general manager, promoted a new "pricing strategy which finds more than half of Chevrolet's 1983 passenger car models carrying lower sticker prices than they did in '82." Some of the reduction, though, was due to elimination of formerly standard equipment, a practice that would become common in the years ahead. The Camaro was named *Motor Trend* "Car of the Year." In a GM reshuffling, Chevrolet became part of the new Chevrolet-Pontiac-GM of Canada Group, which was to emphasize small cars. That group was headed by Lloyd E. Reuss, formerly Buick's general manager. Bob Stempel moved over to the new Buick-Oldsmobile-Cadillac group, which focused on large cars. Model-year sales rose from 148,649 in 1982 to 175,004 in 1983. Calendar-year sales wound up at 178,266 or 8.8 percent of the industry total. Model-year production of 154,381 Camaros represented a 2.72 percent share of the industry's total. The Van Nuys plant reported building 68,810 Camaros (and 37,548 Firebirds). The Norwood factory reported building 85,571 Camaros (and 37,349 Firebirds). Of the Camaros built, 76.7 percent had automatic transmission, 2.5 percent had a four-speed manual transmission, 20.8 percent had a five-speed manual, 6.4 percent had a four-cylinder, 58.4 percent had a V-8 and 35.2 percent had a V-6.

Jerry Heasley photo

**CHEVROLET SOLD MORE THAN 100,000 1984 Z28S —
AN ALL-TIME HIGH NEVER HIT AGAIN.**

1984

The Camaro took off in popularity again in 1984, when 261,591 were made. This included more than 100,000 Z28s — an all-time high never hit again. The Berlinetta gained the most attention in 1984 with its new "space-age instrumentation," including digital readouts, a pivoting pedestal-mounted radio and dual adjustable fingertip control pods that could be moved close to the steering wheel. This Corvette-inspired cockpit also sported a roof console and adjustable low-back seats.

The Camaro's modest "grille" hardly qualified as a grille. It consisted of no more than three side-by-side slots in the front panel. The grille was flanked by rectangular headlamps. Body colors were the same as 1983, but Dark Gold was added to the palette. Buyers could enhance the interior of their Camaro Sport Coupe with an elegant new low-back seating option that came with adjustable head restraints. The stylish striped seat bolsters characterized the standard front reclining bucket seats.

On the mechanical side, Cross-Fire injection was dropped, but the Z28 offered an optional 5.0-liter 190-hp H.O. V-8. It came hooked to either a five-speed manual or four-speed automatic transmission. This engine, introduced in the spring of 1983, was the most powerful carbureted engine offered in an '84 Chevy. The standard 2.5-liter four-cylinder engine featured an electronic fuel injection system that was so advanced it compared in principle to the new Corvette engine. A 173-cid (2.8-liter) V-6 was also a popular option. A hydraulic clutch was now used with all manual gearboxes.

CAMARO SPORT COUPE - SERIES 1F - FOUR/V-6/V-8

Chevrolet promoted the 1984 Camaro as "the best-selling 2+2 on the road." The base Camaro Sport Coupe featured a chassis and suspension configuration derived from the Z28

THE 1984 Z28 HAD NO UPPER GRILLE OPENINGS.

and combined it with clean aesthetics that made it the "purest" Camaro. Steel-belted fourth-generation all-season radial tires were became standard on the Sport Coupe. Base Sport Coupe equipment was otherwise similar to 1983. The standard equipment list included all GM safety, occupant protection, accident avoidance and anti-theft features plus dual black outside rearview mirrors, quad headlamps, a carpeted cargo floor with a storage well, a hinged stowage compartment in the front center console, a power ventilation system, reclining front bucket seats, side window defoggers, a 1.06-in. diameter front stabilizer bar, P195/75R-14 steel-belted radial-ply black sidewall tires, a power front disc/rear drum braking system with audible front wear sensors, fast-ratio power steering, a rear suspension with a torque arm to handle driving and braking forces and 14 x 6-in. body-color wheels with hubcaps.

CAMARO BERLINETTA - SERIES 1F - V-6

Berlinettas could be spotted by their gold-colored body trim. This model got the most attention this year. It had new "space-age instrumentation" that included digital readouts, a pivoting pedestal-mounted radio and dual adjustable fingertip control pods that could be moved close to the steering wheel. The Corvette-inspired cockpit also sported a roof console and adjustable low-back bucket seats. A digital display ahead of the driver showed road speed in miles or kilometers per hour, plus odometer or engine speed. An adjoining vertical-bar tachometer flashed more urgently as engine speed increased, while a monitor farther to the right signaled low fluid levels or other trouble spots. At the left were conventional needle-type gauges. The twin pods contained switches for lights and instrument displays, plus wiper and climate control. Other push-button controls were in the floor console, while the overhead console contained a swivel map light and small storage pouch. A remote-controlled, electronically tuned AM/FM stereo radio with digital clock was standard. Options included a tape player and a graphic equalizer. The radio could swivel for easy operation by either the driver or passenger. Buttons for the optional cruise control were on the Berlinetta's steering wheel, not the steering column.

CAMARO Z28 - SERIES 1F - V-8

The basic 1984 Camaro grille was simple enough, but the Z28 didn't even have slots in its upper panel. The performance model displayed subtle 5.0-Liter H.O. badges on its back bumper, rocker panels and air cleaner. It also had dual tailpipes. Standard features were similar to 1983. On the mechanical side, Crossfire Fuel Injection was dropped, but the Z28 could have an optional high-output 5.0-liter engine (RPO code L69) that was rated at 190 hp. It came hooked to either a five-speed manual gearbox or a four-speed automatic transmission. That H.O. V-8 (introduced in the spring of 1983) was the most powerful carbureted engine offered in a Chevrolet for 1984. It had a higher-lift, longer-duration camshaft, retuned valve system and 9.5:1 compression. The H.O. engine also had a specially calibrated Rochester Quadrajet

carburetor, dual-snorkel cold-air intake, large-diameter exhaust and tailpipes and wide-mouth (Corvette-type) catalytic converter. Z28s could have Berlinetta's roof console for an extra $50, while a locking rear storage cover cost $80. The Z28 standard equipment list included dual body-color sport outside rearview mirrors (left-hand remote controlled), a front air dam and ground effects rocker molding in silver or gold, quad headlamps, a rear deck lid spoiler and 15 x 7-in. five-spoke cast-aluminum wheels with gold, charcoal or silver accent color.

HISTORICAL FOOTNOTES

Introduced: Sept. 22, 1983. Chevrolet Motor Division's model-year sales finished nearly 23 percent higher than the 1983 result, with all lines (except Citation) performing well. To help plan for the enthusiast's market, surveys revealed that nearly two-thirds of Camaro buyers were under age 35. *Road & Track* magazine called the '84 Camaro one of the dozen top enthusiast cars, and it tied with Trans Am for best Sports GT in its price league.

Phil Kunz photo

THE CAMARO BASE COUPE WAS AVAILABLE WITH FOUR-, SIX- AND EIGHT-CYLINDER ENGINES FOR THE THIRD STRAIGHT YEAR IN 1984. THIS CAR HAD A "WINTER OLYMPICS" PACKAGE.

*THE 1985 IROC-Z HAD ROCKER PANEL STRIPING AND
SOME OTHER EXTERIOR FEATURES THAT SET IT APART.*

1985

A hotter IROC-Z version of the Z28 arrived in 1985. It was styled along the lines of the Camaros that competed in the International Race of Champions. Front fog lights, a ground-hugging front air dam, ornamental hood louvers, door decals and rocker panel striping set it off. Special 16 x 8-in. aluminum wheels carried P245-/50VR16 Goodyear Eagle GT unidirectional tires. The chassis featured Delco/Bilstein rear shocks, special struts and springs, a special rear stabilizer and reinforced front frame rails.

Any of three 5.0-liter (305-cid) V-8s were available and the top TPI version came only with a four-speed automatic transmission. Individually tuned runners channeled incoming air to each cylinder and computer-controlled port injectors delivered precisely metered fuel. The Berlinetta got a 2.8-liter MFI V-6 as standard equipment. Also new were body graphics and subtly patterned interior fabrics. The Sport Coupe offered V-6 and V-8 engines. Like the

Z28, it had new styling, a wider selection of sound systems and revised optional instrument cluster graphics. The double-needle speedometer was abandoned.

All Camaros had new "wet arm" windshield wipers with washer outlets on the blades. Split rear seat backs were a new option and Z28-style cast-aluminum wheels were available on the base Camaro.

CAMARO SPORT COUPE - SERIES 1F - FOUR/V-6/V-8

The base Camaro Sport Coupe had new body styling, a wider selection of optional sound systems with electronic-tuning radios and revised optional instrument cluster graphics. Standard equipment included reclining front bucket seats, front disc brake audible wear sensors, a 1.1-in. diameter front stabilizer bar, P195/75R-14 all-season steel-belted radial ply black sidewall tires, a power front disc/rear drum braking sys-

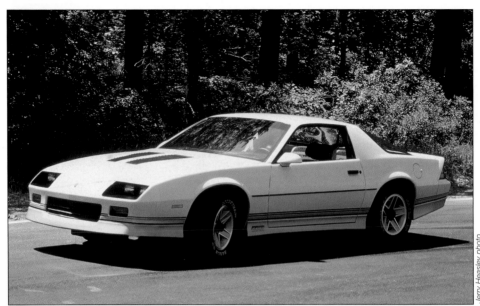

Jerry Heasley photo

THE Z28 SPORTED A FRONT AIR DAM AND "GROUND-EFFECTS" ROCKER MOLDINGS, A REAR DECK LID SPOILER, AND SILVER- OR GOLD-ACCENTED LOWER BODY WITH STRIPING.

tem, power steering, a torque arm rear suspension, an RPO LQ9 2.5-liter inline four-cylinder engine with electronic fuel injection (EFI) and a five-speed manual transmission.

CAMARO BERLINETTA - SERIES 1F - V-6

Chevrolet described the 1985 Camaro Berlinetta as the "fullest expression of poetry in motion." The Berlinetta got a new standard 173-cid (2.8-liter) V-6 with Multiport Fuel Injection and only one engine option: the carbureted 5.0-liter V-8. Also new were body graphics and subtly patterned interior fabrics. The Berlinetta also came standard with body pin striping, a color-accented lower body, a carpeted cargo floor with stowage well, hinged-cover console stowage, an electronically tuned four-speaker AM/FM stereo radio (with swivel remote control, seek-and-scan, digital display and clock, tuning graphs, front coaxial speakers and extended-range rear speakers), reclining front bucket seats, a 2.8-liter Multiport Fuel-Injected V-6, a five-speed manual transmission, a front disc/rear drum

brake system with audible front wear sensors, P205/70R-14 all-season steel-belted radial-ply black sidewall tires, power steering, a torque arm rear suspension and a tachometer.

CAMARO Z28 - SERIES 1F - V-8

The Z28 came with the standard or TPI versions of the 5.0-liter V-8, but not the carbureted H.O. version. Z28s in general had a selection of changes in appearance details, including grille and parking lamps, deeper ground-effects rocker panels, hood louvers, a deeper chin spoiler, three-element taillights, a larger rear bumper fascia and new body nameplates. Inside were new speedometer graphics and a tachometer. Also included as standard Z28 features were dual sport mirrors (left-hand remote control and right-hand manual). A front air dam and "ground-effects" rocker moldings, a rear deck lid spoiler, a Silver- or Gold-accented lower body with striping, an AM radio (could be deleted for credit), a carpeted cargo floor with stowage well, hinged-cover console stowage, reclining front bucket seats, a 5.0-liter four-barrel V-8, a five-speed manual transmission, a front disc/rear drum braking system with audible front break pad wear sensors, a 1.3-in. front stabilizer bar, P215/65R-15 all-season steel-belted radial-ply black sidewall tires, a torque arm rear suspension, power steering and a tachometer.

CAMARO IROC-Z - SERIES 1F - V-8

The most appealing model-option for real Camaro connoisseurs was the new IROC-Z. This car was styled along the lines of the racing models that performed in the International Race of Champions. The IROC-Z was packaged as a Z28 option. In appearance, it could be spotted by twin fog lamps inset in the grille opening (alongside the license plate mount), a low front air dam, ornamental hood louvers and striping at rocker panel level. IROC-Zs had a solid angled front panel between deeply recessed quad head-

lamps, with parking lamps just below the crease line. Deep body-color "ground effects" skirting encircled the entire car. Special 16 x 8-in. aluminum wheels held Corvette-inspired P245-/50VR16 Goodyear Eagle GT unidirectional tires. Near the base of each door were large "IROC-Z" decals. The IROC-Z chassis featured Delco-Bilstein rear shock absorbers, special struts and springs, special rear stabilizer, and reinforced front frame rails. The IROC-Z could have any of three 305-cid (5.0-liter) V-8s. The standard engine had a four-barrel carburetor and five-speed manual gearbox (a four-speed overdrive automatic was available). The other choices were a High Output L69 carbureted V-8 with a five-speed transmission or the new LB9 Tuned Port Injection (TPI) version. The TPI came only with a four-speed automatic transmission. Individually tuned runners channeled incoming air to each cylinder in the TPI V-8, while computer-controlled port injectors delivered precisely

THE IROC-Z WAS THE MUSCLE CAR OF THE CAMARO LINE, AND COULD BE HAD WITH THREE DIFFERENT 305-CID ENGINES.

Chuck Dunlap photo

AN ALL-ORIGINAL 1985 Z/28 WITH T-TOPS AND A FIVE-SPEED LIKE THIS ONE IS A GOOD BET TO BECOME A HIT WITH COLLECTORS.

metered fuel. In limited-production IROC-Z dress, the factory claimed a 0 to 60-mph time in the 7-sec. bracket and 15-sec. quarter-mile acceleration times. Included as standard equipment on the IROC-Z were dual sport mirrors (left-hand remote-control mirror and right-hand manual-adjustable mirror), new extended Z28-type "ground-effects" rocker panels, a larger front air dam, fog lamps, a leather-wrapped steering wheel, a rear deck lid spoiler, an AM radio (could be deleted for credit), a carpeted cargo floor with stowage well, hinged-cover console stowage, reclining front bucket seats, a five-speed manual transmission, a front disc/rear drum braking system with audible front break pad wear sensors, P245/50VR-16 unidirectional high-performance tires (that had been pioneered on the Corvette), 16-in. aluminum wheels, quick-response power steering with 2.5 turns lock to lock and high-effort valving, a modified MacPherson-strut front suspension with increased camber for optimal response,

specific strut valving to provide excellent wheel control, a mass-efficient rear suspension with two short control arms and Bilstein gas shocks, a larger-diameter stabilizer bar, power front disc/rear drum brakes and a tachometer.

HISTORICAL FOOTNOTES

General introduction was Oct. 2, 1984, but the Camaro debuted on Nov. 8. During 1985, Chevrolet capitalized on its involvement with the International Race of Champions by creating the IROC-Z model-option for the Camaro Z28. Model-year sales fell slightly from 207,285 in 1984 to 206,082 in 1985. Calendar-year sales also wound up slightly down at 199,985, or 7.8 percent of the industry total. Model-year production of 180,018 Camaros represented a 2.30 percent share of the industry's total. . A total of 200,091 new Camaros were registered in the U.S. during calendar year 1985. That was up from 198,624 in 1984.

Jerry Heasley photo

THE IROC-Z HAD DISTINCTIVE TWIN FOG LAMPS INSET INTO THE GRILLE OPENING, A LOW FRONT AIR DAM, ORNAMENTAL HOOD LOUVERS AND STRIPING AT THE ROCKER PANEL LEVEL.

1986

Base Camaros could be optioned to look like Z28s this year. When ordered with either the 2.8-liter V-6 or 5.0-liter V-8 they came with a sport suspension, P215/65R15 tires, 15 x 7-in. styled steel wheels and a sport-tone exhaust system. Even four-cylinder Camaros got the sport suspension and 14-in. styled wheels. All Camaros got an air conditioning cutout switch, for use when full power was needed, and an up-shift indicator was added to stick shift models. The rear hatch got a new automatic pull-down latch. Also new was a soft-feel leather steering wheel, shift lever and parking brake lever. Body side moldings now came in eight colors (or black on Sport Coupes).

The IROC-Z and Z28 were virtually un-changed except for new colors. The base coupe included black lower body accents, black wind-shield and drip moldings and color-keyed bum-pers. Berlinettas added an electronic-tuning AM/FM stereo with a digital clock, dual horns, electronic instrumentation, a roof console, full wheel covers and a tachometer.

This was the last time that Camaro pro-duction totals approached the 200,000 level, although they fell short of that goal by nearly 8,000. The figures included 99,608 Sport Coupes, 4,479 Berlinettas, 88,132 Z28s and 49,585 IROC-Zs.

CAMARO SPORT COUPE - SERIES F/P - FOUR/V-6/V-8

The 1986 Camaro Sport Coupe was identi-fied by a new black accent band on the taillights and the use of Chevrolet lettering in place of the Camaro name on the rear fascia. It also gained the F41 sports suspension, P215/656-15 black sidewall steel-belted radial tires with raised white letters, 15 x 7-in. Rally wheels, wheel

Jerry Heasley photo

THE 1986 CAMARO SPORT COUPE RECEIVED A NEW SUSPENSION AND RALLY WHEELS.

trim rings, black sport style outside rearview mirrors, black-out rocker panels, black-out-style fascias, special striping and a "sport tone" exhaust system. The standard interior used in the Sport Coupe featured new solid-tone trim materials and design. Wet-arm windshield wipers were made standard equipment on all Camaros. A new automatic closure feature was adopted for the rear hatch. At the rear, a new center high-mounted stoplight was seen. Black body side moldings were used on the Sport Coupe and all Camaros now had basecoat/clearcoat finish. Standard equipment included a hinged-cover front stowage console, reclining front bucket seats, front disc brake audible wear sensors, a 1.1-in. diameter front stabilizer bar, a power front disc/rear drum braking system, power steering and a torque arm rear suspension. Historical sources indicate that the RPO LQ9 2.5-liter inline four-cylinder engine with electronic fuel injection (EFI) and a five-speed manual transmission was listed as the standard drive train for 1986 Camaros, although produc-

tion totals seem to indicate that no four-cylinder cars were built.

CAMARO BERLINETTA - SERIES 1F/S - V-6

The Berlinetta added a few items to the standard equipment list such as an electronic-tuning AM/FM stereo radio with a digital clock, dual horns, electronic instruments, a locking rear storage cover, dome and map lights, color-keyed sport mirrors (left-hand remote controlled), intermittent windshield wipers, a roof console, full wheel covers and a tachometer. It also featured body-color belt moldings in any of eight colors or black, color-keyed lower accent paint with striping and custom cloth reclining front bucket seats. It lacked rocker panel moldings or a rear stabilizer bar. Other standard equipment for the Berlinetta included a 2.8-liter Multiport Fuel-Injected V-6, a five-speed manual transmission, a front disc/rear drum brake system with audible front wear sensors, P205/70R-14 all-season steel-belted radial-ply black sidewall

THE Z28 (ABOVE) AND IROC-Z MODELS CONTINUED TO BE POPULAR FOR 1986, WITH A COMBINED 88,132 Z-CARS BEING PRODUCED.

tires, power steering and a torque-arm rear suspension.

CAMARO Z28 - SERIES 1F - V-8

The solid-tone interior introduced on the 1986 Camaro Sport Coupe was also new on the Z28, which was technically an option package for the base Camaro. It also offered body side moldings in eight colors and black. Standard equipment included were dual Sport mirrors (left-hand remote control and right-hand manual), a front air dam and "ground effects" rocker moldings, a rear deck lid spoiler, a silver- or gold-accented lower body with striping, an AM radio (could be deleted for credit), a carpeted cargo floor with stowage well, hinged-cover console stowage, reclining front bucket seats, a 5.0-liter four-barrel V-8, a five-speed manual transmission, a front disc/rear drum braking system with audible front break pad wear sensors, a 1.3-in. front stabilizer bar, P215/65R-15 all-season steel-belted radial ply black sidewall tires, a torque arm rear suspension, power steering and a tachometer.

CAMARO IROC-Z - SERIES F/P - V-8

The IROC-Z was once again a Z28 option package. It featured twin fog lamps inset into the grille opening (alongside the license plate mount), a low front air dam, ornamental hood louvers and striping at rocker panel level. IROC-Z had a solid angled front panel between deeply recessed quad headlamps, with parking lamps just below the crease line. Deep body-color "ground effects" skirting encircled the entire car. Special 16 x 8-in. aluminum wheels held Corvette-inspired P245-/50VR16 Goodyear Eagle GT unidirectional tires. Near the base of each door were large "IROC-Z" decals. The IROC-Z chassis featured Delco-Bilstein rear shock absorbers, special struts and springs, special rear stabilizer and reinforced front frame rails. The IROC-Z could have any of three 305-cid (5.0-liter) V-8s: a standard four-barrel with five-speed manual gearbox (four-speed overdrive automatic available), an optional High Output L69 carbureted V-8 with five-speed or the new LB9 Tuned Port Injected (TPI) version. The TPI V-8 came only with four-speed automatic transmission. Individually tuned runners channeled incoming air to each cylinder in the TPI V-8, while computer-controlled port injectors delivered precisely metered fuel. In limited-production IROC-Z dress, the factory claimed a 0 to 60-mph time in the 7-sec. neighborhood and 15-

sec. quarter-mile acceleration times. Standard equipment included new extended Z28-type ground-effects rocker panels, a larger front air dam, fog lamps, special IROC-Z badges inside and out, hood louvers, a leather-wrapped steering wheel, a rear deck lid spoiler, an AM radio (could be deleted for credit), a carpeted cargo floor with stowage well, hinged-cover console stowage, reclining front bucket seats, a five-speed manual transmission, a front disc/rear drum braking system with audible front break pad wear sensors, P245/50VR-16 unidirectional high-performance tires (that had been pioneered on the Corvette), 16-in. aluminum wheels, quick-response power steering with 2.5 turns lock to lock and high-effort valving, a modified MacPherson strut front suspension with increased camber for optimal response, specific strut valving to provide excellent wheel control, a mass-efficient rear suspension with two short control arms and Bilstein gas shocks, a larger-diameter stabilizer bar, power front disc/rear drum brakes and a tachometer.

HISTORY

In 1986, Chevrolet claimed to have America's fastest car (Corvette), most popular car (Cavalier), most popular mid- and full-sized cars (Celebrity and Caprice) and favorite sporty 2 + 2 (Camaro). Low-interest loans (7.7 percent) were offered by GM late in the 1985 model year and 8.8 percent rates arrived for 1986. One Illinois dealer opened experimental operations in a shopping mall in an attempt to lure buyers who might otherwise be missed. A Women's Marketing Committee was formed to develop approaches to attract female buyers, whose role in auto purchasing was gaining steadily by the mid-1980s. Among other innovations was a pre-approved credit plan for women customers through the General Motors Acceptance Corporation. Dealers also held "Car Care Clinics" for women. Model-year sales fell 206,082 in 1985 to 173,674. Calendar-year sales also wound up lower at 163,204, or 6.7 percent of the industry total. Model-year production of 192,219 Camaros represented a 2.43 percent share of the industry's total.

Jerry Heasley photo

THE Z28 FEATURED A REAR DECK LID SPOILER, GROUND EFFECTS ROCKER PANELS, AND LOWER BODY STRIPING.

Scott Moyer photo

THIS 1987 IROC-Z CAME FULLY LOADED WITH LEATHER, AUTOMATIC TRANSMISSION, FOUR-WHEEL DISC BRAKES, POSITRACTION AND A 5.7-LITER V-8.

1987

Camaro coupes changed little in appearance in 1987, but got new wet-arm windshield wipers and a federally required center high-mount stoplight mounted on the rear deck lid spoiler. The biggest news for ragtop fans was the return of a convertible to the lineup. It was built by the Automobile Specialty Co. and didn't appear in the sales catalog because it was introduced very late. However, it was available through dealers on a limited-orders basis.

The arrival of a 5.7-liter (350-cid) V-8 with roller lifters as an option for the IROC-Z was another of this year's exciting changes. Both the four-cylinder engine and the 5.0-liter H.O. V-8 were dropped. Consequently, the 2.8-liter Generation II V-6 became the base power plant.

A new LT model-option replaced the Berlinetta which, ironically, had come into the world as a replacement for the Type LT. A 5.0-liter

165-hp four-barrel V-8 was optional in the Sport Coupe and the LT and standard under the Z28's hood. The Z28 could also be ordered with a 5.0-liter 215-hp TPI V-8.

All 1987 Camaros (except the IROC-Z with the 5.7 liter V-8) could be had with either a five-speed manual gearbox or four-speed overdrive automatic transmission. The big-engined IROC-Z came only with the automatic transmission.

CAMARO SPORT COUPE - SERIES F/P - V-6/V-8

Camaro Sport Coupes could have either a five-speed manual gearbox or four-speed overdrive automatic transmission. Otherwise, Camaros changed little in appearance, aside from the arrival of a convertible. A leather seat option was also available for the first time in years. A Delco-Bose music system was available as a

THE CAMARO
LINEUP FOR
1987 (FROM
LEFT):
THE IROC-Z,
THE LT, THE
SPORT COUPE
AND THE Z28.

premium sound option. All V-8 engines were equipped with friction-reducing roller hydraulic lifters. Standard equipment included the V-6 engine, quad rectangular headlights, black windshield reveal moldings, black concealed windshield wipers, 15 x 7-in. styled steel Rally wheels with trim rings, P215/65R-15 black sidewall steel-belted Eagle GT radial tires, dual black sport mirrors (left-hand remote control), special accent tape stripes, chip-resistant gray or black lower body accent finish, an automatic hatch power pull-down latch, vinyl reclining bucket seats, amber parking light lenses, power steering, power front disc/rear drum brakes,a power ventilation system, the F41 sport suspension and a torque arm rear suspension.

CAMARO LT - SERIES F/P - V-6

A new LT model (actually a set of option packages) replaced the former Berlinetta. A 165-hp carbureted 5.0-liter V-8 was optional in the LT. The V-6 was standard.LT's had specific upper and lower body striping, specific lower accent paint and LT badges on the roof sail panels. A handling suspension was included.

CAMARO Z28 - SERIES 1F - V-8

The 5.0-liter 165-hp four-barrel V-8 that was optional in the Camaro Sport Coupe and Camaro LT was standard under the hood of the Z28. The Z28 could also be ordered with

a TPI version of that V-8 that delivered 215 hp. Standard equipment also included 15 x 7-in. aluminum wheels in Silver, Gold or Charcoal, P215/65R-15 white-outline-lettered steel-belted Eagle GT radial tires, specific wide-accent body striping, an accent color (Silver, Charcoal or Gold) on the lower body, a rear hatch lid spoiler with integral high-mounted stoplight, a front wraparound air dam, ground effects body extensions (on the rocker panels, fenders, doors and quarter panels), simulated hood louvers, a unique front fascia and black grille, dual black sport mirrors (left-hand remote control), side window defoggers, Computer Command Control, a five-speed manual transmission, front disc brake audible wear sensors, a power ventilation system, the F41 sport suspension and a torque arm rear suspension.

CAMARO IROC-Z - SERIES F/P - V-8

Biggest news for Camaro performance fans in 1987 was the arrival of the 350-cid (5.7-liter) V-8 with roller lifters as an option for the IROC-Z. It came only with automatic transmission. Otherwise, Camaros changed little in appearance apart from new wet-arm wipers and the mounting of the required center high-mount stop lamp on the rear spoiler (if a rear spoiler was installed). Standard equipment included 16 x 8-in. aluminum wheels in Argent Silver or Gold, P245/50VR-16 black-letter steel-belted radial tires, specific body striping and color-

THE IROC-Z CONVERTIBLE WAS THE CROWN JEWEL OF THE 1987 CAMARO LINEUP.

coordinated IROC-Z door decals, an accent color (Silver, Charcoal or Gold) on the lower body, a rear hatch lid spoiler with integral high-mounted stoplight, a front wraparound air dam, ground effects body extensions (on the rocker panels, fenders, doors and quarter panels), simulated hood louvers, a unique front fascia, a black grille with Gold or Silver Camaro lettering on it, dual body-color sport mirrors (left-hand remote control), a visor vanity mirror, an automatic hatch power pull-down latch, vinyl reclining bucket seats, special instrumentation with a tachometer, a leather-wrapped steering wheel, amber parking light lenses, power steering, power front disc/rear drum brakes, a headlamp-on warning, an AM radio with clock, basecoat/clearcoat finish, an inside hood re-lease, black or gray finish on headlight openings, a carpeted cargo floor, a deep-well luggage area, a console with hinged-cover storage area, side window defoggers, Computer Command Control, the five-speed manual transmission, front disc brake audible wear sensors, a power ventilation system, a special performance and ride suspension and a torque arm rear suspension.

HISTORY

Model-year sales fell from 173,674 in 1986 to 122,761 in 1987. Calendar year sales also wound up lower at 117,324 or 4.9 percent of the industry total. Model-year production of 137,760 Camaros represented a 1.87 percent share of the industry's total.

THIS Z28 CAME DECKED OUT IN BLACK WITH SILVER.
CHARCOAL AND GOLD WERE THE OTHER TWO ACCENT COLORS FOR 1987.

Paul Plasek photo

THE IROC-Z CONVERTIBLE WENT FOR ABOUT $18,000 IN 1988.

1988

Chevy offered only the base Sport Coupe and the IROC-Z in its 1988 Camaro line. With the demise of the Z28, the base model came with a rear spoiler, aluminum wheels, lower body side panels, and body-color mirrors. It had a standard 2.8-liter 125-hp V-6. The optional 5.0-liter V-8 was standard in the IROC-Z. It now had throttle-body fuel injection and five more horsepower. Two MFI V-8 options were offered for the IROC-Z. They were a 5.0-liter H.O. (which put out 220 hp with a five-speed manual gearbox and 195 hp with automatic transmission) and a 5.7-liter 230-hp edition that came only with four-speed automatic.

Barely 1,000 Camaro convertibles had been produced during the 1987 model year, but the numbers rose to 5,620 in 1988 when the revived body style had its first full-year run.

CAMARO SPORT COUPE - SERIES F/P V-6/V-8

Standard equipment included a 2.8-liter V-6 engine with multiport fuel injection, an AM/FM stereo (with seek-and-scan, a digital clock and an extended-range sound system), basecoat/clearcoat paint, a black windshield molding, black concealed windshield wipers, body tape striping, a carpeted cargo floor, cloth reclining bucket seats, Computer Command Control, a deep-well luggage area, dual color-keyed sport style outside rearview mirrors (left-hand remote and right-hand manual), 15 x 7-in. aluminum wheels in silver or gold, a five-speed manual transmission, a front air dam, ground-effects type rocker panel moldings, front disc brakes with audible wear sensors, hinged cover console stowage, improved corrosion protection including the use of pre-coated steel, power front disc/rear drum brakes, power steering, a power ven-

Jerry Heasley photo

THE CAMARO LINE INCLUDED ONLY THE IROC-Z (LEFT) AND SPORT COUPE FOR 1988.

tilation system, P215/65R-15 steel-belted radial ply tires, a rear deck lid spoiler, a rear hatch with automatic pull-down, side window defoggers, special instrumentation with a tachometer, a Sport suspension, a vinyl-coated shift knob and a vinyl-wrapped steering wheel.

CAMARO IROC-Z - SERIES F/P - V-8

Most noticeable of the Camaro changes this year may have been the absence of a Z28. The IROC-Z was still offered, but was still technically an option for the base Camaro as both were

coded with the F/P designation for car line and series. However, the IROC-Z was promoted as a separate model line in the 1988 Camaro sales catalog. A new 5.0-liter V-8 was standard on the IROC-Z. It had throttle body injection and gained five horsepower over the base 1987 V-8. Two Multiport Fuel Injected V-8 options were also offered for the IROC-Z. The first was a 5.0-liter H.O. V-8 rated at 220 hp with a five-speed manual shift and 195 hp with automatic transmission. The second was the new RPO B2L engine. This was a 350-cid (5.7-liter) TPI V-8 that came only with the four-speed automatic trans-

THE BASE CAMARO CAME AS BOTH A SPORT COUPE AND CONVERTIBLE, AND HAD A CHOICE OF V-6 AND 305-CID V-8 ENGINES.

Daniel B. Lyons photo

THIS IROC-Z T-TOP COUPE CAME IN MEDIUM GRAY METALLIC.

mission. The 5,620 Camaro convertibles made in 1988 included 3,761 IROC-Z ragtops.

Standard equipment included the 5.0-liter V-8 with electronic fuel injection, an AM/FM stereo (with seek-and-scan, a digital clock and an extended-range sound system), basecoat/clearcoat paint, a black windshield molding, black concealed windshield wipers, black-painted headlight openings, body tape striping, black simulated hood louvers, a carpeted cargo floor, cloth reclining bucket seats, Computer Command Control, a deep-well luggage area, dual color-keyed Sport-style outside rearview mirrors (left-hand remote and right-hand manual), a visor-vanity mirror, 15 x 7-in aluminum wheels in silver or gold, a five-speed manual transmission, a front air dam, body-color ground effects panels, specific body striping and color-coordinated IROC-Z door decals. The convertible also had a manually operated cloth top and a flush-fitting fiberglass top boot.

HISTORICAL FOOTNOTES

Robert D. Burger continued as Chevrolet's general manager during 1988. Model-year sales fell from 122,761 in 1987 to 93,617 in 1988. Calendar-year sales were 101,665 units or 3.7 percent of the industry total. Model year production of 96,275 Camaros represented a 1.38 percent share of the industry's total. The Van Nuys, California, plant built all of these cars (and all 62,467 Firebirds made in model year 1988). Of the Camaros built, 80.2 percent had automatic transmission, 19.8 percent had a five-speed manual transmission, 55.5 percent had a fuel-injected V-8, 44.5 percent had a fuel-injected V-6, 100 percent had power steering, 86.1 percent had power front disc brakes, 13.9 percent had power four-wheel disc brakes and 29.5 percent had a limited-slip differential, A total of 99,052 new Camaros were registered in the U.S. during calendar year 1988. That was down from 117,060 in 1987.

Jerry Heasley photo

CAMARO BUYERS COULD PICK BETWEEN THE RS (ABOVE) AND IROC-Z IN 1989.

1989

Two versions of the rear-drive Camaro were available again this year and the less-expensive version was now called the RS. Like the IROC-Z, it came in hatchback coupe or convertible forms. Both models added a PASS-Key theft-deterrent system as standard equipment since the Camaro ranked as the most popular vehicle among car thieves. The RS coupe with a standard 2.8-liter V-6 engine debuted first in California and was designed to lower skyrocketing insurance costs there.

Both IROC-Z models and the RS ragtop had a standard 170-hp V-8. IROC-Z buyers could add the 220-hp 5.0-liter V-8 or the big 5.7-liter V-8 with 230 hp. Chevy built 110,580 Camaros and more than 7,000 had folding tops.

CAMARO RS - SERIES F/P - V-6/V-8

The RS hatchback coupe actually debuted first, in California, as a model intended to keep insurance down. Its standard engine was the 2.8-liter V-6 engine. However, a 170-hp V-8 was standard in the RS convertible. Standard equipment included a PASS-Key vehicle anti-theft (VATS) system, a 2.8-liter V-6 engine with Multiport Fuel Injection, an AM/FM stereo (with seek-and-scan, a digital clock and an extended-range sound system), basecoat/clearcoat paint, a black windshield molding, black concealed windshield wipers, a carpeted cargo floor, cloth reclining bucket seats, dual color-keyed sport style outside rearview mirrors (left-hand remote and right-hand manual), 15 x 7-in. cast-aluminum wheels, a five-speed manual transmission, a front air dam, ground-effects type rocker panel moldings, power front disc brakes with audible wear sensors, power rear drum brakes, power steering, a power ventilation system, P215/65R-15 steel-belted radial-ply touring tires, a rear deck lid spoiler, a rear hatch with automatic pull-down, side window defoggers, special instrumentation with a ta-

Camaro and Firebird: GM's Power Twins – **71**

**CHEVY PRODUCED MORE THAN 83,000 RS CAMAROS IN 1989,
BUT ONLY 3,245 OF THEM WERE CONVERTIBLES.**

chometer and a Sport suspension.

CAMARO IROC-Z - SERIES F/P - V-8

The IROC-Z was back for 1989 and came in hatchback coupe or convertible models, both with the PASS-Key theft-deterrent system as standard equipment. The base engine was the 170-hp V-8. The IROC-Z also had a choice of 220-hp 5.0-liter TPI V-8 or the big 5.7-liter TPI V-8 with 240 hp. Standard equipment included a 5.0-liter V-8 engine with electronic fuel injection, an AM/FM stereo (with seek-and-scan, a digital clock and an extended-range sound system), 15 x 7-in. cast-aluminum wheels, a five-speed manual transmission, a leather-wrapped gearshift knob, specific body striping, color-coordinated IROC-Z door decals, special instrumentation with a tachometer, a front air dam, ground-effects type rocker panel moldings, power front disc brakes with audible wear sensors, power rear drum brakes, power steering, a power ventilation system, P215/65R-15 steel-belted radial-ply touring tires, a rear deck lid spoiler, a rear hatch with automatic pull-down, side window defoggers, a special performance ride and handling suspension, a visor-vanity mirror and specific taillights.

HISTORICAL FOOTNOTES

Sales of Camaros rose from 93,617 in 1988 to 110,034 in 1989. Calendar-year sales were 95,469 units or 3.7 percent of the industry total for the specialty model segment. Model-year production of 110,739 Camaros represented a slightly higher 1.55 percent share of the industry's total than the previous year. The Van Nuys plant built all of these cars (and all 64,406 Firebirds). Of the Camaros built, 79.9 percent had automatic transmission, 20.1 percent had a five-speed manual transmission, 61.5 percent had a fuel-injected V-8, 38.5 percent had a fuel-injected V-6, 100 percent had power steering, 88.4 percent had power front disc brakes, 11.6 percent had power four-wheel disc brakes, 27.9 percent had a limited-slip differential, 100 percent had steel-belted radial tires, 89.7 percent had power door locks, 55.7 percent had power windows, 100 percent had reclining bucket seats, 17.8 percent had a power front driver's seat, 89.9 percent had tilt steering, 99.8 percent had tinted glass, 94.5 percent had manual air conditioning, 58.9 percent had cruise control, and 4.1 percent had a Bose/JBL sound system.

THE 1990 IROC-Z COUPE HAD A BASE PRICE OF $14,145.

1990

With face-lifted '91 Camaros due to arrive in the spring, the 1990 model year was abbreviated and only 35,048 were built. The Camaro RS got a larger 3.1-liter (190-cid) base V-6. All Camaros now incorporated a driver's side airbag. A five-speed manual gearbox remained standard, but Camaros with the optional four-speed overdrive automatic got a modified torque converter with higher lockup points for improved gas mileage.

New standard equipment included halogen headlamps, tinted glass, intermittent wipers and a tilt steering wheel. New 16-in. alloy wheels became standard on the IROC-Z convertible and optional on the coupe. IROC-Z models also had a standard limited-slip differential. Leather upholstery was on the interior options list, while the instrument panel switched to new yellow graphics.

CAMARO RS - SERIES F/P - V-6/V-8

Standard equipment included a PASS-Key vehicle anti-theft system (VATS), a 3.1-liter V-6 engine with Multiport Fuel Injection, an AM/FM stereo (with seek-and-scan, a digital clock and an extended-range sound system), basecoat/clearcoat paint, a black windshield molding, black concealed windshield wipers, body tape striping, a carpeted cargo floor, cloth reclining bucket seats, dual color-keyed sport style outside rearview mirrors (left-hand remote and right-hand manual), 15 x 7-in. cast-aluminum wheels, a front air dam, ground-effects type rocker panel moldings, power front disc brakes with audible wear sensors, power rear drum brakes, power steering, a power ventilation system, P215/65R-15 steel-belted radial-ply touring tires, a rear deck lid spoiler, a rear hatch with automatic pull-down, side window defoggers, special instrumentation with a tachometer and a sport suspension. The 5.0-liter TPI V-8 engine was standard in the RS convertible and optional in the RS coupe.

CAMARO IROC-Z - SERIES F/P - V-8

The IROC-Z got the same new equipment as the Camaro RS including the available four-speed overdrive automatic transmission with a

*THE CAMARO RS RECEIVED A LARGER STANDARD V-6 ENGINE.
CHEVROLET SOLD MORE THAN 28,000 OF THE COUPES
IN AN ABBREVIATED PRODUCTION RUN.*

modified torque converter having higher lock-up points for improved gas mileage. New 16-in. alloy wheels became standard on the IROC-Z convertible and optional on the hatchback coupe. Also new for the IROC-Z was a standard limited-slip differential. Leather was on the interior options list, while the instrument panel (RS and IROC-Z) switched to new yellow graphics. Other standard IROC-Z equipment included a 5.0-liter V-6 engine with electronic fuel injection, an AM/FM stereo (with seek-and-scan, a digital clock and an extended-range sound system), basecoat/clearcoat paint, a black windshield molding, black concealed windshield wipers, body tape striping, a carpeted cargo floor, cloth reclining bucket seats, dual color-keyed sport style outside rearview mirrors (left-hand remote and right-hand manual), 15 x 7-in. cast-aluminum wheels, a five-speed manual transmission, a leather-wrapped gearshift knob, specific body striping, color-coordinated IROC-Z door decals, special instrumentation with a tachometer, a front air dam, ground-effects type rocker panel moldings, power front disc brakes with audible wear sensors, power rear drum brakes, power steering, a power ventilation system, P215/65R-15 steel-belted radial ply touring tires, a rear deck lid spoiler, a rear hatch with automatic pull-down, side window defoggers, a special performance ride and handling suspension, a visor-vanity mirror and specific taillights.

HISTORY

This was an unusual year, with production of 1990 models starting on Aug. 14, 1989, at the Van Nuys, California, factory and ending Dec. 22, 1989. Officially, no 1990 Camaros were actually built in 1990. However, 39 cars were produced in January 1990 before production of 1991 models officially started on Feb. 22, 1990. It is not clear if these cars were 1990 Camaros, 1991 Camaro pilot models or a combination of both. Calendar-year sales of Camaros totaled 77,599 units or 2.4 percent of the domestic total for the specialty model segment. Model-year sales were 78,654 units or 1.2 percent of the industry total. Model-year production totals available for 1990 from various sources reflect a wide variation. The actual number of 1990 Camaros built was around 35,000.

Jerry Heasley photo

THE MUSCULAR NEW 1991 Z28 REPLACED THE IROC-Z IN THE CAMARO LINEUP

1991

The 1991 Camaro lineup debuted in early 1990 and the IROC-Z was replaced by a new Z28. The Z28 and RS series each offered coupe and convertible models. New equipment included 16-in. wheels for the Z28 (optional on the RS), aero-styled rocker panels, a high-profile rear deck lid spoiler for the Z28 and a heavy-duty battery. There were two new exterior colors and the high-mounted stop lamp was relocated.

The RS coupe came standard with a 3.1-liter V-6. A 5.0-liter V-8 was base power plant in the RS convertible and both Z28 models. The 5.7-liter TPI V-8 was optional in Z28s. A five-speed manual transmission was standard, while a four-speed automatic was optional.

CAMARO RS - SERIES F/P - V-6/V-8

Standard equipment included a PASS-Key vehicle anti-theft system (VATS), a 3.1-liter V-6 engine with Multiport Fuel Injection, an AM/FM stereo (with seek-and-scan, a digital clock and an extended-range sound system), basecoat/clearcoat paint, a black windshield molding, black concealed windshield wipers, body tape striping, a carpeted cargo floor, cloth reclining bucket seats, dual color-keyed Sport-style outside rearview mirrors (left-hand remote and right-hand manual), 15 x 7-in. cast-aluminum wheels, a front air dam, ground-effects type rocker panel moldings, power front disc brakes with audible wear sensors, power rear drum brakes, power steering, a power ventilation system, P215/65R-15 steel-belted radial-ply touring tires, a rear deck lid spoiler, a rear hatch with automatic pull-down, side window defoggers, special instrumentation with a tachometer and a sport suspension.

Jerry Heasley photo

**THE RS CONVERTIBLE RETAINED A SPORTY EXTERIOR DESIGN AND
CAME WITH A STANDARD FIVE-SPEED MANUAL TRANSMISSION.**

CAMARO Z28 - SERIES F/P - V-8

Release of the 1991 Camaro marked the return of the Z28. Coupe and convertible models were offered. New equipment included 16-in. wheels for the Z28, aero-styled rocker panels, a high-profile rear spoiler, two new exterior colors, a heavy-duty battery and a relocated high-mounted stop lamp. The 5.0-liter V-8 was the base engine for the Z28 line. The Z28 could also be ordered with the 5.7-liter TPI V-8. Base transmission was the five-speed manual and a four-speed automatic was optional. Removable T-tops were also offered as optional equipment.

HISTORY

Jim C. Perkins was Chevrolet's general manager during 1991. Model-year sales were 51,974 units. Calendar year sales were 54,383 or 1.8 percent of the middle specialty car segment. Model-year production included 92,306 coupes and 8,532 convertibles for a total of 100,838 (excluding 1991 models introduced in the 1990 model year). The Van Nuys, California, plant built all of these cars (and all 50,247 Firebirds). Of the Camaros built, 84.6 percent had automatic transmission

Jerry Heasley photo

**THE Z28 RECEIVED A NEW SPOILER AND ROCKER PANELS,
NEW WHEELS AND TWO NEW EXTERIOR COLORS FOR 1991.**

THIS Z28 CONVERTIBLE WAS ONE OF 1,254 PRODUCED FOR 1992.

1992

Twenty-five years after the debut of the Camaro, Chevrolet marked the anniversary with a "Heritage Edition" package. Consisting primarily of bold hood and rear deck lid striping, it was available on RS and Z28 coupes and convertibles.

Engine and transmission options were basically the same as in 1991. Chevrolet built 66,191 Camaro coupes and 3,816 convertibles and as was the case for the past few years, all were made at the Van Nuys, California, factory.

CAMARO RS - SERIES F/P - V-6/V-8

All Camaros, even those without the Heritage Edition option, had a special "25th Anniversary" instrument panel badge. Both series featured coupe and convertible models. The base engine for the RS line was the 3.1-liter V-6. Other standard equipment included a PASS-Key vehicle anti-theft system (VATS), a 3.1-liter V-6 engine with Multiport Fuel Injection, an AM/FM stereo (with seek-and-scan, a digital clock and an extended-range sound system), basecoat/clearcoat paint, a black windshield molding, black concealed windshield wipers, body tape striping, a carpeted cargo floor, cloth reclining bucket seats, dual color-keyed sport style outside rearview mirrors (left-hand remote and right-hand manual), 15 x 7-in. cast-aluminum wheels, a front air dam, ground-effects type rocker panel moldings, power front disc brakes with audible wear sensors, power rear drum brakes, power steering, a power ventilation system, P215/65R-15 steel-belted radial-ply touring tires, a rear deck lid spoiler, a rear hatch with automatic pull-down, side window defoggers, special instrumentation with a tachometer and a sport suspension.

CAMARO Z28 - SERIES F/P - V-8

The Z28 coupe and convertible offered Black, Bright Red, Polo Green II, Dark Red, Quasar Blue, Arctic White, or Purple Haze

THE FLASHY "HERITAGE EDITION" PACKAGE WAS AVAILABLE AS A CONVERTIBLE OR COUPE AND COULD BE ORDERED ON BOTH THE RS AND Z28 MODELS.

Metallic exterior colors. The 5.0-liter TPI V-8 was the base engine for both the Z28 coupe and the Z28 convertible. Both body styles could also be ordered with the 5.7-liter TPI V-8. The base transmission was the five-speed manual. A four-speed automatic was standard in coupes with the 5.7-liter V-8 and otherwise optional. Removable T-tops were another popular option. Other standard equipment included a 5.0-liter V-8 engine with electronic fuel injection, an AM/FM stereo (with seek-and-scan, a digital clock and an extended-range sound system), basecoat/clearcoat paint, a black windshield molding, black concealed windshield wipers, body tape striping, a carpeted cargo floor, cloth reclining bucket seats, dual color-keyed sport style outside rearview mirrors (left-hand remote and right-hand manual), 16-in. cast-aluminum wheels, P235/55R-16 black-letter steel-belted radial tires, a five-speed manual transmission, a leather-wrapped gearshift knob, specific body striping, special instrumentation with a tachometer, a front air dam, ground-effects type rocker panel moldings, power front disc brakes with audible wear sensors, power rear drum brakes, power steering, a power ventilation system, a rear deck lid spoiler, a rear hatch with automatic pull-down, side window defoggers, a special performance ride and handling suspension, a visor vanity mirror and specific taillights.

CAMARO HERITAGE EDITION - F/P - V-8

The Camaro 25th Anniversary "Heritage Edition" option package was available for all models and body styles. While not truly a separate model, cars with the Heritage Edition package are of particular interest to Camaro collectors. In addition to the standard equipment for each model listed above, the Heritage Edition package added 25th Anniversary emblems, special hood stripes, special rear deck lid stripes, a specific body-color grille, black-finished headlight "pockets" and a body-color treatment on the 16-in. cast-aluminum wheels. The Heritage Edition package was coded as regular produc-

Sarah Werbelow photo

THE 1992 Z28 WAS OFFERED WITH TWO ENGINE CHOICES AND COULD BE ORDERED WITHOUT THE HOOD AND DECK LID STRIPES.

tion option ZO3 and carried a price of $175.

HISTORY

Chevrolet promoted the 1992 Camaro as "a veteran American muscle car on the street and at the racetrack." This turned out to be a fitting description when a Camaro marked its 50th win in Sports Car Club of America Trans-Am Series racing in May of 1992. That victory gave the Camaro the most first-place finishers for any single model in 26 years of Trans-Am competition. Model-year sales were 64,444 units. Calendar-year sales were 54,383.

Jerry Heasley photo

ARCTIC WHITE WAS ONE OF THE EXTERIOR COLORS OFFERED FOR THE 1992 Z28, WHICH ALSO SPORTED TELLTALE STRIPING.

THE FOURTH-GENERATION CAMARO WAS RESIGNED FOR 1993, MAKING IT LONGER AND WIDER THAN IN THE PAST. THERE WERE ONLY TWO OFFERINGS – THE SPORT COUPE (ABOVE) AND THE Z28.

1993

The fourth-generation Camaro was built in a new factory in Ste. Therese, Quebec, Canada, and was a totally new product from nose to tail. It was longer, taller and wider than its third-generation predecessor. Gone were the convertible and RS models, which left the base Sport Coupe and Z28 coupe.

Among the new Camaro's most striking and attractive appearance features were a windshield with a steep 68-degree slope, a low hood line, a smooth roofline and an integral spoiler with a built-in center high-mounted stop lamp. Just forward of the windshield there was a raised cowl panel designed to shield the windshield wipers and reduce turbulence.

Chevrolet made extensive use of dent-resistant, rustproof body panels in the fourth-generation Camaro. The roof, doors, hatchback panel and rear deck spoiler were made of sheet molded compound (SMC) made of chopped glass in a polyester resin. Reaction injection molded (RIM) panels were used in manufacturing the front fenders and front fascia. The rear fascia was polyurethane reinforced with Wollastokup. Rust-resistant two-side galvanized steel was used for the rear quarter and hood panels. A remote hatch release was optional.

Standard features included dual airbags, ABS, a wraparound instrument panel, a state-of-the-art sound system and GM's PASS-Key II theft-deterrent system. The base engine was a 3.4-liter V-6 mated to a five-speed manual transmission. The Z28 got the 5.7-liter LT1 Corvette V-8 fitted with a Borg-Warner T56 six-speed manual transmission. A four-speed automatic was optional in both cars. The '93 Camaro was the first GM car to feature R-134a air conditioning refrigerant.

Also new was a short-and-long arm front suspension. The base coupe had front disc/rear drum brakes, but four-wheel discs were standard on the Z28. A 1993 Camaro Z28 paced the Indy 500 and replicas of the pace car were built and sold to the public.

THE 1993 Z28 COUPE CAME WITH A BASE STICKER PRICE OF ABOUT $16,800.

CAMARO - SERIES 1F - V-6

Standard features included a serpentine belt accessory drive system, four-wheel antilock brakes, a brake/transmission interlock feature with automatic transmission, power front disc/rear drum brakes, 5-mph front and rear energy-absorbing bumpers with body-color fascias, side window defoggers, a stainless steel exhaust system, Solar-Ray tinted glass, miniquad halogen headlights, dual black-finished sport outside rearview mirrors (left-hand remote controlled, right-hand manual), a two-component clearcoat paint system, gas-charged monotube shock absorbers, integral front and rear spoilers, front and rear stabilizer bars, power rack-and-pinion steering, a Firm Ride & Handling suspension, a four-wheel coil spring suspension with computer-selected springs, a front short/long arm (SLA) suspension, the PASS-Key II theft deterrent system, a five-speed manual transmission and 16-in. steel wheels with plastic bolt-on wheel covers. A 3.4-liter SFI V-6 was the only engine available in the base Camaro.

CAMARO Z28 - SERIES 1F - V-8

The Z28 coupe received Corvette's 5.7-liter LT1 V-8 as its only engine. It came fitted with a Borg-Warner T56 six-speed manual transmission. The high-performance engine included platinum-tip spark plugs. Although this engine was basically the same as the Corvette LT1, the Camaro version had some distinctions. It featured two-bolt (instead of four-bolt) main bearing caps. The accessories were mounted on the right, while the Corvette had them on the left. The Camaro version lacked a shield covering the injector nozzles. The exhaust manifolds had rear outlets compared to center outlets on the Corvette version. The Camaro version's exhaust system had a single three-way catalyst, one stainless steel muffler and dual tailpipes. The valve covers were stamped steel rather than composite material. The Camaro's LT1 V-8 did not require synthetic oil like the Corvette type. The location of the A.I.R. pump was on the engine block rather than remote, as in the Corvette.

Scott Moyer photo

Z28 INDY PACE CAR REPLICAS WERE SOLD TO THE PUBLIC.
A TOTAL OF 633 WERE BUILT FOR 1993.

HISTORICAL FOOTNOTES

The Ste. Therese factory, which dated to 1965, was completely revamped to build General Motors' fourth-generation Camaros and Firebirds. The workers were formed into teams, with each department functioning independently, but with the overall goal of producing defect-free automobiles. The North American model-year production (U.S. and Canada) of 1993 Camaros was only 40,224 units due to the new model's late introduction in January.

THE Z28 COUPE HAD ONLY ONE ENGINE OPTION –
THE 5.7-LITER TPI V-8 BORROWED FROM THE CORVETTE.

Jerry Heasley photo

MORE THAN 40,000 NEW Z28S HIT THE STREETS IN 1994.

1994

A convertible returned to the Camaro lineup as a mid-season addition in 1994. Base and Z28 ragtops joined the coupes in both series. New standard features included a keyless entry system, "flood light" interior illumination and a compact disc system with new co-axial speakers. Leather seating surfaces in Grahite and Beige became available late in the production.

The Z28's 5.7-liter V-8 received sequential fuel injection for 1994 to provide a smoother idle and lower emissions. The T56 six-speed transmission utilized Computer-Aided Gear Selection to improve fuel economy. Production rose to 119,934 cars this year and included over 7,200 convertibles.

CAMARO - SERIES 1F - V-6

Coupes utilized the five-speed manual transmission as standard while the convertibles had the 4L60-E electronic four-speed automatic

transmission as base offering. Standard features included P215/60R16 black sidewall tires, a five-speed manual transmission and 16-in. steel bolt-on wheel covers,

CAMARO Z28 - SERIES 1F - V-8

The Z28s again used Corvette's 5.7-liter LT1 V-8 fitted to a Borg-Warner T56 six-speed manual transmission. The four-speed automatic was the optional transmission in Z28s. The Z28's 5.7-liter V-8 received sequential fuel injection for 1994 to provide a smoother idle and lower emissions. The T56 six-speed transmission utilized Computer Aided Gear Selection (CAGS) to improve fuel economy. Standard equipment included the PASS-Key II theft deterrent system, a compact high-pressure spare tire, P235/55R16 black sidewall tires, 16-in. cast-aluminum wheels, a gauge package with 115-mph speedometer and tachometer, a low coolant level indicator system, a low oil level indicator light, a dome light, a day/night inside rearview mirror with dual reading and courtesy lights, an ETR AM/FM stereo radio (with seek-and-scan, digital clock, stereo cassette tape, search-and-repeat and extended-range speakers), a headlamps-on reminder, a driver's four-way seat with manual adjuster, a rear seat with full-folding seatbacks, front reclining bucket seats with cloth trim and integral headrests, a tilt steering wheel, door panel storage compartments, dual covered visor-vanity mirrors and a check-gauges warning light. The convertible also featured a power-operated top that folded flush with the body, a three-piece hard tonneau cover, a full headliner and a heated glass backlight.

HISTORICAL FOOTNOTES

All 1994 Camaro coupes and convertibles were built at the refurbished factory in Ste. Therese, Quebec, Canada. Computer-aided gear selection (or CAGS) was added to the six-speed manual transmission in 1994. It improved fuel economy by directing the driver from first to fourth gear under light acceleration. Rapid acceleration automatically cancelled the 1-to-4 shift. A lamp lit up when the transmission was in "skip shift" mode. The Camaro's model-year sales were 124,121 units. Calendar-year sales were 116,592. The North American model-year production (U.S. and Canada) of 1994 Camaros was 125,244 units. Domestic model-year production (U.S. market only) was 119,799 units and included 112,539 coupes and 7,260 convertibles. The Ste. Therese plant built all of these cars (and all 45,922 Firebirds). Of the Camaros built, 74.9 percent had automatic transmission, 17.8 percent had a five-speed manual transmission, 7.3 percent had a six-speed manual transmission, 65.3 percent had a 3.4-liter SFI V-6 AND 34.7 percent had a 5.7-liter SFI V-8.

BOTH THE BASE CAMARO (ABOVE) AND Z28 WERE AVAILABLE AS CONVERTIBLES FOR 1994.

Jerry Heasley photo

IN 1995, Z28S AGAIN FEATURED THE LT1 V-8 ATTACHED TO A BORG-WARNER T56 SIX-SPEED MANUAL TRANSMISSION, WITH A FOUR-SPEED AUTOMATIC TRANSMISSION OPTIONAL.

1995

Camaro returned in 1995 with the same model lineup. New features included body-colored outside dual sport mirrors on base models, and an optional monochromatic roof treatment on Z28 coupes (and base coupes with T-tops) A speed-rated performance tires package with a 150-mph speedometer and an optional Acceleration Slip Regulation traction-control system was planned for 1995 Z28s, but didn't actually arrive until 1998.

The base coupe was powered by the 3.4-liter V-6 fitted to a five-speed manual transmission. The convertible used the 5.7-liter LT1 V-8 mated to an electronic four-speed automatic transmission. Z28s again featured the LT1 attached to a Borg-Warner T56 six-speed manual transmission, with a four-speed automatic transmission listed as optional equipment.

CAMARO - SERIES 1F - V-6

"Camaro is the American sports machine for people who love to drive and one turn behind the wheel is guaranteed to transform just about anybody into a Camaro enthusiast," stated the 1995 Camaro sales catalog. Camaro returned in 1995 with the same lineup. A coupe and a convertible were offered in both the base and Z28 series. New features included body-colored outside dual Sport mirrors on base models. The base coupe was powered by the 3.4-liter V-6 fitted to a five-speed manual transmission. A 3.8-liter V-6 teamed with an electronically controlled four-speed automatic transmission was a new option. Another new-for-1995 option was a monochromatic roof treatment on base coupes with T-tops. Standard equipment included halogen headlights, a rear deck lid spoiler, auxiliary lighting, carpeted front floor mats, a center console with storage compartment and cupholder, a deep-well luggage area, driver and front passenger-side airbags, an intermittent windshield wiper system, the PASS-Key II theft-deterrent system, Scotchguard protector on fabrics and carpets, cloth-trimmed reclining front bucket seats, special instrumentation with a tachometer, side window defoggers, a tilt adjustable steering wheel, an AM/FM stereo with cassette tape player and a 3.4-liter V-6 with sequential-port fuel injection and a five-speed manual transmission.

CAMARO Z28 - SERIES 1F - V-8

Z28s again featured the LT1 5.7-liter V-8 fitted to the Borg-Warner T56 six-speed manual transmission as standard equipment. The four-speed automatic was optional. New-for-1995 options included a monochromatic roof treatment on Z28 coupes. Also available on the Z28 were speed-rated performance tires (with a 150-mph speedometer). Standard equipment included halogen headlights, a rear deck lid spoiler,

auxiliary lighting, carpeted front floor mats, a center console with storage compartment and cup holder, a deep-well luggage area, driver and front passenger-side airbags, an intermittent windshield wiper system, the PASS-Key II theft-deterrent system, Scotchguard protector on fabrics and carpets, cloth-trimmed reclining front bucket seats, special instrumentation with a tachometer, side window defoggers, a tilt adjustable steering wheel, an AM/FM stereo with cassette tape player, the 5.7-liter V-8 with tuned-port-injection system, a six-speed manual transmission, power four-wheel disc ABS brakes, a limited-slip rear axle, a Delco Freedom II battery, power rack-and-pinion steering, rear-wheel drive, single serpentine belt engine accessory drive, a stainless steel exhaust system, a Performance Ride & Handling suspension, 16 x 8-in. cast-aluminum wheels and P235/55R-16 touring tires. The convertible also had a standard rear window defogger, a fully lined power-operated folding top and a form-fitting three-piece tonneau cover for a sleek top-down appearance.

Jerry Heasley photo

THE 1995 Z28S COUPE RECEIVED A NEW OPTIONAL MONOCHROMATIC ROOF TREATMENT.

Daniel B. Lyons photo

*THE 1995 Z28 CONVERTIBLE HAD A STANDARD REAR WINDOW DEFOGGER,
A FULLY LINED POWER-OPERATED FOLDING TOP
AND A FORM-FITTING THREE-PIECE TONNEAU COVER.*

HISTORICAL FOOTNOTES

Jim C. Perkins was the general manager of Chevrolet Motor Division as the 1995 model year began, but he was soon to be followed by John G. Middlebrook, who would hold the title by 1996. The Camaro's model-year sales were 98.806 units. Calendar-year sales were 97,525. Industry trade journals reported model-year production of 115,365 coupes and 7,360 convertibles for a total of 122,725 units. The Ste.

Therese, Quebec, plant built all of these cars (and all 50,986 Firebirds). Of the Camaros built, 77.8 percent had automatic transmission, 13.8 percent had a five-speed manual transmission, 8.4 percent had a six-speed manual transmission, 66.5 percent had a 3.4-liter SFI V-6, 0.4 percent had a 3.8-liter SFI V-6 and 33.1 percent had a 5.7-liter SFI V-8. A total of 98,938 new Camaros were registered in the U.S. during calendar year 1995.

THE BASE CAMARO COUPE CAME WITH TWO DIFFERENT V-6 ENGINES IN 1995.

Jerry Heasley photo

THE SS RETURNED TO THE CAMARO LINEUP FOR THE FIRST TIME IN 24 YEARS IN 1996. SLP ENGINEERING TEAMED UP WITH GM TO PRODUCE 2,410 CARS WITH THE SS PACKAGE, WHICH WAS OPTIONAL FOR THE Z28.

1996

In 1996, Camaro buyers had their choice of three Camaro coupes and three convertibles in base, RS or Z28 trim. They shared a new standard 3.8-liter Series II 3800 V-6 with base Camaros. A new V-6 Performance Handling package was offered for these cars and V-6 Camaros with automatic transmission got a new second gear select switch that allowed second gear starting for an improved "launch" on slippery surfaces. The base line featured a five-speed manual transmission as standard equipment. A four-speed automatic transmission was optional. T-tops were again available as optional equipment on coupes and an antitheft system was also available for all Camaro models.

To keep enthusiasts happy, an SS performance package for the Z28 was introduced at midyear. The first Camaro SS in 24 years was actually a team effort by Chevrolet Motor Division and SLP Engineering of Troy, Michigan. "SLP" originally stood for "Street Legal Performance" and this car was marketed through Chevy dealers for those who appreciated muscle cars.

CAMARO - SERIES 1F - V-6

Standard equipment included manual lap and shoulder safety belts, driver and front the PASS-Key II theft-deterrent system, Scotchguard protector on fabrics and carpets, cloth-trimmed reclining front bucket seats, special instrumentation with a tachometer, side window defoggers, a tilt adjustable steering wheel, an AM/FM stereo with cassette tape player, a 3.8-liter V-6 with sequential-port fuel injection, a five-speed manual transmission, power front disc/rear drum ABS brakes, a Delco Freedom II battery, power rack-and-pinion steering, rear-wheel drive, single serpentine belt engine accessory drive, a stainless steel exhaust system, a Firm Ride & Handling suspension, 16 x 7 1/2-in. wheels with bolt-on wheel covers and P215/60R-16 touring tires. The convertible also had a standard rear window defogger, a fully lined power-operated folding top, air conditioning, a full headliner, rear seat and trunk courtesy lamps, a glass rear window and a form-fitting three-piece hard boot with storage bag.

THE BRICKYARD 400 GOT THE Z28 AS A PACE CAR IN 1996.

CAMARO RS - SERIES 1F - V-6

The Camaro RS, with its "ground effects" lower body panels, was a new model for 1996. The standard power plant for RS models was the 3.8-liter V-6. The new V-6 Performance Handling package was offered for the RS, as was the new second gear select switch for V-6s with automatic transmissions. In addition to or in place of standard equipment on the base Camaro, the RS coupe and convertible featured the ground effects package, air conditioning, P235/55R16 tires and 16-in. aluminum wheels.

Jerry Heasley photo

THE Z28 HAD A STANDARD 5.7-LITER V-8 ATTACHED TO A SIX-SPEED MANUAL TRANSMISSION. IT ALSO FEATURED A HIGH-PERFORMANCE SUSPENSION, FOUR-WHEEL ABS, A LIMITED-SLIP REAR END AND 150-MPH SPEEDOMETER.

CAMARO Z28 - SERIES 1F - V-8

The Z28 again used the 5.7-liter V-8 as its standard engine. It came standard linked to a six-speed manual transmission. The four-speed automatic was optional. In addition to or in place of base Camaro equipment, the Z28 featured air conditioning, a limited-slip rear axle, four-wheel power ABS disc brakes, the 5.7-liter sequential fuel injected V-8, a low-coolant-level indicator, two way manual seat adjustment, platinum tip spark plugs, a special coupe roof treatment with black mirrors, a 150-mph speedometer. A Performance Ride & Handling suspension, P235/55R16 black sidewall radial tires, a high-pressure compact spare tire, a six-speed manual transmission and 16-in. aluminum wheels.

CAMARO SS - SERIES 1F - V-8

A Michigan company named SLP Engineering teamed up with General Motors to issue an all-new Camaro SS model in 1996. SLP (which originally stood for Street Legal Performance) was founded by ex-drag racer Ed Hamburger and began specializing in modifying Pontiac Firebirds in the 1970s. SLP worked hand in hand with both Pontiac and Chevrolet to create super-high-performance versions of both F-cars based on new Camaros and Firebirds. The modifications gave the 1996 Camaro SS extra horsepower and gave the car appearance, handling and braking upgrades to go along with the added power. The new Camaro SS was featured in 35 automotive publications during 1996 and appeared on the cover of 17 leading magazines. The base engine was a 305-hp LT1 V-8. An optional performance exhaust system added 5 hp. Other standard Camaro SS coupe content included an underhood forced-air induction system, a restyled rear deck lid spoiler, a restyled suspension on coupe and T-top models, B.F. Goodrich Comp T/A tires (size P275/40ZR17), 17 x 9-in. ZR-1 styled cast-aluminum alloy wheels,

Quaker State Synquest synthetic engine oil, exterior SS badges replacing Z28 logos and a Camaro SS interior plaque. Camaro SS convertibles retained the Camaro Z-28 suspension and had 16-in. B.F. Goodrich Comp T/A tires and 16 x 8-in. styled cast-aluminum wheels.

HISTORICAL FOOTNOTES

The Camaro's model-year sales were 75,336 units. Calendar-year sales were 66,866. Model-year production was 54,525 coupes and 6,837 convertibles for a total of 61,362 units. The Ste. Therese, Quebec, plant built all of these cars (and all 30,937 Firebirds). Of the Camaros built, 71.7 percent had automatic transmission, 16.4 percent had a five-speed manual transmission, 11.1 percent had a six-speed manual transmission, 70.5 percent had a 3.8-liter SFI V-6, 29.5 percent had a 5.7-liter MFI V-8, 11.3 percent had traction control, 100 percent had power steering, 100 percent had ABS brakes, 26 percent had a limited-slip differential, 100 percent had steel-belted radial tires, 76.8 percent had power door locks, 70.9 percent had power windows, 100 percent had reclining bucket seats, 46.4 percent had a power seats, 27.4 percent had leather seats, 100 percent had dual front airbags, 100 percent had tilt steering, 100 percent had tinted glass, 99.2 percent had manual air conditioning, 95.7 percent had cruise control, 100 percent had delay windshield wipers, 42.8 percent had a ETR stereo cassette player, 15.9 percent had a Bose/JBL sound system, 34.1 percent had a Bose/JBL sound system with CD, 7.2 percent had another brand CD, 65.4 percent had an electric rear window defogger, 29.2 percent had a manual remote-control left-hand outside rearview mirror, 70.8 percent had power rearview mirrors, 27.8 percent had a power right-hand rearview mirror, 88.1 percent had aluminum styled wheels, 70.5 percent had remote keyless entry and 43.8 percent had T-tops. A total of 68,106 new Camaros were registered in the U.S. during calendar year 1996.

**THE 1997 RS CAME WITH A GROUND EFFECTS PACKAGE,
AIR CONDITIONING AND ALUMINUM WHEELS.**

1997

The Camaro observed its 30th anniversary in 1997 and Chevrolet marked the occasion by offering an orange-striped 30th Anniversary package for Z28s. Standard features on all Camaros now included automatic daytime running lamps, four-wheel ABS disc brakes, dual airbags, an electronically controlled AM/FM stereo with cassette player (and extended range speakers) and a reinforced steel safety cage with steel side-door beams and front and rear crush zones. The standard power plant of the base model was a 200-hp V-6.

The Camaro model lineup was unchanged, but there were numerous technical refinements. A new instrument panel and floor console featured built-in power outlets and cupholders, coupes got a new 200-watt sound system, taillamps were switched to an international tri-color design, new uplevel five-spoke wheels were introduced and automatic transmission became standard equipment in Z28s.

CAMARO - SERIES 1F - V-6

The Camaro lineup again was comprised of three coupes and three convertibles offered in base, RS or Z28 trim. Standard equipment included four-wheel disc ABS brakes, a brake/transmission shift interlock (with automatic transmission), basecoat/clearcoat paint, dual Sport mirrors (left-hand remote controlled), a front air dam, halogen headlights, a rear deck lid spoiler, auxiliary lighting, carpeted front floor mats, a center console with storage compartment and cupholder, a deep-well luggage area, driver and front passenger side airbags, an intermittent windshield wiper system, the PASS-Key II theft-deterrent system, Scotchguard protector on fabrics and carpets, cloth-trimmed reclining front bucket seats, special instrumentation with a tachometer, side window defoggers, a tilt adjustable steering wheel, an ETR AM/FM stereo with cassette tape player with extended-range speakers, a 3.8-liter V-6 with sequential port fuel injection, a five-speed manual transmission, power front disc/rear drum ABS brakes, a Delco Freedom II battery, power rack-and-pinion steering, rear-wheel drive, single serpentine belt engine accessory drive, a stainless steel exhaust system, a Firm Ride & Handling suspension, 16 x 7 1/2-in. wheels with bolt-on wheel covers, P215/60R-16 touring tires and a reinforced steel safety cage that included steel side-door beams and front and rear crush zones. The convertible also had a standard rear window defogger, a fully lined power-operated folding top, air conditioning, a full headliner, rear seat and trunk courtesy lamps, a glass rear window and a form-fitting three-piece hard boot with storage bag.

CAMARO RS - SERIES 1F - V-6

The power plant for Camaro RS models was the 3.8-liter V-6. In addition to or in place of standard equipment on the base Camaro, the RS coupe and convertible featured a ground effects package, air conditioning, P235/55R16 tires and 16-in. aluminum wheels.

CAMARO Z28 - SERIES 1F - V-8

The Camaro observed its 30th anniversary in 1997 and Chevrolet marked the occasion by offering a 30th Anniversary Package for the Z28. The package consisted of a paint scheme that used Arctic White with Hugger Orange stripes that was reminiscent of the package on the Camaro that paced the 1969 Indianapolis 500. Also part of the package were door handles finished in white, white five-spoke aluminum wheels and a white front fascia intake. Seats in this anniversary Z28 were also Arctic White with cloth black-and-white houndstooth inserts. In addition, the floor mats and headrests had 30th Anniversary five-color embroidery. The Z28 again used the 5.7-liter V-8 as its standard engine. It came standard linked to a six-speed manual transmission. In addition to, or in place of base Camaro equipment, the Z28 featured air conditioning, a limited-slip rear axle, four-wheel power ABS disc brakes, the 5.7-liter SFI V-8, a low-coolant-level indicator, two-way manual seat adjustment, platinum tip spark plugs, a spe-

THE BASE CAMARO COUPE RECEIVED A FEW UPGRADES, LIKE DAYTIME RUNNING LAMPS AND FOUR-WHEEL ABS, AND CAME STANDARD WITH A 200-HP V-6.

**THE 1997 Z28 COUPE WAS LARGELY UNCHANGED FROM 1996,
BUT AUTOMATIC TRANSMISSION BECAME STANDARD EQUIPMENT.**

cial coupe roof treatment with black mirrors, a 150-mph speedometer, a Performance Ride & Handling suspension, P235/55R16 black sidewall radial tires, a high-pressure compact spare tire, a six-speed manual transmission and 16-in. aluminum wheels.

CAMARO SS - SERIES 1F - V-8

Chevrolet built Camaros and SLP Engineering, of Troy, Michigan, turned new Camaro coupes and convertibles into a Camaro SS. SLP offered a choice of two engines, beginning with a 305-hp version of the LT1 V-8. This could be boosted to 310 hp with the addition of an optional performance exhaust system. Other standard Camaro SS coupe content included an underhood forced-air induction system, a restyled rear deck lid spoiler, a restyled suspension on coupe and T-top models, B.F. Goodrich Comp T/A tires (size P275/40ZR17), 17 x 9-in. ZR-1 styled cast-aluminum alloy wheels, Quaker State Synquest synthetic engine oil, exterior SS badges replacing Z28 logos and a Camaro SS interior plaque. Camaro SS convertibles retained the stock Camaro suspension and had 16-

in. B.F. Goodrich Comp T/A tires and 16 x 8-in. styled cast-aluminum wheels. The Camaro SS was offered in standard exterior colors of Artic White, Black, Bright Red and Polo Green. Sebring Silver Metallic finish was optional. All colors were available with Dark Gray or Medium Gray interiors. All but Sebring Silver cars could have a neutral color interior and all but Polo Green cars could have a red interior. Also available was a new special edition, low-volume "30th Anniversary SS" with Artic White finish, bold Hugger Orange dual stripes on the hood, roof, deck lid and rear spoiler, white SS wheels, exterior SS emblems, a commemorative dash plaque, two key fobs and a premium quality car cover with locking cable and tote bag. The 30th Anniversary SS option required Chevrolet options 1SJ, Z4C and AG1 on coupes and 1SM, Z4C and AG1 on convertibles. SLP Engineering projected that it would build a total of 3,000 Camaro Z28s with the SS package (coupes and convertibles combined) in 1997 and that 1,000 of them would receive the "30th Anniversary SS" option, but actual production fell short of these goals.

THE "30TH ANNIVERSARY" CAMAROS WERE WHITE-AND-ORANGE SS MODELS THAT WERE DESTINED TO BE COLLECTOR CARS.

HISTORICAL FOOTNOTES

The Camaro's model-year sales were 58,152 units. Calendar-year sales were 55,973. According to industry trade journals domestic model-year production was 48,292 coupes and 6,680 convertibles for a total of 54,972 units. The Ste. Therese, Quebec, plant built all of these cars (and all 30,754 Firebirds). Of the Camaros built, 71.5 percent had automatic transmission, 14.9 percent had a five-speed manual transmission, 13.6 percent had a six-speed manual transmission, 66 percent had a 3.8-liter SFI V-6, 34 percent had a 5.7-liter MFI V-8, 13.7 percent had traction control, 100 percent had power steering, 100 percent had ABS brakes, 27.4 percent had a limited-slip differential, 100 percent had steel-belted radial tires, 81.3 percent had power door locks, 78.8 percent had power windows, 100 percent had reclining bucket seats, 47.3 percent had a power seats, 22 percent had leather seats, 100 percent had dual front airbags, 100 percent had tilt steering, 100 percent had tinted glass, 99.2 percent had manual air conditioning, 93.4 percent had cruise control, 100 percent had delay windshield wipers, 30 percent had a ETR stereo cassette player, 15.9 percent had a name brand sound system, 3.8 percent had a name brand sound system with CD, 20.3 percent had another brand CD, 64 percent had an electric rear window defogger, 29.2 percent had a manual remote-control left-hand outside rearview mirror, 70.8 percent had power rearview mirrors, 27.8 percent had a power right-hand rearview mirror, 18 percent had chrome styled wheels, 82 percent had aluminum styled wheels, 76.6 percent had remote keyless entry and 43.3 percent had T-tops. A total of 55,437 new Camaros were registered in the U.S. during calendar year 1997.

Jerry Heasley photo

THE 1998 Z28 CONVERTIBLE CARRIED A PRICE TAG OF $27,975.

1998

The big news for 1998 was a restyled front end for all Camaros and a new Corvette-derived LS1 V-8 engine in SS and Z28 models. Chevy dropped both RS Camaros in 1998 and offered an optional Sport Appearance package instead. It was available for all Camaros except SS models. A factory-direct SS Performance/Appearance package replaced the previous limited-edition performance car made at SLP Engineering.

Exterior revisions included a redesigned hood, front fenders and front fascia, composite headlamps with reflector optics and optional fog lamps. A new four-wheel disc brake system was standard on all Camaros, as was a one-piece all-welded exhaust system.

The Z28 received a Gen III 5.7-liter 305-hp LS1 "Corvette" aluminum-block V-8. Base Camaros again featured the 3.8-liter V-6 and a five-speed manual transmission. The 4L60-E four-speed automatic was standard in Z28s and optional in base Camaros. Z28s offered an optional six-speed manual transmission.

CAMARO - SERIES 1F - V-6

New features for the first-rung F-car included four-wheel disc brakes, a standard PASS-Key II anti-theft system, the new front end styling, body-color door handles and new colors of Sport Gold and Navy Blue. Standard equipment for the base Camaro coupe included a 3.8-liter V-6, a five-speed overdrive manual gearbox, a battery with run-down protection, rear-wheel drive, a 3.23:1 rear axle ratio, a stainless steel exhaust system, a firm ride suspension, independent front suspension with an anti-roll bar, front coil springs, front shocks, a rear suspension with an anti-roll bar, rear coil springs, rear shocks, power rack-and-pinion steering, four-wheel disc ABS brakes, a 15.5-gal. fuel tank, a rear wing spoiler, body-color front and rear bumpers, and monotone body paint. The base convertible featured an electrically operated lined convertible top, automatic halogen sealed beam headlights, daytime running lamps, a center high-mounted stoplight, a manual remote control left-hand outside rearview mirror, 16 x 7.5-in. steel wheels,

THE Z28 FEATURED A VERSION OF THE CORVETTE LS1 5.7-LITER V-8 FOR 1998.

THE CAMARO SS AGAIN HAD SEVERAL PERFORMANCE AND APPEARANCE UPGRADES.

full wheel covers, P215/60SR16 black sidewall tires and black door handles.

CAMARO Z28 - SERIES 1F - V-8

The Z28 got a slightly de-tuned version of the Corvette LS1 engine for 1998. This V-8 replaced the LT1 used from 1995 through 1997. The Z28 also had the new front-end styling, a black roof treatment and the same two new colors. Standard equipment for the Camaro Z28 coupe included a 5.7-liter V-8, a four-speed electronic overdrive transmission, a battery with run-down protection, rear-wheel drive, a limited-slip differential, a 2.73 rear axle ratio, a stainless steel exhaust system with chrome tips, a Sport ride suspension, independent front suspension with an anti-roll bar, front coil springs, front shocks, a rear suspension with an anti-roll bar and rear coil springs. The Camaro Z28 convertible featured traction control, an electrically operated fully lined convertible top, a glass rear window, a sound system with four performance speakers, a rear window defroster and a carpeted cargo floor.

CAMARO SS - SERIES 1F - V-8

Chevrolet built Camaros and SLP Engineering, of Troy, Michigan, turned new Camaro coupes and convertibles into a Camaro SS with the WU8 "SS Performance & Appearance" option. SLP offered a choice of two engines beginning with a 315-hp version of the LS1 V-8. This could be boosted to 320 hp with the addition of an optional performance exhaust system. Other standard Camaro SS coupe content included an under-hood forced-air induction system, a unique spoiler and a high performance suspension package.

HISTORICAL FOOTNOTES

The Camaro's model-year sales were 48,806 units. Calendar-year sales were 47,577. According to industry trade journals domestic model-year production was 45,630 coupes and 3,858 convertibles for a total of 49,218 units. The Ste. Therese, Quebec plant built all of these cars (and all 32,157 Firebirds). Of the Camaros built, 72.9 percent had automatic transmission, 13.8 percent had a five-speed manual transmission, 13.3 percent had a six-speed manual transmission, 63.5 percent had a 3.8-liter SFI V-6 and 36.5 percent had a 5.7-liter MFI V-8A total of 47,624 new Camaros were registered in the U.S. during calendar year 1998.

ALL 1998 CAMAROS, INCLUDING THE Z28, GOT RESTYLED FRONT ENDS.

*A TOTAL OF 38,800 CAMARO COUPES WERE BUILT IN 1999,
STARTING AT A PRICE OF $16,625.*

1999

The big change for 1999 Camaros was a Zexel Torsen differential to replace all limited-slip rear axle applications. Traction control was made available with the 3800 V-6 engine and a Monsoon premium sound system was added to the convertible's options list. A new electronic throttle control was featured with V-6 Camaros and a new telltale light that monitored oil life was incorporated into the instrument cluster in all Camaros. Another change was a larger fuel tank so that Camaro lovers could go further on a tank of gas.

"Why settle for just any sports car, when you can get something with attitude?" asked Chevrolet's 1999 Camaro sales catalog. "That's what the Camaro is all about."

CAMARO - SERIES 1F - V-6

Standard equipment for the base Camaro coupe included the 3.8-liter 200-hp V-6, a five-speed overdrive manual gearbox, dent resistant body panels (doors, roof, hatch lid and front fenders), a left-hand remote control Sport-style outside rearview mirror, a right-hand manual Sport-style rearview mirror, composite headlights with automatic exterior lamp control, CFC-free air conditioning, battery run-down protection, carpeted front floor mats, full instrumentation with a tachometer, next-generation dual airbags, the PASS-Key II theft-deterrent system, retained power accessory, cloth-trimmed reclining frona Firm Ride & Handling suspension, 16-in. bolt-on wheel covers and P215/60R-16 black sidewall touring tires. The convertible added a fully lined power top (in White, Neutral or Black), a three-piece hard tonneau cover and a glass rear window with an electric defogger. A new option for V-6 powered base Camaros was traction control.

CAMARO Z28 - SERIES 1F - V-8

The Z28 boasted four-wheel disc brakes with ABS, a new heavy-duty Torsen limited-

Leonard Goffe photo

THIS 1999 Z28 CONVERTIBLE CAME IN MYSTIQUE TEAL WITH CHROME WHEELS.

slip differential, a special Sport suspension and the LS-1 V-8 as standard equipment. A four-speed automatic transmission was standard, but a six-speed manual transmission was a no-cost option.

CAMARO SS - SERIES 1F - V-8

Technically, the Camaro SS was a Z28 performance/appearance option sourced from SLP Engineering, of Troy, Michigan. "Think of it as the extreme Z28," said the 1999 Camaro sales brochure. This WU8 "SS Performance & Appearance" option pumped the LS1 V-8 up to 320 hp. Other standard Camaro SS coupe content included a forced air induction system, a special air scoop hood, a new low-restriction exhaust system, a Torsen limited-slip performance axle, an exclusive high-level rear spoiler, a high-performance ride & handling suspension package, speed-rated P275/40ZR17 Goodyear Eagle F1 tires, 17-in. lightweight cast-aluminum alloy wheels. Exterior SS badges replaced Z28 logos and the interior featured a Camaro SS interior plaque. The Camaro SS convertible was based

on the Z28 convertible, but shared the 320-hp V-8, 17-in. wheels and functional hood scoop with the SS coupe.

HISTORICAL FOOTNOTES

The Camaro's model-year sales were 41,412 units. Calendar-year sales were 40,7267. According to industry trade journals domestic model-year production was 38,800 coupes and 3,298 convertibles for a total of 42,098 units. The Ste. Therese, Quebec, plant built all of these cars (and all 41,226 Firebirds). Of the Camaros built, 70.8 percent had automatic transmission, 11.8 percent had a five-speed manual transmission, 17.4 percent had a six-speed manual transmission, 58.7 percent had a 3.8-liter SFI V-6, 41.3 percent had a 5.7-liter SFI V-8, 100 percent had power steering, 100 percent had four-wheel disc brakes with ABS, 33.9 percent had traction control, 100 percent had automatic headlamps (DRLs), 12.6 percent had a limited-slip differential. and 56.8 percent had T-tops. A total of 39,384 new Camaros were registered in the U.S. during calendar year 1999.

Jerry Heasley photo

*NEW BODY-COLOR SIDE MIRRORS WERE
ONE OF THE ONLY CHANGES FOR THE 2000 Z28.*

2000

The Canadian-built Camaro continued as one of North America's top-selling sports cars in 2000. A new Monterey Maroon Metallic body color was added to the Camaro's palette. The Z28 also got new body-colored outside rearview mirrors on both sides of the car, plus a leather-wrapped steering wheel with "redundant" radio controls inside. Integrated child seat tether anchors were added to all models. The car also had new 16-in. aluminum wheels came standard with painted finish or with optional polished finish.

On the inside, an ebony-colored interior selection replaced dark gray to provide a "true" black interior. A medium gray cloth interior replaced the former Artic White leather option and accent interior cloth replaced red accent. New cloth fabrics were used on the seats and door trim. Also new was a redundant radio control steering wheel. The Monsoon radio with CD player was made to be compatible with the trunk-mounted 12-disc CD changer. Both the V-6 and V-8 engines were revised to meet Low Emission Vehicle regulations in California and states requiring California emissions.

In the spirit of the original 1967-1969 Camaro Z28, Chevrolet Motor Division and Westech Automotive teamed up to build a new "302 Camaro" show car that appeared at the 2000 SEMA show. It featured a high-revving 302-cid LS1-based V-8. SLP Engineering, which teamed with Chevrolet to build the Camaro SS, contributed a lightweight flywheel, an aluminum differential cooler and a heavy-duty axle assembly. The 302 also featured a carbon fiber driveshaft and its chassis was stiffened with

THE SS SPORT COUPE USED A 320-HP VERSION OF THE LS1 V-8, FORCED-AIR INDUCTION, AND A SPECIAL FIBERGLASS (SMC) AIR SCOOP HOOD.

Hotchkiss springs, sway bars, rear control arms, a panhard bar and a strut tower brace.

Koni double adjustable shocks and Baer Racing 14-in. cross-drilled brake rotors and PBR calipers helped the 302 corner at high speeds. The interior was complete with an L.G. Motorsports roll bar, special Recaro seats with five-point safety belts and a Billet Hurst six-speed shifter. The exterior featured an SLP "Bow Tie" grille assembly and special striping and "302" badging. The show car rode on 18-in. American Racing Torq-Thrust II wheels with B.F. Goodrich Z-rated ultra-high performance tires.

CAMARO - SERIES 1F - V-6

Standard equipment for the base Camaro coupe included driver and front passenger airbags, CFC-free air conditioning, a center console with cupholders and storage provisions, an engine oil life monitor, cloth-trimmed reclining front bucket seats, a full-folding rear seat, a tilt steering wheel, daytime running lamps (DRLs) with automatic exterior lamp control, a body-color left-hand remote-control outside rearview mirror, a body-color manual right-hand outside rearview mirror, P215/60R-16 touring tires, 16-in. steel bolt-on wheel covers, power four-wheel disc brakes with ABS, a 3800 SFI V-6 engine, power rack-and-pinion steering, a Firm Ride and Handling suspension, the PASS-Key II theft-deterrent system and a five-speed manual transmission. In addition to, or in place of, the above equipment, the Camaro convertible also featured power door locks, an electric rear window defogger, a leather-wrapped steering wheel with redundant radio controls, remote keyless entry, a 200-watt Monsoon ETR AM/FM premium sound system (with cassette player, seek-and-scan, digital clock, TheftLock, speed-compensated volume and Automatic Tone Control), power windows with driver's side "express down," fog lamps, twin power mirrors, carpeted rear floor mats, body-color body side moldings, a remote trunk release, a power convertible top (in Artic White, black or neutral colors), a tonneau cover, a tonneau cover storage bag and cruise control.

CAMARO Z28 - SERIES 1F - V-8

The 2000 Camaro Z28 was Chevrolet's "modern muscle car." New Z28s got body-color outside rearview mirrors. Standard equipment for the Camaro Z28 Sport Coupe included 16-in. aluminum wheels, power four-wheel disc brakes with ABS, a 5.7-liter LS1 SFI V-8 engine, a dual-outlet exhaust system, a limited-slip rear axle with Zexel Torsen differential, power rack-and-pinion steering, a Performance Handling suspension package, the PASS-Key II theft-deterrent system, a four-speed electronically controlled automatic transmission (or six-speed manual transmission at no extra cost), theatre lighting, carpeted front floor mats, a gauge package with a 155-mph speedometer and tachometer and digital odometer.

CAMARO SS - SERIES 1F - V-8

Technically, the Camaro SS was a Z28 performance/appearance option sourced from SLP Engineering. It had a base price of $3,700, but the actual cost of each car depended upon individual buyer's preferences in equipment and trim. This so-called WU8 "SS Performance & Appearance" option included a 320-hp version of the LS1 V-8, forced-air induction with a special fiberglass (SMC) air scoop hood, a low-restriction exhaust system with dual 2 3/4-in. tailpipes, a Torsen limited-slip performance axle, an exclusive high-level rear spoiler, a high-performance ride & handling suspension package, speed-rated P275/40ZR17 Goodyear Eagle F1 tires, 17-in. lightweight cast-aluminum alloy wheels, a power steering cooler, Quaker State Synquest synthetic engine oil, exterior SS badges replacing Z28 logos and a Camaro SS interior plaque. The Camaro SS convertible was based on the Z28 convertible, but shared the 320-hp V-8, 17-in. wheels and functional hood scoop with the SS coupe.

HISTORICAL FOOTNOTES

The Camaro's model-year sales were 41,962 units. Calendar-year sales were 42,131. Domestic model-year production was 41,825 coupes and 3,636 convertibles for a total of 45,461 units. The Ste. Therese, Quebec, plant built all of these cars (and all 31,826 Firebirds). Of the Camaros built, 69.3 percent had automatic transmission, 10.9 percent had a five-speed manual transmission, 19.8 percent had a six-speed manual transmission, 55.1 percent had a 3.8-liter SFI V-6, 44.9 percent had a 5.7-liter MFI V-8, 100 percent had power steering, 100 percent had four-wheel disc brakes with ABS, 50 percent had traction control, 100 percent had automatic headlamps (DRLs), 44.9 percent had a limited-slip differential, 100 percent had steel-belted radial tires, 84 percent had power door locks, 84 percent had power windows, 100 percent had reclining bucket seats, 61.1 percent had a power seats, 41 percent had leather seats, 100 percent had dual front airbags, 100 percent had tilt steering, 100 percent had tinted glass, 100 percent had manual air conditioning, 88.1 percent had cruise control, 100 percent had delay windshield wipers, 18.1 percent had a ETR stereo cassette player, 63 percent had a name brand sound system with CD, 68.5 percent had another brand CD, 82.7 percent had an electric rear window defogger, 24 percent had a manual remote-control left-hand outside rearview mirror, 76 percent had power rearview mirrors, 27.8 percent had a power right-hand rearview mirror, 10.8 percent had chrome styled wheels, 79.6 percent had aluminum styled wheels, 78 percent had remote keyless entry, 78 percent had an anti-theft device and 58 percent had T-tops. A total of 42,006 new Camaros were registered in the U.S. during calendar year 2000.

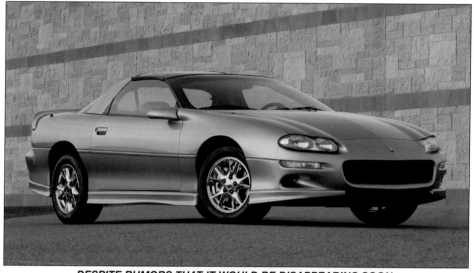

DESPITE RUMORS THAT IT WOULD BE DISAPPEARING SOON, THE 2001 CAMARO APPEARED IN THE CHEVROLET LINEUP.

2001

By early 2001, rumors that the Camaro was getting near the end of the line were flying and they ultimately proved to be true. Sales of Chevrolet's hot sporty car were on the decline and it seemed that only contracts with Canadian autoworkers at the Camaro assembly plant would keep the car alive through 2002.

With GM planning to discontinue the nameplate after 2002, there was little motivation to make major product changes. A new "de-contented" Z28 package was introduced and a few alterations in color schemes were made. The latter changes included the addition of a new Sunset Orange Metallic exterior color and the discontinuation of Sebring Silver Metallic. A total of 29,009 Camaros were built for worldwide distribution this year. That included 5,328 ragtops and 6,332 Camaro SS models.

On September 26 (the same day the Camaro was introduced in 1967), national newspapers announced that GM would stop making Camaros and Firebirds. "GM loses some old muscle," said the headline in *The Detroit News* that morning.

CAMARO - SERIES 1F - V-6

The base model got a new 16-in. chrome wheels option, re-valved shock absorbers and new Sunset Orange Metallic paint choice. Standard equipment for the base Camaro coupe included the 3.8-liter 200-hp V-6, rear-wheel drive, 16-in. steel wheel rims, P215/60R16 tires, a Space-Saver spare tire on a steel spare wheel, full wheel covers, front independent suspension, front and rear stabilizer bars, front disc/rear drum ABS brakes, child seat anchors, and an anti-theft system with an engine immobilize. The base convertible included front fog lights, a power convertible roof, a glass rear window, a rear window defogger, remote power door locks, one-touch power windows and a Bose premium brand 500-watts stereo system with eight speakers.

CAMARO Z28 - SERIES 1F - V-8

For 2001 the Z28 had the same changes as the base model (re-valved shocks, Sunset Orange Metallic paint choice and 16-in. chrome wheel option), plus more horsepower to help it compete better with the rival Mustang. Its 5.7-liter LS1 V-8 churned out 310 hp at 5200 rpm, 50 more than the Mustang's 5.0-liter V-8. A four-speed automatic transmission was standard, but a six-speed manual transmission was a no-cost option. Standard equipment for the Camaro Z28 coupe included the LS1 V-8, four-speed automatic transmission and a Bose premium brand 500-watts stereo system with eight speakers

CAMARO SS - SERIES 1F - V-8

Camaro buyers who checked off the SS performance option got a real muscle car that delivered 325 hp thanks to its functional hood scoop, forced-air induction system and big, fat exhausts. The SS ran from 0 to 60 mph in a tad over 5 seconds and could do the quarter mile in 13.5 seconds. The complete contents of this WU8 SS Performance/Appearance package included the 325-hp engine, the forced-air induction hood, a specific SS spoiler, 17-in. aluminum wheels, P275/40ZR17 Goodyear Eagle F1 tires, a high-performance ride and handling package, a power steering cooler, a low-restriction dual outlet exhaust system and SS badging. The package also included a 3.23:1 ratio rear axle with the MX0 automatic transmission or a 3.42:1 ratio rear axle with the MN6 six-speed manual transmission. It was available for Z28s, but was not available with the Y3F Sport Appearance package.

HISTORICAL FOOTNOTES

The 2001 model year saw a total of 29,009 Camaros built for distribution throughout the world. This included 12,652 cars with the LS1 V-8 and 16,357 cars with the 3800 V-6. A total of 1,697 of the V-6 Camaros had the Y87 package. A total of 398 Camaros were ordered with the Y3B SLP Rally Sport package. According to Camaro expert Tony Hossain, there was little interest among collectors and enthusiasts in the RS package, since they were more excited about the SS model with SLP options plus the 35th Anniversary SS option that was due in 2002. On Sept. 26, 2001, General Motors surprised no one by announcing that it would stop making, at least for the time being, the Chevrolet Camaro and Pontiac Firebird. GM also said that it would shut down the Canadian plant where both cars were made.

A REAR DECK LID SPOILER WAS USED TO SET OFF THE SPORTY LOOKS OF ALL THE 2001 CAMAROS.

*A SPECIAL 2002 LIMITED EDITION 35TH ANNIVERSARY SS
WAS PRODUCED TO MARK THE CAMARO'S FAREWELL YEAR.*

2002

In the fall of 2001, Chevrolet Motor Division announced that production of the Camaro would end after the 2002 model year, although the gate was left open for the development of a new type of Camaro sometime in the future.

Returning this year was Sebring Silver Metallic finish. A new limited-edition Camaro 35th Anniversary package was introduced for cars with the SS package. Its special features included Rally Red paint, unique badging and striping, a unique grille and tail panel appliqué, special 17-in. wheels, embroidery on the front seat headrests and front floor mats and a luxurious Ebony leather interior.

The second-gear start feature was eliminated on Camaro base coupes and convertibles equipped with the V-6 engine and automatic transmission. An eight-speaker Monsoon stereo system became standard and convertibles with a manual trunk got a new entrapment release handle. P245/55R16 tires were made standard on Z28 coupes and convertibles, while both base models got P235/55R16 tires.

CAMARO - SERIES 1F - V-6

Standard equipment for the base Camaro coupe included the 3.8-liter 200-hp V-6, a five-speed manual transmission, rear-wheel drive, 16-in. aluminum wheels, P235/55R16 tires, a Space-Saver spare tire on a steel spare wheel, full wheel covers, front independent suspension, front and rear stabilizer bars and ventilated front disc/solid rear disc ABS brakes. The base convertible included a remote anti-theft system, front fog lights, a power convertible roof, a glass rear window, a rear window defogger, remote power door locks, one-touch power windows, Monsoon premium brand 500-watts stereo system with eight speakers, cruise control, audio and cruise control buttons on the steer-

Erick Lieder photo

GM AND SLP ENGINEERING AGAIN TEAMED UP TO BUILD THE 2002 CAMARO SS.
THIS COUPE WAS LOADED WITH OPTIONS, PRODUCED 325 HP
AND CARRIED A WINDOW PRICE OF $35,515.

ing wheel, a remote trunk release, a leather-wrapped steering wheel and a leather-trimmed gearshift knob.

CAMARO Z28 - SERIES 1F/P - V-8

Standard equipment for the base Z28 coupe included the 5.7-liter 310-hp V-8, a four-speed automatic transmission, rear-wheel drive, 16-in. aluminum wheels, P245/50ZR16 tires, a Space-Saver spare tire on a steel spare wheel, full wheel covers, front independent suspension, front and rear stabilizer bars and ventilated front disc/solid rear disc ABS brakes. Standard equipment for the base Z28 convertible also included a remote anti-theft system, front fog lights, a power convertible roof, a glass rear window, a rear window defogger, remote power door locks, one-touch power windows, cruise control, audio and cruise control buttons on the steering wheel, a remote trunk release, P245/50ZR16

tires, a six-way power driver's seat, a height-adjustable driver's seat and a rear spoiler.

CAMARO SS - SERIES 1F - V-8

At the 2002 Chicago Auto Show the "final" Camaro SS received heavy promotion. The code WU8 SS Performance and Appearance package was a $3,625 option for the Z28. The contents of this option package included a 5.7-liter 325-hp V-8, a forced-air induction hood, a specific SS spoiler, 17-in. aluminum wheels, P275/40ZR17 Goodyear Eagle F1 tires, a high-performance ride and handling package, a power steering cooler, a low-restriction dual outlet exhaust system and SS badging. The package also included a 3.23:1 ratio rear axle with the MX0 automatic transmission or a 3.42:1 ratio rear axle with the MN6 six-speed manual transmission. It was available for Z28s, but was not available with the Y3F Sport Appearance package. A special limited-edition 35th anniversary

THE SS INTERIOR HAD ALL THE BEST FEATURES GM COULD OFFER.

A CAMARO WITH THE SLP OPTION PACKAGE WAS ALL MUSCLE FROM ANY ANGLE.

model was the big news for Camaro SS fans in 2002. It was actually a $2,500 option for the Camaro Z28 coupe and convertible with the SS package only.

HISTORICAL FOOTNOTES

The Camaro entered its final year of availability – at least for now – in the fall of 2001. Generating the most excitement for the 2002 model year were three specialty models created as a joint effort between Chevrolet Motor Division and SLP Engineering. The 2002 Camaro RS package offered by SLP could be added to V-6-powered Camaros for $849. It was available for cars finished in Artic White, Light Pewter Metallic, Silver Metallic, Navy Blue Metallic, Onyx Black, Monterey Maroon Metallic, Sun-

set Orange Metallic, Mystic Teal Metallic and Bright Rally Red. The RS content included a front grille with the Chevrolet bow-tie logo, an interior plaque with RS badge, three exterior RS badges, a dual-outlet exhaust system with a high-performance muffler (adds 5 hp and a throaty exhaust note) and black or silver striping. The black striping was not available for Oynx Black or Navy Blue cars and the silver striping was not available for Light Pewter or Sunset Orange cars. SLP also offered the SS package (with a new 345-hp option available at extra cost), plus the 35th anniversary package listed with 2002 options. The latter was available only for the Camaro Z28 with the SS package and was on display at the 2002 Chicago Automobile Show in February.

THE 2010 CAMARO WAS THREE YEARS IN THE MAKING.

2010

It was three years in the making, but to fans of the Camaro it was an eternity. When Chevrolet debuted its Camaro concept coupe at the 2006 North American International Auto Show in Detroit, it filled the void among enthusiasts of the General Motors pony car that had ceased production at the conclusion of the 2002 model year.

That fourth-generation Camaro suffered from slowing sales from the beginning of the 2000s — averaging fewer than 46,000 for 2000, 29,009 for '01 and 41,776 in '02 — and the plug was pulled on producing a 2003 version.

(Production of Camaro's Pontiac counterpart, the Firebird, was also dropped.)

After 35 years of continuous production from the Camaro's debut on Sept. 29, 1966, as a '67 model and direct competitor to Ford's Mustang, it was difficult to understand the Camaro's sales decline. But the decreasing numbers did not lie. Possibly, even at that low point, Chevrolet, armed with the knowledge that the Camaro had significant name value and buyer loyalty in the marketplace, understood that a production hiatus might spur a renewed interest in the pony car after a few years away.

The Camaro concept coupe's unveiling in 2006 followed in '07 by a concept convertible were well received by both the motoring press and the public. This acceptance, which could be loosely translated to sales success of a production Camaro, spurred Chevrolet to authorize production of its new pony car.

On March 16, 2009, production began at Ontario, Canada's Oshawa Car Assembly plant of the 2010 Camaro. The fifth-generation coupe had familiar lines, as its design was inspired by the first-gen Camaro of the late 1960s. This retro-styled Camaro was again expected to assume the role of sales competitor to not only Ford's Mustang, but also Dodge's Challenger, both also designed with a retro appearance reminiscent, respectively, of their late-'60s and early-'70s design.

MODEL LINEUP

The Camaro staple of two-door, four-place, front-engine, rear-drive pony car was retained for the fifth-gen's format. The initial coupe-only Camaro was offered in LS, LT and SS versions.

THE NEW-GENERATION CAMARO'S COZY INTERIOR FEATURES TWO GUAGE PODS IN THE CENTER OF THE LARGE, THICK STEERING WHEEL.

DRIVETRAIN

Powertrain for the LS/LT was a dual overhead cam 3.6-liter V-6, rated at 304-hp, with a 11.3:1 compression ratio. It was linked to either a Hydra-Matic six-speed automatic transmission with TAPshift or Aisin-Warner

An AY6 six-speed manual transmission was standard. The SS came with the multi-port fuel-injected LS3 V-8 (426-hp) coupled to the TR6060 six-speed manual trans or the L99 V-8 (400-hp) mated to the Hydra-Matic. The LS3 had a compression ratio of 10.7:1 while the L99's was 10.4:1.

The V-6-powered LS or LT ran on regular unleaded and produced 273 lbs.-ft. of torque at 5200 rpm. Both of the V-8s in the SS demanded premium fuel and offered torque ratings of 420 lb.-ft. at 4600 rpm or 410 lbs.-ft. at 4300 rpm, respectively.

FEATURES

Key features of the 2010 Camaro included a fully independent four-wheel suspension system, four-wheel disc brakes (four-piston Brembo calipers on SS models) and an RS appearance package available on LT and SS trim

AN RS APPEARANCE PACKAGE WAS AVAILABLE FOR THE LT AND SS MODELS.

THE 2010 CAMARO COULD BE HAD WITH A 300-HP V-6,
OR WITH A TIRE-WRECKING 426-HP V-8.

levels that offered a spoiler and RS-specific tail lamps and wheels. Rally and "hockey" stripe packages were available in several different colors as well.

Standard safety features included anti-lock brakes, airbags (comprised of driver, passenger, side and curtain both front and rear), engine immobilizer, StabiliTrak electronic traction control (with additional Competitive/Sport modes on SS). The OnStar communications system was optional.

Creature comforts that were standard equipment included air conditioning, cruise control, power steering/windows/locks/mirrors, remote keyless entry, tilt steering wheel, rear window defroster and tachometer.

SPECIFICATIONS

Camaro was based on General Motors' Zeta platform comprised of unitized body/frame construction. Dimensions: 112.3-inch wheelbase, 190.4-inch overall length, 75.5-inch width and 54.2-inch height. Curb weight: LS w/automatic 3,769 lbs. w/manual 3,780 lbs.; LT w/automatic

3,750, w/manual 3,741; SS w/automatic 3,913, w/manual 3,860. Weight balance was 52 percent front and 48 percent rear.

Utilizing a 16.1:1 steering ratio, Camaro had a 37.7-foot turning radius. It used a 3.27 standard axle ratio. Fuel tank capacity was 19 gallons.

SPECIAL EDITIONS

Camaro offered three limited edition models: Transformers, Synergy and Indianapolis 500 Pace Car editions.

Transformers Special Edition: It was available only on LT and SS versions ordered in Rally Yellow exterior finish. It could be had with or without the optional RS package. For an additional $995 (RPO code: CTH), the Transformers appearance package consisted of Autobot shield badging on side panels under Camaro nameplate, Autobot shield on wheel center caps and embroidered on interior console, Transformers logo on driver and passenger door sill plates (replacing Camaro labeled plates) and a black centered rally stripe with Transformers

THE 2010 CAMARO SS IN FIBER GRAY METALLIC WITH THE RS PACKAGE.

ghost logo embedded.

Synergy Special Edition: Using RPO code GHS, the Synergy production Camaro (costing $26,790) was based on the Synergy concept Camaro shown at the 2009 SEMA show. It could be ordered only on the LT version, and could not be ordered in conjunction with the optional RS package. The package included the limited-edition Synergy Green exterior paint accented with Cyber Grey rally striping, rear spoiler from the RS and SS option packages, 19-inch Sterling Silver painted wheels with P245/50R19 tires, Synergy Green instrument panel and door inserts and Synergy Green stitching on the Jet Black cloth seats, steering wheel, shift knob and center console.

Indianapolis 500 Pace Car Limited Edition: Costing $41,950 and having a production run of just 295 units, the Indianapolis 500 Pace Car edition Camaro was based on the SS version equipped with the 6.2-liter V-8 and automatic transmission. It featured Inferno Orange exterior paint with White Diamond rally striping. Indianapolis 500 Speedway logo decals were added to each door as was unique badging on front body panels under the Camaro nameplate. The package also included premium accented floor mats and Inferno Orange accented interior trim kit and engine cover. The SS grille was replaced with a [3]heritage[2] grille made available from General Motors as an aftermarket accessory.

HISTORICAL FOOTNOTES

Chevrolet sold 61,648 2010 Camaros in 2009 (April to December). Camaros paced both the 2009 Daytona 500 and Indianapolis 500 and the 2010 Indy 500.

It earned both the 2010 World Car Design of the Year and World Car of the Year awards.

CRITICS APPLAUDED THE 2011 CAMARO FOR ITS HEAD-TURNING LOOKS, ACCELERATION, HANDLING AND BANG-FOR-THE BUCK VALUE.

2011

The initial sales success of Chevrolet's re-launch of the Camaro in 2010 kept changes to a minimum for 2011. One of the most anticipated changes was the announcement that Camaro would broaden its coupe-only status and include a convertible, beginning in spring of 2011.

Other changes of note included the OnStar communications system becoming standard equipment and 21-inch wheels offered as an option across the Camaro line. A Head-Up Display (HUD) became standard on LT and SS models, and featured important vehicle data such as speed, navigation directions and diagnostics projected directly onto the windshield.

MODEL LINEUP

Camaro was again a two-door, four-place, front-engine, rear-drive pony car offered in LS, LT and SS versions.

DRIVETRAIN

The LS and LT versions were powered by a dual overhead cam 3.6-liter V-6, now rated at 312-hp, an 8-hp bump from 2010, with a 11.3:1 compression ratio. It was linked to either a Hydra-Matic six-speed automatic transmission with TAPshift or Aisin-Warner AY6 six-speed manual transmission (standard). The SS came with the multi-port fuel-injected LS3 V-8 (426-hp) coupled to the TR6060 six-speed manual trans or the L99 V-8 (400-hp) mated to the Hydra-Matic. The LS3 had a compression ratio of 10.7:1 while the L99's was 10.4:1.

The V-6-powered LS or LT ran on regular un-

THE OPTIONAL CONSOLE-MOUNTED GAUGE PACKAGE FEATURES OIL TEMPERATURE, VOLTS, TRANSMISSION FLUID TEMPERATURE AND OIL PRESSURE MONITORING.

leaded and produced 278 lb.-ft. of torque at 5200 rpm (a 5 lb.-ft. boost over 2010's V-6). Both of the V-8s in the SS demanded premium fuel and offered torque ratings of 420 lb.-ft. at 4600 rpm or 410 lb.-ft. at 4300 rpm, respectively.

HISTORY

Just as Ford's Mustang launched a series of retro versions such as Boss, Mach 1, Shelby, etc., the Camaro rumor mill was buzzing with conjecture that a return of the Z28 for 2012 was on the drawing board. It was expected to be powered by a supercharged 6.2-liter V-8 backed by a six-speed automatic transmission.

THE POWER SUNROOF RETURNED AS AN OPTION FOR 2011.

WHILE COMPETING MODELS SUCH AS THE MUSTANG AND CHALLENGER WERE DESIGNED TO MORE CLOSELY RESEMBLE THEIR 1960S AND '70S ANCESTORS, THE NEW-GENERATION CAMARO CLEARLY TOOK A DIFFERENT TRACK, WITH A LOW ROOFLINE, MODERN CREASES AND BODY ANGLES, AND A FROWNING FRONT END THAT HAS QUICKLY BECOME A TRADEMARK FEATURE.

A.C. Bogarty photo

THIS GOLD COUPE WAS ONE OF MORE THAN 64,000 1967 FIREBIRDS EQUIPPED WITH A V-8.

1967

Ford rocked the automotive world with its mid-1964 introduction of the Mustang and took the industry by surprise. General Motors wasn't able to field a true competitor until three years later, when it introduced the Firebird on Feb. 23. It was Pontiac's version of Chevy's new Camaro dressed up with a Poncho-style split grille, different engines and transmissions and a few suspension tweaks.

Pontiac offered the sporty "shorty" in five flavors – base, Sprint, 326, 326 H.O. and 400 — created by tacking regular production options onto the same basic car. The options created distinctive packages that were merchandised as separate models. Bucket seats were standard in all Firebirds. Design characteristics of the '67s included vent windows and three vertical air slots on the rear fenders.

Sprints featured a 215-hp overhead cam six with a four-barrel carburetor. A floor-mounted three-speed manual gearbox and heavy-duty suspension were standard. A Firebird Sprint convertible cost $3,019 and a coupe was $2,782.

Firebird 326s featured a 250-hp version of the 326-cid Tempest V-8 with two-barrel carburetion. The convertible cost $2,998 and the coupe was $2,761. Firebird 326-H.O.s used a 285-hp version of the same V-8 with a 10.5:1 compression ratio and four-barrel carburetor. A column-shift three-speed manual transmission, dual exhausts, H.O. stripes, a heavy-duty battery and wide-oval tires were standard. The H.O. convertible cost $3,062 and the coupe cost $2,825.

The performance version of the 1967 Firebird was the 400. It featured a 325-hp version of the 400-cid GTO V-8. Standard equipment included a dual-scoop hood, chrome engine parts, three-speed heavy-duty floor shift and sport-type suspension. Prices were about $100 higher than a comparable 326 H.O. Options included Ram-Air induction, which gave 325 hp and cost over $600.

BASE FIREBIRD - OHC-6 - SERIES 223

Standard equipment included bucket seats,

THE BASE
400 ENGINE
PRODUCED
325 HP.

A.C. Bogarty photo

vinyl upholstery, nylon-blend carpets, wood-grain dash trim and E70-14 wide oval tires. The base engine was a regular-fuel OHC six with a monojet carburetor. Two body styles were offered and came with any of the Tempest or GTO power trains. However, the two body styles were marketed in five "models" created by adding regular production options (UPCs) in specific combinations. The models were the base Firebird, Firebird Sprint, Firebird 326, Firebird 326 H.O. and the Firebird 400.

FIREBIRD SPRINT - OHC-6 - SERIES 23

Sprint models featured a 215-hp OHC six with a four-barrel carburetor. A floor-mounted three-speed manual gearbox and heavy-duty suspension were standard. The Sprint version of the OHC six also featured a racier cam and a tuned exhaust manifold. Body still moldings with "3.8-Litre Overhead Cam" emblems were seen. Body side racing stripes were a popular and heavily-promoted Sprint option.

FIREBIRD 326 - V-8 - SERIES 223

Firebird 326s featured a 250-hp version of the base Tempest V-8 with two-barrel carburetion. A three-speed transmission with column-

mounted shifter was standard equipment. The 326 V-8 also used lettering on the rear edge of the hood bulge for model identification. In this case the model call-outs read "326." E70-14 tires were standard.

FIREBIRD 326 H.O. - V-8 - SERIES 223

Firebird 326 H.O. models featured a 285-hp version of the base Tempest V-8 with 10.5:1 compression and four-barrel carburetion. A three-speed manual transmission with column shift, a dual exhaust system, H.O. side stripes, a heavy-duty battery and F70 x 14 wide oval tires were standard. The Firebird 326 H.O. convertible was priced $3,062 and the Firebird 326 H.O. coupe was priced $2,825.

FIREBIRD 400 - V-8 - SERIES 223

Firebird 400s used a 325-hp version of the GTO V-8 with four-barrel carburetion. Standard equipment included a dual scoop hood, chrome engine parts, a three-speed heavy-duty floor shifter and a sport-type suspension. The letters "400" appeared on the right-hand side of the deck lid. Options included a Ram Air induction setup that gave 325 hp at a higher rpm peak and cost over $600 extra.

PONTIAC BUILT MORE THAN 82,000 BEAUTIFUL NEW FIREBIRDS IN 1967.

PONTIAC SOLD 15,528 NEW FIREBIRD CONVERTIBLES IN 1967.

HISTORICAL FOOTNOTES

Racecar builder and driver John Fitch marketed a performance-oriented "Fitchbird" package. In magazine road tests, the stock 1967 Firebird Sprint hardtop with 215 hp did 0 to 60 mph in 10 seconds and the quarter mile in 17.5 seconds. With the 325-hp Firebird 400 option, the times went down to 6.4 and 14.3 seconds. A second test driver clocked the Firebird 400 hardtop with the 325-hp motor at 14.7 seconds and 98 mph in the quarter mile.

Jim Thomson photo

THE FIREBIRD 400 CONVERTIBLE WAS A HEAD TURNER IN 1968.

1968

The Firebird arrived so late in 1967, Pontiac had no time to make big changes for 1968. Or maybe they didn't want to. The vent windows went the way of the do-do bird and were replaced by one-piece side glass. Suspension upgrades included bias-mounted rear shocks and multi-leaf rear springs. Pontiac built 90,152 coupes (base price $2,781) and 16,960 ragtops (base price $2,996).

The $116 Sprint option included a three-speed manual gearbox with floor shift, an overhead-cam six, Sprint emblems, body sill moldings and four F70 x 14 tires. The 250-cid engine had a single four-barrel carburetor and 215 hp.

The appeal of the new $106 Firebird 350 option was a 265-hp V-8. The 350 H.O. option included three-speed manual transmission with column shift, dual exhausts, H.O. side stripes, a heavy-duty battery and four F70 x 14 tires.

Jim Thomson photo

THE TWIN HOOD SCOOPS IDENTIFIED THE 400 ENGINE. MOST OF THE STYLING WAS UNCHANGED FROM 1967.

The Firebird 400 option ($351-$435) added chrome engine parts, a sports suspension, dual exhausts, 400 emblems and a dual-scoop hood. Its 400-cid four-barrel V-8 produced 330 hp. The Ram Air 400 was about the same, except for its de-clutching fan and functional hood scoops. The Ram Air V-8 produced 335 hp and did 0 to 60 in 7.6 seconds. A quarter mile took 15.4 seconds.

THE BASE FIREBIRD AND SPRINT CAME WITH AN OVERHEAD CAM STRAIGHT SIX.

FIREBIRD - OHC-6 - SERIES 223

Base Firebird equipment included the standard GM safety features, front bucket seats, vinyl upholstery, a simulated burl woodgrain dashboard, an outside rearview mirror, side marker lights, E70 x 14 black sidewall wide-oval tires with a Space Saver spare and a larger-displacement 250-cid, 175-hp OHC six-cylinder engine. Styling was nearly identical to the 1967 1/2 Firebird except that the 1967 model's vent windows were replaced with one-piece side door glass. Technical changes included bias-mounted rear shock absorbers and multi-leaf rear springs.

FIREBIRD SPRINT - OHC-6 - SERIES 223

Sprint models featured a 215-hp OHC six with a four-barrel carburetor. A floor-mounted three-speed manual gearbox and heavy-duty suspension were standard. The Sprint version of the OHC six also featured a racier cam. Body still moldings with "3.8 Litre Overhead Cam" emblems were seen. Body side racing stripes were a popular and heavily-promoted Sprint option.

FIREBIRD 350 - V-8 - SERIES 223

The new Firebird 350 model featured a three-speed manual transmission with column shift and F70 x 14 tires. The 350-cid V-8 had a 3.88 x 3.75 bore and stroke, a 9.2:1 compression ratio, a Rochester two-barrel carburetor and 265 hp at 4600 rpm. Although the Pontiac V-8 heads had the same compression ratio, they had been redesigned with deeper, smoother combustion chambers and larger, more upright valves to promote a controlled combustion environment. They were part of Pontiac's emissions program, as was a new, thermostatically controlled carburetor pre-heating system.

FIREBIRD 350 H.O. - V-8 - SERIES 223

Standard equipment on the hot-performing H.O. version of the Firebird 350 included a three-speed manual transmission with column shift, a dual exhaust system, H.O. side stripes, a heavy-duty battery and four F70 x 14 tires. The engine was a 350-cid V-8 with 10.5:1 compression, a Rochester four-barrel carburetor and 320 hp at 5100 rpm. The price of the 350 H.O. was $181 over base model cost.

FIREBIRD 400 - V-8 - SERIES 223

The Firebird 400's standard equipment included a three-speed manual transmission with floor-mounted gear shifter, a chrome air

A.C. Bogarty photo

*A FIREBIRD COUPE WITH THE 350 V-8 CAME WITH A
BASE PRICE OF $2,887 WHEN IT WAS NEW.*

Dee Sherrow photo

*THIS SHARP 1968 SPRINT CONVERTIBLE FEATURES A WOOD STEERING WHEEL, POWER
TOP, DUAL EXHAUST, FOUR-BARREL OHC SIX AND RALLYE II WHEELS.*

cleaner, chrome rocker arm covers, a chrome oil cap, sports type springs and shock absorbers, a heavy-duty battery, dual exhausts, a hood emblem and dual scoop hood, F70 x 14 red line or white sidewall tires and a Power Flex variable pitch cooling fan.

FIREBIRD RAM AIR 400 - V-8 - SERIES 223

The Ram Air 400 model had the same inclusions as the Firebird 400, except for the addition of a de-clutching cooling fan and twin functional hood scoops. The engine was a 400-cid V-8

with 10.75:1 compression ratio, a Rochester four-barrel carburetor and 335 hp at 5000 rpm. It had a special high-lift camshaft, forged aluminum pistons, an Armasteel crankshaft, new push rods and guides, tulip-head valves and dual high-rate valve springs.

HISTORICAL FOOTNOTES

Production started Aug. 21, 1967. The model introductions were Sept. 21, 1967. Model year output was 107,112 Firebirds. Model year sales stood at 96,510 Firebirds. Calendar year sales hit 91,813 Firebirds

THIS CAR WAS A PILOT VERSION OF THE SOON-TO-BE-RELEASED 1969 TRANS AM.

1969

Flatter wheel openings, front fender wind splits, new rooflines and a creased lower belt-line characterized 1969 Firebirds. The gas filler moved behind the rear license plate and a rectangular Pontiac-style split bumper grille was used. Square body-colored Endura bezels held the headlamps. Headlines were made when the Trans Am arrived March 8, 1969, at the Chicago Auto Show. It was the slinkiest Firebird model-option up to this point.

Standard equipment for Firebirds included vinyl bucket seats, grained dashboards, carpeting, outside mirrors and side marker lamps. The hardtop listed for $2,831 and the ragtop for $3,045. Model options included Sprint ($121 extra), 350 ($111 extra), 350 H.O. ($186 extra), 400 ($275-$358 extra), 400 H.O. ($351-$435 extra) and Ram Air 400 ($832 extra), plus the Trans Am.

The features of each model were similar to 1968. The Trans Am included a heavy-duty three-speed manual gear box with floor shifter, 3.55:1 axle, glass-belted tires, heavy-duty

shocks and springs, 1-inch stabilizer bar, power front disc brakes, variable-ratio power steering, engine-air extractors, a rear-deck air foil, a black-textured grille, full-length body stripes, white-and-blue finish, a leather-covered steering wheel and special identification decals. The new Trans Am hardtop had a base price of $3,556 and a production run of just 689 units. The convertible cost some $150 additional and only eight were built.

The Trans Am grew out of the Sports Car Club of America's Trans-American sedan racing series. Pontiac paid the SCCA a $5 royalty per car to use the name. The T/A was originally planned with a special super-high-performance 303-cid small-block V-8 that would have made it race eligible. About 25 cars were fitted with the short-stroke 303-cid tunnel-port V-8s, but these were used exclusively for SCCA Trans-Am racing. Production models could have either a 335-hp 400 H.O. (a.k.a. Ram Air III) V-8 or an optional 345-hp Ram Air IV engine. Quarter-miles times for Trans Ams were in the

FIREBIRD COUPES COULD STILL BE HAD FOR LESS THAN $3,000 IN 1969.

14- to 14.5-second bracket.

BASE FIREBIRD - OHC-6 - SERIES 223

Standard equipment for base Firebirds included vinyl bucket seats, a camera case grained dashboard, carpeting, outside mirrors, a heater and defroster, side marker lamps, small hubcaps, a 250-cid OHC six-cylinder engine, a three-speed manual transmission with column-mounted gearshift, E70 x 14 tires and a Space Saver spare tire. An optional Custom Trim package added breathable knit-style vinyl upholstery, bright roof rail interior moldings, woodgrain dashboard trim, a molded trunk mat, integral front armrests, padded door panels, a passenger assist grip and assorted interior and exterior trim items.

FIREBIRD SPRINT - OHC-6 - SERIES 223

The Sprint Six package was an extra-cost option UPC 342. It included the UPC W53 Sprint version of the 250-cid OHC six-cylinder engine (with a higher compression ratio, larger valves, a hotter cam grind and a four-barrel carburetor), a low-restriction exhaust system, a three-speed manual transmission with floor-mounted shifter, red Sprint badges on the rocker panel moldings and a heavy-duty suspension..

FIREBIRD 350 - V-8 - SERIES 223

The Firebird 350 option (UPC L30) included a three-speed manual transmission with column shift and F70 x 14 tires. The engine was a 350-cid V-8 with a 9.2:1 compression ratio, a Rochester two-barrel carburetor and 265 hp at 4600 rpm.

FIREBIRD 350 H.O. - V-8 - SERIES 223

This option package (UPC 344; engine code L-76) included a three-speed manual transmission with column shift, a dual exhaust system and a heavy-duty battery. Side stripes were no longer available for cars with the H.O. option. The engine was a 350-cid V-8 with a 10.5:1 compression ratio, a Rochester four-barrel carburetor and 325 hp at 5100 rpm.

THE 1969 TRANS AM WAS A BOLD NEW FIRST-YEAR 'BIRD.

FIREBIRD 400 - V-8 - SERIES 223

This option package (UPC 345; engine code WS6) included chrome engine parts, a dual exhaust system, a heavy-duty battery, a three-speed manual transmission with floor shifter, F70 x 14 red stripe or white sidewall tires and a variable pitch cooling fan. The engine was a 400-cid V-8 with a 10.75:1 compression ratio, a Rochester four-barrel carburetor and 330 hp at 4800 rpm. A special hood is used on the Firebird 400 and incorporates non-functional air scoops. Also, a Ride & Handling package was required. Price: $275-$358 over base model cost depending on transmission.

FIREBIRD RAM AIR 400 - V-8 SERIES 223

This option (UPC 348; engine code L-74) included the same features as the Firebird 400, except for addition of de-clutching cooling fan and twin functional hood scoops with operating mechanism. The package price was $558.20.

FIREBIRD RAM AIR IV - V-8 - SERIES 223

This option (UPC 347; engine code L-67) includes the same features as the Ram Air 400, plus special hood scoop emblems. The engine is a 400-cid V-8 with a special camshaft and valve train, a 10.75:1 compression ratio, a Rochester four-barrel carburetor and 345 hp at 5400 rpm. Price: $832 over base model cost. Specific transmissions were required. A 3.90:1 ratio rear axle was standard and a 4.33:1 ratio rear axle was optional.

TRANS AM - V-8 - SERIES 223

The option (sales code 322; UPC WS4; engine code L74) included a heavy-duty three-speed manual gearbox with a floor-mounted gearshift, a 3.55:1 rear axle, fiberglass-belted tires, heavy-duty shock absorbers, heavy-duty springs, a one-inch stabilizer bar, power front disc brakes, variable ratio power steering, engine air exhaust louvers on sides of fender, a rear deck lid air foil, a black textured grille,

THIS FIREBIRD 400 CONVERTIBLE INCLUDED A SPECIAL HOOD WITH TWIN AIR SCOOPS, WHICH WERE FUNCTIONAL ON THE 400 H.O. MODEL.

full-length body stripes, white and blue finish, a leather covered steering wheel and special identification decals. The engine was the UPC L74 400 H.O. V-8 with 335 hp. Certain features listed as "standard equipment" in the first printing of sales litreature were not used on production Trans Ams. They included a driver-controlled hood scoop, a chrome air cleaner cover and a leather-grained sport steering wheel. The price listed on the Pontiac build sheet for a standard Trans Am was $1,025 over base model cost. Apparently, the retail price of the Trans Am over the Firebird 400 was $1,163.74. That included $508.70 for the Ram Air V-8, $232.76 for mandatory options including power front disc brakes, variable-ratio power steering and a 3.55:1 ratio rear axle and $421.28 for the other Trans Am goodies.

HISTORICAL FOOTNOTES

Calendar-year sales of Firebirds came to 55,402 cars for a 0.65 percent market share. The high-performance Trans Am was introduced March 8, 1969. Because of slow sales and late introductions of next-year models, 1969 Firebirds left in stock were carried over and sold through the following fall. A total of 87,709 Firebirds and Trans Ams were built during the 1969 model year. Of these: 20,840 Firebirds and Trans Ams had synchromesh transmission and 66,868 had automatic transmission. 114 Trans Ams had the L-74 Ram Air III V-8 and Turbo-Hydra-Matic. 520 Trans Ams had the L-74 Ram Air V-8 and synchromesh. Eight Trans Am convertibles were made. All Trans Am convertibles had the L74 V-8; four had manual transmission. Nine Trans Am coupes had the L67 Ram Air IV engine and Turbo-Hydra-Matic transmission. Forty-six Trans Am coupes had the L67 Ram Air IV engine and manual transmission.

THE TRANS AMS HAD PLENTY OF POWER WITH EITHER THE RAM AIR III OR IV 400 ENGINES.

1970

The 1970 Firebirds arrived late, but were worth the wait. Car magazines raved about the Maserati-inspired Endura nose with twin recessed grilles. Standard equipment on base Firebirds included a 250-cid, 155-hp six, glass-belted tires, front bucket seats, vinyl upholstery, a woodgrained dash, carpeting, an outside mirror, manual front disc brakes, wide wheel rims and door pockets. There was only a hardtop model with a $2,875 base price and 18,874 were built.

Styling changes for the 1970 Firebird began at the front, where there was a new Endura rubber front end with dual recessed grilles and single headlights. Split side marker lamps, enlarged wheel openings, flush door handles and smooth, clean, curvy body panels brought Pontiac's sports-compact car up to date. Firebird lettering and engine badges were behind the front wheel cutouts.

A new Firebird model had chrome "Esprit" signatures on its roof pillars, knit-vinyl upholstery, a deluxe steering wheel, dual sport mirrors, concealed wipers and antenna, trunk floor mats, wheel trim rings, decor moldings and a 350-cid two-barrel V-8. Esprits sold for $3,241 and 18,961 were built.

The performance-oriented Firebird 400 became the Formula 400. It included fat stabilizer bars, high-rate springs, wind-up rear axle controls, bias-belted tires, extra-wide wheel rims, manual front disc brakes and rear drums, carpet, vinyl interiors, front and rear bucket type seats, dual outside sport mirrors, concealed wipers and antennas and a deluxe steering wheel. Power came from a 400-cid four-barrel V-8 with 10.25:1 compression and 265 hp and a three-speed Hurst floor shift. The Formula 400 had extra-long twin hood scoops and model nameplates. It sold for $3,370 and just 7,708 were built.

The second Trans Am was all new, but basically similar in features to the 1969 1/2 version. Front air dams, front and rear spoilers, a shaker hood, side air extractors, a rear-end spoiler and aerodynamic outside mirrors gave it an exotic sports car look. It included front and rear stabilizers, heavy-duty shock absorbers and springs, engine-turned dash inserts, a rally gauge cluster, concealed wipers, bucket seats, carpets, vinyl upholstery, power brakes and steering and 11-inch wide, 15-inch diameter Rally rims with wide F60-15 white-letter tires. Trans Ams had white or blue finish with contrasting racing stripes. They were base priced at $4,305 and had a production run of 3,196 units.

The standard V-8 in the new Trans Am was a 400-cid 335-hp Ram Air HO (Ram Air III) V-8. An improved Ram Air IV with 370 hp was avail-

AS IN 1969, TRANS AMS WERE AVAILABLE ONLY IN BLUE WITH WHITE STRIPES, OR WHITE WITH BLUE STRIPES FOR 1970, AND AGAIN HAD PLENTY OF EXTERIOR GOODIES TO SET THEM APART.

able for $390. A wide-ratio four-speed manual gearbox with Hurst floor shift was standard. The Ram Air III T/A did 0 to 60 mph in 6.0 seconds and the quarter mile in 14.6. *Hot Rod* magazine road tested a white 1970 Trans Am with the 400-cid Ram Air IV V-8, a four-speed manual transmission and 3.73:1 gears and recorded a 13.90-second quarter mile at 102 mph.

BASE FIREBIRD - SIX/V-8 - SERIES 223

Styling changes included Endura rubber front ends with dual recessed grilles, single headlights, split side marker lamps, enlarged wheel openings, flush door handles and smooth, clean, curvy body panels. Firebird lettering and engine badges appeared behind front wheel cutouts. The only body type offered was a sleek-looking sports coupe. Standard equipment on base Firebirds included a 250-cid 155-hp six, an Endura front bumper, E78-14 black sidewall fiberglass tires, front bucket seats, rear bucket type seats, a front stabilizer bar, side marker lights, all-vinyl upholstery, a woodgrained dashboard, carpeting, an outside rearview mirror, manual front disc/rear drum brakes, six-

inch wheel rims and door storage pockets. A 350-cid 255-hp V-8 was optional.

FIREBIRD ESPRIT - V-8 - SERIES 224

The Esprit was outwardly identified by model script on the rear roof pillar, bright roof rail and wheel opening moldings, V-8 displacement badges under front fender Firebird lettering and bird emblems above the grille. Standard equipment included all found on base models, plus custom interior option with knit vinyl upholstery, a vinyl-covered deluxe steering wheel, dual body-color outside sport mirrors, concealed windshield wipers, a concealed radio antenna, trunk floor mats, wheel trim rings, custom trim, decor moldings, higher rate springs and a 350-cid two-barrel V-8 with 8.8:1 compression and 255-hp at 4600 rpm. A three-speed manual gearbox with floor-mounted shift lever was regular equipment.

FIREBIRD FORMULA 400 - V-8 - SERIES 226

Standard equipment on the Formula 400 included all GM safety features, fiberglass twin hood scoop, 1 1/8- front and 5/8-in. rear stabilizer bars, F70 x 14 bias-belted black sidewall tires, 7-inch wheel rims, manual front disc/rear drum brakes, carpets, an all-vinyl interior, front bucket seats, rear bucket type seats, dual outside sport mirrors, concealed windshield wipers, a concealed radio antenna and a deluxe steering wheel. The Formula had the same springs as the base Firebird with heavy-duty "Firm Control" shocks. The Trans Am suspension was optional. Power came from a 400-cid four-barrel V-8 with 10.25:1 compression and 330 hp at 4800 rpm. The base engine was linked to a three-speed Hurst floor shift. External distinctions included extra-long twin hood scoops and Formula 400 nameplates. The 335-hp L74 Ram Air III V-8 was optional. No Formulas were equipped with the Ram Air IV V-8.

TRANS AM - V-8 - SERIES 228

The Trans Am had all GM safety features, plus front air dams, front and rear spoilers, a shaker hood, side air extractors, a rear deck lid spoiler, aerodynamically styled outside mirrors with left-hand remote contro, a 1 1/4-in. front stabilizer bar, a 7/8-in. rear stabilizer bar, heavy-duty Firm Control shock absorbers, heavy-duty springs, an engine-turned instrument panel insert, a Rally gauge cluster, concealed windshield wipers, bucket seats, carpets, all-vinyl upholstery, power brakes, power steering, 15 x 7-in. Rally wheel rims and F60-15 white letter tires. The standard V-8 in the Trans Am was a 335-hp Ram Air 400 engine. The factory called this the Ram Air H.O., but it is best known as the Ram Air III V-8. It had a 10.5:1 compression ratio and developed peak power at 5000 rpm. The base transmission was a wide-ratio four-speed manual gearbox with Hurst floor shift. The Trans Am came only with white or blue finish with contrasting racing stripes.

HISTORICAL FOOTNOTES

Pontiacs were introduced Sept. 18, 1969, and the all-new second-generation Firebird bowed Feb. 26, 1970. Calendar-year output was 422,212 Pontiacs, giving the company sixth place in the sales rankings. James McDonald became the new general manager of Pontiac Motor Division, replacing John Z. DeLorean, who moved to Chevrolet.

THE "CHICKEN" LOGO WAS RIGHT UP FRONT IN 1970.

VINYL WAS STILL THE MATERIAL OF CHOICE FOR FIREBIRD INTERIORS FOR 1970.

THE 1971 455 H.O. TRANS AM WAS THE MOST MUSCULAR PONTIAC AROUND.

1971

There was no need to change the beautiful Firebird for 1971, and Pontiac hardly did. A careful look would reveal new high-back seats and new wheel covers (except on Trans Ams). Simulated louvers appeared behind the front wheel cutouts.

Base Firebird prices started at $3,047 and 23,022 were built. Some 20,185 buyers paid $400 more to get an Esprit coupe. Formula prices started in the Esprit bracket, but only 7,802 examples of this model were made.

Standard equipment on Trans Ams was about the same as 1970. The exotic sports car version of the Firebird got the new high-back seats, revised grille trim, new optional honeycomb wheels and a rarely ordered rear console. A chrome engine dress-up kit was no longer standard. A new LS5 455 HO engine with four-barrel carburetion and 8.4:1 compression producing 335 hp was standard with a heavy-duty three-speed manual gearbox and floor shifter. The Trans Am price tag started at $4,594 and only 2,116 T/As were built.

BASE FIREBIRD - SIX/V-8 - SERIES 223

Standard equipment on the basic Firebird included vinyl bucket seats, a woodgrain instrument panel insert, a deluxe steering wheel, an Endura front bumper, bright grille moldings, standard hubcaps, narrow rocker panel moldings, front disc/rear drum brakes and E78-14 tires. An inline 250-cid 145-hp overhead-valve six-cylinder Chevrolet-built engine and three-speed manual transmission were standard.

FIREBIRD ESPRIT - V-8 - SERIES 224

Esprits included custom trim features with knit vinyl upholstery, a custom cushion steering wheel, a trunk mat, bright roof drip moldings, wheel opening moldings, concealed windshield wipers, twin body-colored outside rearview mirrors, wheel trim rings and dual horns as standard extras. Power was supplied by the two-barrel 350-cid V-8 with 8.0:1 compression and 250 hp at 4400 rpm. A floor-mounted three-speed manual transmission was the standard gearbox.

*TRANS AMS WENT LARGELY UNCHANGED
IN THE LOOKS DEPARTMENT FOR 1971.*

FIREBIRD FORMULA - V-8 - SERIES 226

Standard equipment on Formula Firebirds included a handling package, dual exhausts with chrome extensions and a heavy-duty three-speed manual transmission. Also featured were standard hubcaps, F70-14 black sidewall tires and Formula 350 or 400 or 455 identification. Engine choices were the two-barrel 350-cid V-8, the four-barrel 400-cid V-8, the four-barrel 455-cid V-8 and the 455 H.O. V-8.

TRANS AM - V-8 - SERIES 228

Standard equipment on Trans Ams included all-vinyl bucket seats, a Rally gauge cluster (with a clock and a tachometer), an Endura front bumper, a Formula steering wheel, twin body-color outside rearview mirrors (left-hand mirror remote controlled), special honeycomb wheels, functional front fender air extractors, a rear deck lid spoiler, a black textured grille insert, bright grille moldings, front and rear wheel opening air spoilers, concealed windshield wipers, Trans Am identification markings, a performance dual exhaust system with tailpipe extensions, a special air cleaner with rear-facing cold air intake on hood controlled by throttle, a power-flex cooling fan, power steering, a Saf-

T-Track differential, a handling package, dual horns, power front disc/rear drum brakes and F60-15 white lettered tires. The UPC LS5 455 H.O. engine with four-barrel carburetion, 8.4:1 compression and 335 hp at 4800 rpm was standard in all Trans Ams, as was a four-speed manual gearbox with floor shifter. As in the past, the Trans Am was offered only in a limited number of exterior finish colors. Cars done in "Cameo White" had blue stripes on a black base. Also available was "Lucerne Blue" body finish with white stripes on a black base. One minor change was the absence of a chrome engine dress-up kit on the standard equipment list.

HISTORICAL FOOTNOTES

Production of the 1971 models started Aug. 10, 1970. Model year production was 53,125 Firebirds. That included 46,655 cars with automatic transmission and 6,470 cars with manual transmission. Firebird sales were 49,078 for the model year and 55,462 for the calendar year. Firebird sales and production totals were pulled down by a United Auto workers strike that began Sept. 14, 1970, and lasted 67 days. A Trans Am-based racecar nicknamed the "Tirebird" was campaigned this year. Driven by John Cordts and sponsored by the B.F. Goodrich Tire Co., it took a third overall at Watkins Glen.

THE TRANS AM WAS STILL IN PRODUCTION IN 1972, BUT IT WAS ALMOST IDENTICAL TO THE TWO PREVIOUS YEARS.

1972

It was nearly a wrap for the Firebird in 1972. A 174-day-long U.A.W. strike at the Norwood, Ohio, factory created all kinds of problems. By the time it was over, federal laws had changed and the cars left sitting on the assembly line had to be trashed. GM seriously thought about killing the Firebird (and Camaro). This kept product changes minimal. A honeycomb grille, new interiors and restyled hubcaps and wheel covers were among the few alterations.

Standard equipment in base models included front bucket seats, rear bucket-style seats, vinyl trim, carpets, an Endura nose and a small full-width front air dam. The base engine was a Chevy inline six-banger. Prices ranged upwards from $2,838. Pontiac reported making 12,000 base coupes.

The Esprit had name scripts on its roof pillars, custom cloth-and-Morrokide trim, distinctive door panels, a perforated headliner and other slightly upscale trim features for about $300 ad-

ditional. Pontiac made 11,415 of this model and most of them probably had the base two-barrel 350-cid V-8 and optional Turbo-Hydra-Matic.

The Formula retained a street-performance car image with a twin air scoops on its fiberglass hood, a thick front stabilizer, firm shocks, fat tires and dual exhausts with chrome tips. A four-barrel 350-cid V-8 was standard, but 400-cid and 455 H.O. V-8s could also be ordered. Model year output was 5,250 cars.

Trans Ams had a street-racer look with a Formula steering wheel, engine-turned dash, rally gauges, air dams, flares and spoilers. They included fast-rate power steering, fat stabilizers, high-rate springs, a Safe-T-Track axle and a 300-hp 455 H.O. V-8 with cold-air induction and a four-speed close-ratio gear box with floor shift. Turbo-Hydra-Matic was a no-cost option. Only 1,286 were built.

The 1972 Trans Am with a four-speed manual transmission could do the quarter mile in 14.3 seconds at 98 mph. *High Performance Cars* magazine tested the same 455 H.O. in two different states of tune in its September and October issues. The car had a four-speed gearbox and 3.42:1 rear axle. In stock trim it turned the quarter mile in 14.58 seconds at 98 mph. For the later test it was tuned by Nunzi's Automotive, a Brooklyn, N.Y, Pontiac specialty shop. This upgrade resulted in a 14.04-second quarter mile at 103.22 mph.

BASE FIREBIRD - SIX/V-8 - SERIES 2S

There was a new honeycomb mesh grille insert, new interior trims, redesigned hubcaps and restyled wheel covers. Standard equipment in the basic model included front bucket seats, rear bucket type seats, all-vinyl seat trim, solid foam seat cushions with integral springs, loop-pile carpet, a deluxe steering wheel, an upper-level ventilation system, woodgrained dashboard accents, an ashtray light, an Endura front bumper, a small full-width front air dam, hubcaps, a windshield radio antenna, bright moldings on the windshield, rear window and grille, thin body sill moldings, front disc/rear drum brakes, a three-speed manual transmission with column-mounted gearshift lever on six-cylinder cars (floor-mounted gearshift lever on cars with V-8s) and E78-14 black sidewall tires.

FIREBIRD ESPRIT - V-8 - SERIES 2T

The Esprit had model signature script moldings on the roof pillars. Standard equipment was the same as in basic Firebirds, plus custom cloth and Morrokide interior trim, distinctive door trim panels, a perforated vinyl headliner, added sound insulation, a custom cushion steering wheel, rear armrest ashtrays, a molded trunk mat, a dashboard assist grip, wheel trim rings, body-color sport style outside rearview mirrors (left-hand remote-controlled), body-color door handle inserts, concealed windshield wipers, bright roof rail trim, window sill moldings, rear hood edge accents, wheel opening moldings

and wide rocker panel accent strips. A three-speed manual transmission with floor-mounted gearshift lever was also included.

FIREBIRD FORMULA - V-8 - SERIES 2U

Formula Firebirds had the same equipment features as the base Firebird, plus a fiberglass hood with forward-mounted twin air scoops, a custom cushion steering wheel, body-color outside rearview mirrors, special Formula identification, a 1-1/8-in. front stabilizer bar, firm control shock absorbers, a dual exhaust system with chrome tailpipe extensions, a 1-1/8-in. front stabilizer bar, a 5/8-in. rear stabilizer bar and F70-14 tires. A power-flex fan was standard with the 400- and 455-cid engines.

FIREBIRD TRANS AM - V-8 - SERIES 2V

The Trans Am had the same standard features as the Firebird, plus a 455 H.O. V-8, a Formula steering wheel, engine-turned dashboard trim, a Rally gauge cluster with clock and tachometer, a front air dam, front and rear wheel opening flares, a full-width rear deck spoiler, engine air extractors, a shaker hood, 15-in. Rally II wheel rims with trim rings, black-textured grille inserts, fast-rate power steering, power brakes with front discs and rear drums, a 1 1/4-in. front stabilizer bar, a 7/8-in. rear stabilizer bar, special high-rate rear springs, a Safe-T-Track differential, an air cleaner with rear-facing cold air induction system, a power-flex cooling fan, performance dual exhausts with chrome extensions, four-speed close-ratio manual transmission with floor-mounted gearshift (or Turbo-Hydra-Matic) and F60-15 white lettered tires. The Trans Am again came only in "Cameo White" with blue racing stripes or "Lucerne Blue" finish with white racing stripes.

HISTORICAL FOOTNOTES

Production of the 1972 models started Aug. 12, 1971. Firebird sales were 31,204 for the model year and 22,865 for the calendar year.

Jerry Heasley photo

**THE 1973 TRANS AM SD 455 COUPE CLOCKED A
13.54-SECOND QUARTER MILE IN ONE MAGAZINE TEST.**

1973

This was the year to add performance, but the appearance of the Firebird changed only modestly. There was a new grille with rows of boxes you could store eggs in. GM also had to work out some affordable changes to the Endura nose to make it meet government crash standards. Prices rose modestly and production climbed to 14,096.

Firebird Esprits could be identified by the chrome model "signatures" on their roof pillars. Standard equipment included a custom interior, concealed wipers, twin body-color mirrors and African crossfire mahogany interior accents. A 150-hp version of the 350-cid V-8 with a two-barrel carburetor was standard. This model gained additional buyers in 1973 and 17,249 were made.

Formula Firebirds could again be identified by the special twin-scoop hoods. Other features included a custom cushion steering wheel, heavy-duty suspension, black-textured grille,

Jerry Heasley photo

THE '73 WAS NICELY APPOINTED INSIDE.

Jerry Heasley photo

THE BUCCANEER RED T/A MADE A BOLD STATEMENT.

175-hp Formula 350 V-8 with dual exhausts, and F70-14 tires. Engine options up to 310 hp were offered. The popularity of the Formula nearly doubled as its model year production rose to 10,166.

The most significant 1973 Trans Am changes were the addition of stylized Firebird graphics on the hood and the release of a "Super-Duty" 455-cid V-8, which was also available in Formulas. Stylist John Schinella created the so-called "chicken" hood decal, a modernized rendition of the legendary Indian symbol.

The SD-455 V-8 evolved from the Trans-Am racing program of the early 1970s. It represented a low-compression, extra-horsepower option made available in limited quantities. It featured a special block with reinforced webbing, large forged-steel connecting rods, special aluminum pistons, a heavy-duty oiling system with dry sump pump provision, a high-lift camshaft, four-bolt main bearing caps, special valve train components, dual exhausts and a special intake manifold. The SD-455 heads were a variation on Pontiac's Ram Air IV heads. They had 1.77-in. exhaust valves and 2.11-in. intake valves with special cupped heads and swirl-polish finish. The SD-455's free-flowing, cast-iron, round-

port headers were designed for performance, too. An SD-455 Trans Am was capable of 0 to 60 mph in 7.3 seconds and did the quarter mile in 15 seconds.

Standard Trans Am equipment was the same as 1972, plus the new "chicken" hood graphics. For the model year, a total of 4,802 Trans Ams were built. Production of SD-455 Trans Ams totaled 252, of which 180 had automatic and 72 had stick shift. Fifty Formula Firebirds also had the SD-455 V-8.

BASE FIREBIRD - SIX/V-8
- SERIES 2FS

Standard equipment in the basic model included front bucket seats, rear bucket type seats, all-vinyl seat trim, solid foam seat cushions with integral springs, loop-pile carpet, a deluxe steering wheel, an upper-level ventilation system, woodgrain dashboard accents, an ashtray light, an Endura front bumper, a small full-width front air dam, hubcaps, a windshield radio antenna, bright moldings on the windshield, rear window and grille, thin body sill moldings, front disc/rear drum brakes, a three-speed manual transmission with floor shift and E78-14 black sidewall tires.

FIREBIRD ESPRIT - V-8 - SERIES 2FT

The Firebird Esprit could be most easily identified by the model signature scripts on the roof pillars. Also considered standard equipment were a custom interior, concealed windshield wipers, twin body-color outside rearview mirrors (left-hand remote-control), dual horns, deluxe wheel covers, all-vinyl or cloth-and-vinyl custom interior trim, African crossfire mahogany dash and console accent panels, a 350-cid 150-nhp two-barrel V-8 and a three-speed manual transmission.

FIREBIRD FORMULA - V-8 - SERIES 2FU

Formula Firebirds could again be identified by the special twin-scoop hoods. Other features included a custom cushion steering wheel, heavy-duty suspension, black-textured grille, dual exhausts and F70-14 tires, plus all items included on lower-priced lines. This year Formula Firebird owners initially had a choice of three V-8 engines, the 350 cid, the 400 cid and the 455 cid. Late in the year, the Super-Duty version of the 455-cid V-8 was also offered to Formula buyers. See the Trans Am section for information about this engine. The "SD-455" was used in only 43 Formula Firebirds in 1973.

FIREBIRD TRANS AM - V-8 - SERIES 2FV

The most significant change to the Firebird Trans Am this season was the addition of the optional, but very popular, "chicken" or "big bird" graphics treatment for the hood. Stylist John Schinella created this modernized rendition of the legendary Indian symbol. Standard equipment included a Formula steering wheel, a Rally gauge cluster with clock and tachometer, a full-width rear deck spoiler, power steering, power front disc/rear drum brakes, a Safe-T-Track differential, wheel opening flares, front fender air extractors, dual exhausts with chrome extensions, heavy-duty underpinnings, Rally II

wheels with trim rings, dual body-color outside rearview mirrors (left-hand remote-controlled), F60-15 white-lettered tires and a choice of Turbo-Hydra-Matic or four-speed manual transmission. The Super-Duty 455 V-8 engine was an option that evolved from Pontiac's Trans Am racing program of the early 1970s. It represented a low-compression, extra-horsepower option made available in extremely limited quantities. The "SD-455" featured a special block with reinforced webbing, large forged-steel connecting rods, special aluminum pistons, a heavy-duty oiling system (with dry sump pump provisions), a high-performance camshaft, special round port cylinder heads, four-bolt main bearing caps, a special intake manifold, a special dual exhausts system and high-performance valve train components. The SD-455 Trans Am could do the quarter mile in 13.54 seconds at 104.29 mph. A pre-production version of the SD-455 had a 310-hp motor, but all SD-455s sold to the public had 290 hp. The SD-455 was available in cars with only three colors: Brewster Green, Cameo White and Buccaneer Red.

HISTORICAL FOOTNOTES

Model year production of all Firebirds was 46,313. Model year sales were 43,869 units and calendar year sales stood at 52,219 units. A "Buccaneer Red" pre-production version of the SD-455 with the 308/320 "K" camshaft and 310 hp, TH400 transmission and 3.42:1 gears was tested by *Hot Rod* magazine in June 1973. It did 0 to 60 mph in 7.3 seconds and the quarter mile in 13.54 seconds at 104.29 mph. At midyear, the Environmental Protection Agency issued an order to remove a time-delay emissions system from Pontiac engines. All engines built after March 15 with serial numbers above 532727 were so modified, along with 700 earlier engines. Power plants having this change were painted a darker-than-normal shade of blue. They also had two thermal valves tapped into the intake manifold and no exhaust gas recirculation (EGR) system solenoid.

Jerry Heasley photo

THIS ULTRA-RARE 1974 TRANS AM SD-455 SHARED THE YEAR'S NEW FRONT-END STYLING

1974

By 1974, it was time to give the Firebird a "facial." The new front end had shovel-nose styling and twin-slot grilles with vertical fins. At the rear, the taillights took the form of long, horizontal slots. Stylists lowered the rear fender line. The new image was not warmly embraced by the car-buying public and only 26,372 Firebirds rolled out of the factory in Ohio.

As usual, model badges decorated the Esprit's roof. Standard on this line were trim and convenience-feature upgrades. Production was up to 22,583 units.

In addition to equipment standard in Esprits, Formulas featured hubcaps, dual-scoop fiberglass hoods, special heavy-duty suspension, black-textured grilles, dual exhausts and F70-14 tires. Available model options included Formula 350, Formula 400, and Formula 455. Production was 14,519 cars.

Standard equipment on Trans Ams included a formula steering wheel, Rally gauges with clock and tachometer, swirl-grain dash trim, full-width rear deck lid spoiler, power steering

and front disc brakes, limited-slip differential, wheel opening air flares, front fender air extractors, dual exhausts with chrome extensions, Rally II wheels with trim rings, special heavy-duty suspension, four-speed manual transmission (or M40 Turbo-Hydra-Matic), dual outside racing mirrors and F60-15 white-lettered tires. Production climbed to 10,255.

The SD-455 V-8 went into 212 Firebirds, most of which were Trans Ams. Despite this low number, PMD did great publicizing the SD-455's outstanding performance. Several car magazines reported that Firebirds with this option were faster and quicker than a Corvette. Publicity like that enhanced PMD's performance image and attracted many Firebird buyers to Pontiac showrooms.

BASE FIREBIRD - SIX/V-8 SERIES - 2FS

New Firebird styling changes included a shovel-nosed Endura front end, a horizontal slotted taillight treatment, a lowered rear fender line and twin horizontal rectangular grille inserts with vertical blades. All Firebird models had ashtrays, lamps, nylon carpeting, high/low ventilation, Endura styling and a windshield radio antenna. The basic Firebird also featured a deluxe two-spoke steering wheel, a single-buckle seat and shoulder belt arrangement, narrow rocker panel moldings and E78-14 tires. A reduced compression ratio gave the base six-cylinder engine 10 less horsepower. A 350-cid V-8 with a two-barrel carburetor was optional. Cars with this engine got "350" engine callouts on the front fenders. Firebird interiors were carried over from 1973, except for new color schemes. Buyers could order multi-color combinations such as white seats with red door panels, dashboard and carpeting. Also, the fabric formerly known as Bravo bolster cloth was renamed Bravado bolster cloth.

FIREBIRD ESPRIT - V-8 - SERIES 2FT

As usual, the model name in chrome script on the rear roof pillar was a trait of the Firebird Esprit. Standard extras on this line included a custom cushion steering wheel, a custom interior package, body-color door handle inserts, concealed wipers with articulated left arm, deluxe wheel covers, dual horns, body-colored dual outside rearview sport mirrors (left-hand remote-controlled), roof drip and wheel opening moldings, wide body sill moldings, window sill and rear hood edge moldings, a three-speed manual floor shift (with base engine only), a safety belt warning system and E78-14 tires. A 350-cid V-8 with a two-barrel carburetor and single exhaust was the standard engine. A 400-cid V-8 with a two-barrel carburetor and automatic transmission attachment was optional.

THE TRANS AM AGAIN CAME WITH MULTIPLE ENGINE OPTIONS FOR 1974, INCLUDING AN S-D 445 VERSION.

THE '74 T/A WAS NOT LACKING IN BELLS AND WHISTLES. THE EXTERIOR GOODIES INCLUDED A HOOD SCOOP, FLARED WHEEL WELLS, DUAL EXHAUST AND SPORT MIRRORS.

PONTIAC SOLD MORE THAN 10,000 1974 TRANS AMS.

FORMULA FIREBIRD - V-8 - SERIES 2FU

In addition to equipment standard in the base Firebird, the Formula featured hubcaps, a dual-scoop fiberglass hood, a special heavy-duty suspension, black-textured grilles, a dual exhaust system, a custom cushion steering wheel and F70-14 tires. Available model options included Formula 350, Formula 400 and Formula 455, as well as the rare Formula SD-455.

FIREBIRD TRANS AM - V-8 - SERIES 2FV

Standard equipment on Trans Am included a formula steering wheel, a Rally gauge cluster with clock and dash panel tachometer, swirl grain dashboard trim, a full-width rear deck lid spoiler, power steering, power front disc/rear drum brakes, a limited-slip differential, wheel opening air deflectors (flares), front fender air extractors, dual exhausts with chrome extensions, Rally II wheels with trim rings, a special heavy-duty suspension, a four-speed manual transmission (or M40 Turbo-Hydra-Matic), dual outside racing mirrors and F60-15 white-lettered tires. The standard engine was a 400-cid 225-nhp V-8 with a four-barrel carburetor. The 455-cid 250-nhp L75 engine was optional. A rare option was the SD-455 engine.

HISTORICAL FOOTNOTES

The 1974 Pontiacs were introduced on Sept. 20, 1973. Model year production of Firebirds rose to 73,729 vehicles of which 66,126 had V-8 engines. A total of 1,008 Trans Ams were built with LS2 SD-455 engines. Sales came in at 66,350 units for the model year and 67,391 for the calendar year. *Motor Trend* nominated the Firebird for its "Car of the Year" award and described the car as the "best combination available of pure performance and handling in the U.S. Grand Touring market." In one survey, *Motor Trend* asked 1,500 Japanese car enthusiasts to pick the best car in the world. The Firebird came out ahead of the Mustang by a slight margin and well ahead of the Corvette. *Super Stock* magazine (June 1974) put an SD-455 Trans Am through its paces. The car had the TH-400 transmission and 3.08:1 rear axle. It did the quarter mile in 14.25 seconds at 100.93 mph.

Jerry Heasley photo

FLARED WHEEL WELLS, HOOD SCOOP AND
SPOILER MADE THE T/A EASILY RECOGNIZABLE.

1975

Firebird sales picked up in 1975, although the cars continued to look much the same as before. The biggest update was a new rear window that wrapped around the corners of the roof to give the driver improved vision. GM's HEI electronic ignition system was added to the equipment list along with a radial tuned suspension system. The base Firebirds were the plainest-looking and had visible windshield wipers. Esprits had concealed wipers, dressy moldings, body-color door handle inserts and chrome "Esprit" signatures on the roof. Formulas featured were ready for some street action with their heavy-duty underpinnings and dual hood scoops. The Trans Am was ready to go sports-car racing with its bolt-on flares, spoilers, engine air extractors, shaker hood scoop and "chicken" decals.

There were some technical changes. The Espirit's base engine became the Chevy-built six instead of the 350-cid two-barrel V-8. At the start of the year, the biggest Trans Am engine was the 400-cid V-8. At midyear, the 455-cid V-8 was reinstated, but with single exhausts and a catalytic converter. Due to decreased horsepower, the M38 Turbo-Hydra-Matic was the only automatic used. All Firebirds certified for sale in California were required to use this transmission.

Model-year production included 22,293 Firebirds, 20,826 Espirits, 13,670 Formula Firebirds and 27,274 Trans Ams. Only 8,314 Firebirds were built with the in-line six-cylinder engine. Most (26,417) Trans Ams had the 400-cid 185-hp L78 four-barrel V-8. Only 857 Trans Ams were built with the 455-cid 200-hp L75 four-barrel V-8. Road testers found the 1975 Trans Am with the L78 drive train capable of 0 to 60 mph in 9.8 seconds and the quarter mile in 16.8 seconds.

BASE FIREBIRD - SIX/V-8 - SERIES 2FS

This was the year that GM added performance-robbing catalytic converters to all of its cars, including the Firebird. Firebirds continued to look much the same as in 1974, except for a new roofline with a 10 percent larger wrap-around backlight. The grille had new rectangular running lamps and turn signal lamps. High Energy Ignition and Radial Tuned Suspension systems were added to the equipment list. As usual, base models had conventional wipers, "baby moon" hubcaps, a deluxe two-spoke steering wheel and minimal bright work. Inside the standard Madrid Morrokide bucket seat interior came in black, white or saddle regular combinations. Options included black or saddle interiors with white seats or four special combinations. The standard 250-cid overhead valve in-line six was up to 105 hp. Three-speed manual transmission was standard in 49 states and a Turbo-Hydra-Matic 350 (THM-350) transmission was standard in cars sold in California. A four-speed manual transmission was optional. The 350-cid two-barrel V-8 was $130 extra and required installation of Turbo-Hydra-Matic transmission as a separate $237 option.

FIREBIRD ESPRIT - SIX/V-8 - SERIES 2FT

Esprits had all of the same standard features as the base Firebird, plus concealed windshield wipers, a custom interior, decor moldings, colored vinyl door handle inserts, wide rocker moldings, deluxe wheel covers, dual horns, "Esprit" roof pillar signature scripts and an "Esprit" script on the right-hand corner of the rear deck lid. The base power plant in Esprit was now the Chevy-built six. The 350-cid two-barrel V-8 was available at the same price as in base Firebirds and the Turbo-Hydra-Matic 350 was the only transmission available

FORMULA FIREBIRD - V-8 - SERIES 2FU

Formula Firebirds featured heavy-duty chassis components, wider front and rear tracks and a distinctive twin scoop hood. The base engine was a 350-cid V-8 with a four-barrel carburetor and dual outlet "splitter" exhausts. The standard transmission was either a four-speed manual with a floor-mounted gearshift or Turbo-Hydra-Matic, also with a floor-mounted gearshift. The THM-350 was required for cars sold in California.

TRANS AM - V-8 - SERIES 2FV

The Trans Am had flares, front and rear air dams, extractors, shaker hood scoop, Firebird decals, a rear deck lid spoiler, rally gauges, rally wheel rims and a shaker hood scoop. There were some changes in a technical sense. At the beginning of the year, the biggest engine for the 1975 Trans Am was a 400-cid, 185-hp V-8 that included a four-barrel carburetor and a dual outlet "splitter" exhaust system. At midyear, a 455-cid, 200-hp four-barrel V-8 was reinstated. Labeled the 455 H.O., it included a tuned exhaust setup with pipes that branched into dual "splitters" behind the catalytic converter. The 445 H.O. option also included a 3.23:1 performance rear axle and semi-metallic disc brakes. Trans Am colors were Sterling Silver, Stellar Blue, Buccaneer Red and Cameo White.

HISTORICAL FOOTNOTES

The 1975 Firebirds appeared in showrooms on Sept. 27, 1974. Model year output was 84,063 cars. Sales came out as 75,565 in the model year and 82,652 in the calendar year. Road testers found the 1975 Trans Am with the 185-nhp V-8 capable of 0 to 60 mph in 9.8 seconds and the quarter mile in 16.8 seconds. *Car and Driver* magazine (September 1975) tested a Trans Am with the 455-cid V-8, four-speed manual transmission and 3.23:1 gears. It did the quarter mile in 16.1 seconds at 88.8 mph. In March of 1975 *Road Test* magazine put a Trans Am with a 400-cid V-8, a THM-350 and 2.56:1 gears through its paces and recorded quarter-mile performance of 17.99 seconds at 79.36 mph.

THE '76 LIMITED EDITION TRANS AM CAME ONLY IN STARLIGHT BLACK.

1976

The "chrome-bumper" Firebird had disappeared! This year all four Pontiac F-cars wore body-colored urethane bumpers front and rear. For a little bit extra, buyers could add a new canopy-style vinyl top. Other product innovations included a Formula appearance package and a fuel economy indicator. Stylists recessed the square, single headlamps into the front fenders and topped things off with a traditional Pontiac split grille. It had a mesh pattern insert.

Firebird/Esprit equipment included the 250-cid six with three-speed manual gearbox, power steering and radial-tuned suspension. Esprits added sport mirrors and deluxe wheel covers. Formula had a 350-cid two-barrel V-8, a choice of four-speed manual or Turbo-Hydra-Matic transmission and a full-length console. Trans Am added an air dam, a rear spoiler, a shaker hood, Rally II wheels, Rally gauges, fat GR70 x 15 tires and a 400-cid four-barrel V-8.

A special Trans Am that created excitement and sales was introduced at the 1976 Chicago Auto Show. This "Limited Edition" model featured Starlight black finish with gold striping, gold interior accents, gold honeycomb wheels and a super-sized version of the "chicken" hood decal. This original Limited Edition T/A commemorated PMD's 50th anniversary and was actually modified with a T-top conversion installed by Hurst. A total of 2,590 were made.

The overall popularity of Firebird and Esprit models remained much the same as the previous year with 21,209 base models and 22,252 Esprits leaving the factory in 1976. However, the Formula was becoming a hotter product with 20,613 assemblies and the Trans Am was on fire with 46,701 built. That was a production increase of 51 percent for Formulas and 71 percent for Trans Ams!

FIREBIRD - SIX/V-8 - SERIES 2FS

The 1976 Firebird again had a twin-section grille with a mesh pattern insert set into a sloping front panel. The single round headlamps were recessed into square bezels. The parking and signal lamps were located at each end of a wide, slot-like opening below the bumper strip. Another styling change was that all Firebirds featured body-colored urethane bumpers at both ends. New-for-1976 options included a canopy-style vinyl half-top, a new appearance package for Formula models and a fuel economy indicator. Brake systems on all Firebirds were refined to meet federal standards, axle ratios were lowered to promote better fuel economy and V-8 engines idled slower for the same reason. There were improvements to the cooling and air-conditioning system.

FIREBIRD ESPRIT - SIX/V-8 SERIES 2FT

Standard Firebird Esprit equipment included a Chevrolet-built 250-cid inline six with a three-speed manual transmission. The custom interior that was standard in the Esprit featured wider vertical ribs than the standard interior. On the seatbacks the ribs were bordered by a "horse col-lar" and on the seat cushions they ran right down to the floor. Custom door panels were the same as the 1975 design.

FORMULA FIREBIRD - V-8 - SERIES 2FU

Standard Formula Firebird equipment included 350-cid (5.7-liter) V-8 engine, a Turbo-Hydra-Matic or close-ratio four-speed manual (code M-21 Borg-Warner Super T-10) transmission, a new all-steel duct-type dual scoop hood and power steering,. The two-barrel 350-cid V-8 (available only with the THM-350 transmission) was not legal in California and buyers there had to order the four-barrel version as a mandatory option. It came only with Turbo-Hydra-Matic drive. The 400-cid V-8 was available nationwide for $118 extra. The new W50 Formula Appearance package was an option that included contrasting finish on the lower body perimeter and air scoops and "Formula" graphics on the lower body sides. At first the W50 package came only with a yellow main body and black body side and scoop finish, but it was later available in four color combinations C, N, T and V. Over 85 percent of Formula customers ordered this option. The 455-cid V-8 wasn't offered in the Formula.

PONTIAC SOLD MORE THAN 20,000 FORMULA VERSIONS OF ITS FIREBIRD IN 1976.

R. Boone photo

FIRETHORN RED WITH A BLACK INTERIOR WAS A NICE COLOR COMBINATION FOR THE 1976 TRANS AM. THIS WAS ONE OF ABOUT 5,400 400 FOUR-SPEEDS BUILT THAT YEAR.

FIREBIRD TRANS AM - V-8 - SERIES 2FW

Standard Trans Am equipment included all federally mandated safety, anti-theft, convenience and emissions control features, a 400-cid (6.6-litre) V-8 engine, an M-21 close-ratio four-speed manual transmission (Turbo-Hydra-Matic was optional), a shaker hood scoop and air cleaner, a front air dam, concealed windshield wipers, front fender air extractors, rear wheel opening air deflectors, power steering, Rally gauges with a clock and tachometer, front disc/rear drum brakes, a heater, a defroster, carpeting, windshield moldings, a formula steering wheel, dual sport mirrors with left-hand remote controlled, dual horns, a rear deck lid spoiler, chrome side-splitter tailpipe extensions, Rally II wheels with trim rings, GR70-15 raised white letter tires and a Radial Tuned Suspension. Trans Am color choices for 1976 were: Firethorn Red, Sterling Silver, Starlight Black, Carousel Red, Goldenrod Yellow and Cameo White.

FIREBIRD TRANS AM LIMITED EDITION - V-8 - SERIES 2W/Y81/Y82

In February 1976, at the Chicago Automobile Show, Pontiac introduced the Limited Edition Trans Am. This package featured Starlight Black exterior body finish, gold pin striping, gold interior accents (including gold anodized instrument panel appliqués and gold steering wheel spokes), gold grilles, gold headlight liners, gold honeycomb wheel rims and a host of other special distinctions. The car was promoted as a commemorative edition for Pontiac Motor Division's 50th anniversary. The 1976 Limited Edition models were inspired by a 1974 show car that took its theme from the black-and-gold John Player racing cars. The package was designed by John Schinella and featured a gold version of his trademark "screaming chicken" decal on the hood. Pontiac built the entire car and then sent it to Hurst Corp. for modifications such as having "T-tops" installed. Hurst Hatch T-top roofs were installed on 643 cars. This T-top design was originally devised for the 50th Anniversary Grand Prix and there were problems adapting it to the Firebird body. Production did not start until April of 1976 and Hurst Hatch roofs were used on only about 25 percent of the Limited Editions made that year.

HISTORICAL FOOTNOTES

Introduced September 25, 1975. Model-year production of Firebirds was 110,775, an all-time record and the first six-figure year since 1968. Sales totals stood at 98,405 Firebirds for the model year and 108,348 Firebirds for the calendar year, both of which were records for the nameplate. *CARS* magazine named the 1976 Trans Am "Top Performance Car of the Year."

THE 1977 ESPIRIT CAME WITH THREE ENGINE CHOICES: V-6, 301 V-8 AND 350 V-8.

1977

By the late '70s the wisdom of keeping the Firebird in the Pontiac line was becoming evident with sales numbers zooming and profit levels rising thanks to the second-generation F-car's longevity. For 1977, the designers favored a front end with four rectangular headlights and "honeycomb" grille texture. The grille insert was recessed and it jutted out at the bottom, in the center, to give the vertical center divider a more aggressive V shape.

Four models were offered: base, Esprit, and performance Formula and Trans Am. Formula's had a new hood with simulated air scoops and a rear-deck-lid spoiler. Engine choices ranged from a Buick-built 231-cid (3.8-liter) V-6 to an Oldsmobile-built 403-cid (6.6-liter) V-8. Esprit buyers could order a new blue "Sky Bird" appearance package with blue velour seating, a subtle two-tone blue body finish and blue cast-aluminum wheels. A new 301-cid (5.0-liter) two-barrel V-8 was standard in Formulas, which also had black-out trim and large "For-

mula" graphics on the lower part of the doors. Trans Ams had a new shaker hood and came with a standard 400- or 403-cid V-8. Also available was an optional "T/A 6.6" version of the Pontiac-built 400-cid power plant with an 8.0:1 compression ratio and 200 hp. Cars so-equipped could do 0 to 60 in 9.3 seconds and had a top speed approaching 110 mph.

The Trans Am could again be ordered with an extra-cost package, which was called the Special Edition rather than Limited Edition. It was available in Y81 coupe and Y82 Hurst Hatch (or T-top) models. Custom gold decals and gold snowflake wheels really set off this well-integrated appearance option. PMD records indicate that 15,567 Special Edition Trans Ams were built in 1977.

While performance may have been down somewhat from earlier years, the Trans Am still had a hot, sexy sports-racing-car image that drove the Firebird's popularity higher. Model year production totals included 30,642 base

Firebirds, 34,548 Esprits, 21,801 Formulas and 68,745 high-profit-margin Trans Ams. To put the Firebird's success in perspective, remember that less than 30,000 were made just five years earlier, when the model's future seemed dim.

FIREBIRD - V-6/V-8 - SERIES 2FS

New front-end styling for the Firebird coupe featured quad rectangular headlamps and an "aggressive" grille. The wheelbase was 108 in. and engine choices ranged from a 231-cid two-barrel (3.8-liter) V-6 to the 350-cid four-barrel (5.7-liter) V-8. Firebird's new grille was deeply recessed, directly in line with the quad rectangular headlamps. Its simple pattern consisted of a series of round-like (hexagonal) holes that resembled fencing more than a customary grille. A "Pontiac" nameplate went on the driver's side of the grille. Crossbar-trimmed amber parking and signal lamps were also recessed, but into the outer ends of twin air intake slots positioned in the bumper valance panel, on either side of a solid and "veed" center section. The "nose" of the Firebird protruded forward to a slight point and held a V-shaped Pontiac emblem in the center, but the sides were more sharply angled than the prior version. Standard engine in the base Firebird was now the 231-cid (3.8-liter) V-6 with a two-barrel carburetor. A Chevrolet-built 301-cid (5.0-liter) two-barrel V-8 was a new engine for the base Firebird and Esprit that became available about Feb. 1, 1977. Other engine options for these models — in all regions of the country — included the 350-cid (5.7-liter) four-barrel V-8. A three-speed manual transmission was used with the base engine.

FIREBIRD ESPRIT - V-6/V-8 - SERIES 2FT

The Esprit could have a new blue "Skybird" appearance package with blue velour seating, two-tone blue body, a dark blue rear panel, dark blue grille panels, accent stripes, special identification and blue cast-aluminum wheels. Esprit engine choices were the same as those for the base Firebird. A three-speed manual transmission was used with the base engine.

FORMULA FIREBIRD - V-8 - SERIES 2FU

Standard engine in the Formula in 49 states was a 301-cid (5.0-liter) two-barrel V-8 made by Pontiac. In California and "high-altitude" counties a 350-cid (5.7-liter) four-barrel V-8 was standard. Other options included the 5.7-liter four-barrel V-8 in "federal" areas, two versions of a 400-cid Pontiac four-barrel V-8 and a 403-cid Oldsmobile four-barrel V-8. Some engines were not available in California and others were available only in California. A power-flex radiator fan was used with 6.6-liter V-8s. A four-speed manual transmission was available with the 301-cid (5.0-liter) V-8 and the T/A 6.6-liter (400-cid) engines. Turbo-Hydra-Matic transmission was optional. Standard Formula equipment included the new black-out grille, a new steel hood with twin simulated air scoops, integral body-colored bumpers, new rectangular headlamps, bright windshield and rear window moldings, bright grille moldings, Firebird emblems on the sail panel and rear deck lid, a rear deck lid spoiler, dual horns, front bucket seats, bucket-type rear seats, all-Morrokide bucket seats and a full-length front console. Buyers who ordered the optional Formula Appearance package got a blacked-out lower body and hood scoops, multi-color stripes and large "Formula" super graphics on the body sides.

FIREBIRD TRANS AM - V-8 - SERIES 2FW

The Trans Am equipment list started off with all federally mandated safety, anti-theft, convenience and emissions control features. A 400-cid (6.6-liter) V-8 engine was standard in 49 states and a 403-cid (6.6-liter) V-8 was standard in California or high-altitude counties. The T/A 6.6-liter (400-cid) V-8 was optional. Other standard equipment included a Turbo-Hydra-Matic transmission (or four-speed manual transmission with the optional T/A 6.6-liter V-8), a

Trans Am wraparound rear deck spoiler decal, a front center air dam, rear wheel opening air deflectors, a shaker hood scoop and air cleaner, concealed windshield wipers, front fender air extractors, power steering, a Power-Flex radiator fan, Rally gauges with a clock and tachometer, a front seat console, power front disc/rear drum brakes, a heater, a defroster, a rear deck lid spoiler, dual chrome splitter tailpipe extensions, 15 x 7-in. Rally II wheels with trim rings, a Safe-T-Track limited-slip differential, GR70-15 black sidewall steel-belted radial tires and a Radial Tuned Suspension with larger front and rear stabilizer bars.

FIREBIRD TRANS AM BLACK SPECIAL EDITION - V-8 - SERIES FW/Y81/Y82

The 1977 Special Edition package was similar to the 1976 Limited Edition package. Its standard equipment started off with all federally mandated safety, anti-theft, convenience and emissions control features. The 400-cid (6.6-liter) V-8 was standard in 49 states and the 403-cid (6.6-liter) V-8 was standard in California or high-altitude counties. The T/A 6.6-liter (400-cid) V-8 was optional. .

HISTORICAL FOOTNOTES

Motor Trend road tested a 1977 Firebird Formula with the base 301-cid V-8 and four-speed manual transmission and concluded "Detroit's putting some of the fun back." The car did 0 to 60 mph in 12 seconds and covered the quarter mile in 17.9 seconds at 75.2 mph while providing 20.9 mpg fuel economy. Total model-year production of Firebirds rose to a record 155,736 units.

THE BLACK SPECIAL EDITION TRANS AM WAS THE STAR OF THE FIREBIRD LINE FOR THE SECOND STRAIGHT YEAR.

*THERE WERE FEW MAJOR CHANGES IN THE TRANS AM
(ABOVE) AND FIREBIRD LINEUP FOR 1978.*

1978

With Pontiac dealers struggling to accommodate hoards of Firebird buyers, GM saw no reason to make any sweeping changes in the 1978 models. Small changes were seen, including a couple of new engine options, redesigned seats and an expanded list of extra-cost items with some midyear additions.

Base engine was the 3.8-liter V-6 with three-speed shift. Formulas had a new 305-cid (5.0-liter) V-8, while the Trans Am included a 400-cid (6.6-liter) four-barrel V-8. Firebirds had Endura bumpers, small hubcaps and bucket seats were standard. Esprits added wheel covers, sport mirrors, bright hood and wheel opening moldings and custom pedal trim. Esprit buyers were offered a new "Red Bird" package that was similar to the Sky Bird option, except in red. The blue Sky Bird option also returned. Formulas again had black-out trim and large "Formula" graphics on the lower doors. Trans Am included a front air dam, black grille, rear spoiler, sport mirrors, rear wheel air deflectors, Rally II wheels, a "shaker" hood and air cleaner and rally instrument panel with tachometer. Au-

tomatic transmission was standard on Formulas and Trans Ams, but Formula could have a four-speed manual at no extra cost.

It was another good year for Firebirds, with production of 32,672 base Firebirds, 36,926 Esprits, 24,346 Formulas and 93,341 Trans Ams. Pontiac's calendar-year sales of 896,980 cars were the highest in its history up to the point and the booming popularity of the F-car was a big reason for this achievement.

FIREBIRD - V-6/V-8 - SERIES 2FS

The appearance of the 1978 Firebird was similar to 1977, with rectangular quad headlamps and a dark grille. The wide three-row taillights had back-up lights at the inner ends, close to the license plate. Taillight ribs filled most of the back panel. The base Firebird engine was a 3.8-liter (231-cid) V-6 with a two-barrel carburetor. The new 5.0-liter V-8 with 305 cid replaced the 301-cid V-8 used last year. It cost $117 extra in base Firebirds and Turbo-Hydra-Matic transmission was standard with any V-8.

A four-speed manual gearbox was optional. The 5.7-liter (350-cid) V-8 was also available for $265. A three-speed manual transmission was used with the base V-6.

FIREBIRD ESPRIT - V-6/V-8 SERIES 2FT

In the early part of the 1978 model year Esprit buyers could still order the blue "Sky Bird" appearance package with a choice of code 30 Lombard Blue cloth upholstery with 24N1 Blue Doeskin trim or 24B1 Blue Lombardy trim, a two-tone blue body, a dark blue rear panel, dark blue grille panels, accent stripes, special identification and blue cast aluminum wheels. At midyear, the Sky Bird was replaced by a new "Red Bird" package that included two-tone Red paint, Carmine Red custom interior trim, a red Formula steering wheel, red grille liners and taillight bezels and red-trimmed snowflake aluminum wheel rims. There were also special "Red Bird" decals for the sail panels, but these were gold, as were the lower-body-perimeter pinstripes. Standard engine in the Esprit was the 3.8-liter (231-cid) V-6 with a two-barrel carburetor. The new 305-cid 5.0-liter V-8 was optional for $117 with a Turbo-Hydra-Matic transmission or a four-speed manual gearbox in Federal areas only. The 5.7-liter (350-cid) V-8 was also available for $265 with a Turbo-Hydra-Matic transmission or a four-speed manual gearbox in Federal areas only. The three-speed manual transmission was used with the base engine.

FORMULA FIREBIRD - V-8 SERIES 2FU

Standard engine in the Formula was the Chevrolet 5.0-liter (305-cid) V-8 with a two-barrel carburetor. Other engine options included a 5.7-liter (350-cid) four-barrel V-8 in "federal" areas, two 6.6-liter (400-cid) Pontiac V-8s and a 403-cid Oldsmobile four-barrel V-8. Some engines were not available in California and others were available only in California. A Power-Flex radiator fan was used with 6.6-liter V-8s. A four-speed manual transmission was available

with the base engine and Turbo-Hydra-Matic was optional. The optional Formula Appearance package included a blacked-out lower body and hood scoops, multi-color stripes and large "Formula" super graphics on the body sides.

FIREBIRD TRANS AM - V-8 SERIES 2FW

Standard Trans Am equipment included a 400- or 403-cid (both called "6.6-liter") V-8, a Turbo-Hydra-Matic transmission, a Trans Am front fender decal, a black-out grille, a Trans Am wraparound rear deck spoiler decal, a front center air dam, rear wheel opening air deflectors, a shaker hood scoop and air cleaner, concealed windshield wipers, front fender air extractors, power steering, a Power-Flex radiator fan, Rally gauges with a clock and tachometer, a front seat console, power front disc/rear drum brakes, a heater, a defroster, carpeting, windshield moldings, an aluminum machine-turned instrument panel trim plate, a formula steering wheel, dual sport mirrors with left-hand remote controlled, dual horns, a rear deck lid spoiler, dual chrome splitter tailpipe extensions, 15 x 7-in. Rally II wheels with trim rings, a Safe-T-Track limited-slip differential, GR70-15 black sidewall steel-belted radial tires and a radial-tuned suspension with heavy front and rear stabilizer bars. Trans Ams were available in only seven colors, Cameo White, Platinum, Starlight Black, Martinique Blue, Solar Gold, Chesterfield Brown, Mayan Red and (early in the year) a Sundance Yellow. During early 1978 production, Trans Ams with the WS6 Special Performance package included the UPC W72 "T/A 6.6-Liter" V-8, so early 1978 Trans Ams with the W72 engine also had the WS6 package and a combined package price of $324. Later in the model year, the W72 engine could be ordered in Trans Ams without the WS6 package for $75 extra.

FIREBIRD TRANS AM BLACK SPECIAL EDITION - V-8 SERIES 2FW/Y82/Y84

The original 1978 Black Special Edition

THE OPTIONAL FORMULA APPEARANCE PACKAGE
FEATURED "FORMULA SUPER GRAPHICS."

package was similar to the 1977 Special Edition package. a Radial-Tuned Suspension with larger front and rear stabilizer bars, Starlight Black exterior body finish, gold body striping, gold interior and exterior accents, gold aluminum wheels and a removable hatch roof made by Hurst or GM's Fisher Body Div. During early 1978 production Trans Ams with the WS6 Special Performance package included the UPC W72 "T/A 6.6-Liter" V-8, so early 1978 Trans Ams with the W72 engine also had the WS6 package and a combined package price of $324. Later in the model year, the W72 engine could be ordered in Trans Ams without the WS6 package for $75 extra.

FIREBIRD TRANS AM GOLD SPECIAL EDITION - V-8 - SERIES 2FW/Y88

The 1978 Gold Special Edition package was released at midyear. It came only with the new Fisher T-top roof. Standard Trans Am Gold Special Edition equipment included a Solar Gold exterior body finish, dark gold body striping, a dark gold and bronze "big bird" hood decal, a Camel Tan interior, gold snowflake aluminum wheels and the removable hatch roof. Late in the model year, when the Gold Special Edition cars were offered, the W72 engine could be ordered in Trans Ams without the WS6 package for $75 extra.

HISTORICAL FOOTNOTES

Car and Driver road tested a 1978 Firebird Trans Am with the 400-cid 200-nhp V-8 and Turbo-Hydra-Matic transmission and concluded it was "very sophisticated and impeccably well mannered." The car was fitted with non-stock 2.56:1 gears to produce a 130-mph top speed. It did 0 to 110 mph in 34.8 seconds. A better representation of stock Trans Am performance is found in the spring 1978 issue of *Road Test* magazine. This publication put a Trans Am with the W72 "T/A 6.6-liter" V-8 and a four-speed manual gearbox through its paces. The testers recorded a 7.2 second 0-to-60 performance and a 15.2-second quarter mile at 93 mph. Total model-year production of Firebirds rose to another new record of 187,285 units. Sales stood at 175,607 for the model year and 209,536 for the calendar year.

FORMULA FIREBIRDS LIKE THIS ONE SHARED A NEW FRONT-END LOOK WITH THE BASE FIREBIRDS AND TRANS AMS IN 1979.

1979

Sales were racing and Firebirds were pacing some leading races this year. A special model to celebrate a milestone in Trans Am history didn't hurt the excitement level one bit. The frontal appearance got a nice facelift with square headlights set into individually recessed housings on each side of a wider center panel. Horizontal ribbing was in vogue this year and the stylists used it for grilles below each set of headlights and across the rear end panel. The standard equipment list and model-option offerings were similar to those in 1977.

The Red Bird package was back and the new front-end look seemed to enhance its sophisticated image. A dressy new Custom cloth trim was offered to Esprit buyers. You could get the 1979 Formula without a rear spoiler and with a new Formula steering wheel, instead of the previous Custom Cushion style.

While regular Trans Ams had few alterations, an exciting 10th Anniversary option was new. It included a large "bird" on the hood, silver finish, charcoal gray roof and special 10th anniversary decals. One of these $11,000 cars paced the Daytona 500. The gold-and-black Special Edition package was offered again.

By 1979, the price of a base V-6 Firebird was $4,825 and 38,642 were built. Esprit prices began at $5,193 and 30,853 were produced. Now costing just over $6,000, the Formula had a production run of 24,851 units. Really amazing was the Trans Am, which listed for about $300 more than a Formula and still had 117,108 total assemblies. This added up to more than 211,000 Firebirds built.

FIREBIRD - V-6/V-8 - SERIES 2FS

The third and last facelift for the second-generation Firebird came in 1979. Pontiac literature described the new grilleless look as "a broad new forefront cast in durable urethane." The treatment was used on all Firebird models. It featured a more gently contoured, slanted front nose panel with twin, rectangular-shaped headlights set into squarish ports at either end. The center of the panel came to a V-shaped peak. Below this was another bumper panel with a large license plate recess in its center and two long, thin, horizontal openings on either side. The openings were filled with six grille louvers and white-lensed parking lights. Base Firebirds and

Esprits had full-width taillights with dark-finished bezels, but they lacked the black, opaque covers over the red lenses to create a "blacked-out" look. Exterior color choices were reduced from 18 to 13, but the Trans Am gained one and now had nine. The base Firebird came with a 231-cid two-barrel V-6 engine, a three-speed manual transmission and power steering. The V-6 was not available in high-altitude counties. Instead, a 350-cid four-barrel V-8 was a required extra-cost option, adding $428 to the car's price and requiring a Turbo-Hydra-Matic transmission attachment at additional cost.

FIREBIRD ESPRIT - V-6/V-8 - SERIES 2FT

The styling changes seen on the base Firebird were also characteristic of the 1979 Esprit. This year the two-tone blue Sky Bird package was not available, but the UPC W68 Red Bird package was back with the Hobnail velour cloth trim version priced at $491 and the doeskin vinyl trim version priced at $449. The Esprit came with a 231-cid two-barrel V-6 engine and a three-speed manual transmission. As was the case with the base Firebird, the V-6 was not available in Esprits sold in designated high-altitude counties. Instead, the 350-cid four-barrel V-8 was a required extra-cost option, adding $428 to the car's price and requiring Turbo-Hydra-Matic transmission attachment at additional extra cost.

FORMULA FIREBIRD - V-8 - SERIES 2FU

The Formula came with a 4.9-liter (301-cid) two-barrel V-8. Four-wheel disc brakes were a new Formula option. A 5.0-liter (305-cid) V-8 was a required option in California cars and a 5.7-liter (350-cid) V-8 was the required option in designated high-altitude counties. Sales catalogs said that the W50 Formula Appearance package "brought the brawn to the surface." It included contrasting lower-body perimeter finish with the color break line accentuated with a broad stripe of a third color, which was repeated along the bottom of the taillight panel.

Only with this option was a rear deck lid spoiler standard on 1979 Formula Firebirds.

FIREBIRD TRANS AM - V-8 - SERIES 2FW

The styling changes seen on the base Firebird were also characteristic of the 1979 Trans Am. Standard Trans Am equipment included a 403-cid (6.6-liter) V-8 engine, a Turbo-Hydra-Matic or four-speed manual transmission. Four-wheel disc brakes were a new Trans Am option. In a return to the past, but a change from 1978, raised white letter tires could be ordered as a separate option without ordering the WS6 package. Engine options included the 4.9-liter four-barrel V-8 for a credit and the higher-performance T/A 6.6-liter four-barrel V-8 as a $90 option.

FIREBIRD TRANS AM BLACK SPECIAL EDITION - V-8 - SERIES 2FW/Y84

The Y84 Black Special Edition package with gold graphics and accents was available for $674 without hatch roof panels or for $1,329 with the Fisher Hatch Roof. Standard Trans Am Black Special Edition equipment included a 403-cid (6.6-liter) V-8 engine, a radial-tuned suspension with larger front and rear stabilizer bars, Starlight Black exterior body finish, gold body striping, gold interior and exterior accents, gold aluminum wheels and a removable hatch roof made by GM's Fisher Body Division.

FIREBIRD TRANS AM 10TH ANNIVERSARY - V-8 - SERIES 2FX

The first Trans Am was a 1969 1/2 model, so 1979 was the model's 10th anniversary. A special 10th Anniversary model was announced on Jan. 26, 1979, and made its initial public appearance at the Chicago Automobile Show on Feb. 24. The car was displayed there with four special concept cars and a Trans Am with a rear-mounted jet engine that was used in the movie "Hooper." The package included all standard Trans Am features, plus a host of special

THIS 10TH ANNIVERSARY '79 TRANS AM WAS DECKED OUT IN PLATINUM.

appearance and performance extras as regular equipment. Since this was an all-inclusive deal, the 10th Anniversary Trans Am was considered a separate model, rather than an option package. You took all the equipment and laid out $10,619 for the privilege (if you bought at full sticker price). The standard goodies included a larger-than-normal "super bird" hood decal, a front air dam with bolder styling, special cast-aluminum turbo-air-flow wheel rims with finned perimeter openings and knock-off style hubs and a complete complement of convenience features-These cars came only in Platinum Silver with a silver hatch roof and charcoal accents on the shaker-style hood scoop, the bumper panel, the windowsills, the rear window surround and portions of the roof. Red, white and charcoal pinstripes accented numerous body panels. Behind the front wheel openings were red Trans Am lettering and 10th Anniversary Limited Edition decals. Most 10th Anniversary Trans Ams had the base L80 (403-cid) V-8 with Turbo-Hydra-Matic attachment. A few were produced with the T/A 6.6 V-8 linked to a four-speed manual transmission.

FIREBIRD TRANS AM 10TH ANNIVERSARY DAYTONA PACE CAR - V-8 - SERIES 2FX

Some historical sources indicate that a limited number of 10th Anniversary Trans Ams were turned out as Official Pace Car Replicas patterned after the car that paced the Daytona 500 stock car race on Feb. 18, 1979. According to John Witzke, Historian and Pontiac Oakland Club International (POCI) Technical Advisor for the 1977-1979 W72 Performance Package, this information has not been confirmed. Firebird expert Dave Doern confirms that Daytona 500 decals were made available through the Pontiac parts department as a dealer-installed decal package.

HISTORICAL FOOTNOTES

Car and Driver road tested a 1979 Firebird with the "T/A 6.6-liter" V-8 in a January 1979. The car did 0 to 60 mph in 6.7 seconds and traveled down the quarter mile in 15.3 seconds at 96.6 mph. Total model-year production of Firebirds rose to another new record of 211,454 cars.

THE INDY PACE CAR TRANS AM FEATURED THE 4.9-LITER TURBO ENGINE.

1980

New options and engineering refinements were the big changes in 1980 Firebirds. A drastic dip in production was seen for the first time in eight years. The output of Firebirds, Esprits, Formulas and Trans Ams was almost half what it had been the previous season.

Up front, a center console was now standard in all models. A dozen new body colors were offered, plus a new upholstery selection — dark blue. Dual exhaust systems made of lightweight alloys were introduced. Optional new four-speaker ETR sound systems were introduced. Tungsten halogen headlamps were optional.

A new Yellow Bird package with gold accent striping replaced the Red Bird for Esprits. On Oct. 16 1979, Pontiac announced that the Trans Am had been selected to pace the 64th Indianapolis 500 race the next May. To commemorate this, a Trans Am Indy Pace Car replica was issued as a separate model.

The Indy Pace Car replicas came only with a 4.9-liter 210-hp turbo V-8. They were two-toned with white upper bodies and charcoal gray bottoms set off by tri-color stripes. Oyster-colored vinyl bucket seats with matching hobnail cloth inserts were standard. These $11,200-and-up cars came basically fully loaded and 5,700 were built. Turbo graphics were on the hood and spoiler. PMD said the Indy Pacer was the first domestic car to have a standard turbo engine.

The turbocharger was made by AiResearch Corporation. It was exclusive to Trans Ams, but not pace cars. It could be added to any model. All Turbo Trans Ams included a unique hood and special bird hood decals. Road testers registered a 0-to-60 time of 8.2 seconds and a top speed of 116 mph for the turbo. The quarter mile took 16.7 seconds at 86 mph.

Trans Am buyers could again get a black-painted Special Edition package, either with or without a hatch roof. It could be had with conventional 4.9- and 5.0-liter V-8s as well as with the 4.9-liter turbo. New color combinations for regular Trans Ams included bronze/burgundy and a revised red/gold combination.

Model-year production included 29,811 Firebirds, 17,277 Esprits, 9,356 Formulas and 50,896 Trans Ams. Some Firebirds were rare. For instance, only 12 Special Edition Trans Ams were made with the 5.0-liter LG4 V-8.

THE NAME OF THE YELLOW BIRD PACKAGE APPEARED ON THE REAR PANEL.

FIREBIRD - V-6/V-8 - SERIES 2FS

For 1980, engineering improvements and new options headlined the changes in Firebird land. The technical upgrades included a lightweight dual exhaust system, the use of low-friction ball joints, revised engine offerings and the deletion of a four-speed manual gear box. The bucket seats had smooth—rather than pleated—headrests and could be had in a new dark blue trim combination. A front console was added to the standard equipment list. Twelve new exterior paint colors were offered. New options included dual front radio speakers, extended-range dual rear speakers and an electronically controlled radio with seek/scan feature. During the year a wheel cover locking package and audio power booster were added to the options list. The electric clock now had a quartz mechanism and after Nov. 20, 1979, a roof rack was available for the Firebird as a dealer-installed option. The base Firebird came with a 231-cid two-barrel V-6 engine (305-cid two-barrel V-8 at extra cost in California) and a three-speed manual transmission (Turbo-Hydra-Matic at extra cost in California)

FIREBIRD ESPRIT - V-6/V-8 SERIES 2FT

The changes for the base Firebird were the same for the Esprit. A new Esprit feature was the addition of wide rocker panel moldings to the standard equipment list. The Esprit came with a 231-cid two-barrel V-6 engine (305-cid two-barrel V-8 at extra cost in California) and a three-speed manual transmission (Turbo-Hydra-Matic at extra cost in California). A new Yellow Bird option package replaced the Red Bird package. It added basically the same features in a different color scheme, but black-out style taillights were added.

FORMULA FIREBIRD - V-8 SERIES 2FV

The changes seen on the base Firebird were also characteristic of the 1980 Formula Firebird. The Formula came with a 4.9-liter (301-cid) four-barrel V-8 engine, Turbo-Hydra-Matic transmission, a lower body accent color with striping, black-out style taillights, a splitter exhaust system, a machine-turned instrument panel trim plate and 225/70R-15 black sidewall steel-belted radial tires. A 5.0-liter (305-cid) four-barrel V-8 was a required option in California cars. A new option in Formula Firebirds was a turbocharged 301-cid V-8.

FIREBIRD FORMULA TURBO 4.9 V-8 - SERIES 2FW/LU8

The Turbo 4.9 Formula Firebird came with

a 301-cid (4.9-liter) V-8 engine with a TBO305 AiResearch Corp. turbocharger, a Turbo-Hydra-Matic transmission, a lower-body accent color with striping, a specific hood with an off-center power bulge designed to accommodate the turbocharger (with "Turbo 4.9 lettering on the left-hand side), outside sport mirrors (left-hand remote controlled/right-hand manual convex), Formula identification, Rally II wheel rims with trim rings and a Formula steering wheel.

FIREBIRD TRANS AM - V-8 - SERIES 2FW

Standard Trans Am equipment included a 4.9-liter E/C (301-cid) four-barrel V-8 engine, a Turbo-Hydra-Matic transmission, a Trans Am front fender decal, a blacked-out grille, blacked-out taillights, a Trans Am grille panel decal, a Trans Am wraparound rear deck spoiler decal and a Radial Tuned Suspension with heavy front and rear stabilizer bars. Engine options included the Formula's base L37 4.9-liter four-barrel V-8 for a $180 credit (and no dual resonator tailpipes), the 5.0-liter V-8 in California cars and the 4.9-liter Turbo V-8.

FIREBIRD TRANS AM BLACK SPECIAL EDITION - V-8 - SERIES 2FW/Y84

The Y84 Black Special Edition package returned with slightly gaudier gold graphics and accents. It was available for $748 without hatch roof panels or for $1,443 with the Fisher Hatch Roof. Standard Trans Am Black Special Edition equipment included a 301-cid (4.9-liter) V-8 engine, a Turbo-Hydra-Matic transmission, a Trans Am front fender decal, a blacked-out grille, blacked-out taillights, a Trans Am grille panel decal, a Trans Am wraparound rear deck spoiler decal, Starlight Black exterior body finish, gold body striping, gold interior and exterior accents, gold aluminum wheels and a removable hatch roof made by GM's Fisher Body Division.

FIREBIRD TRANS AM TURBO 4.9 - V-8 - SERIES 2FW/LU8

Trans Am Turbo 4.9 equipment included a 301-cid (4.9-liter) V-8 engine with a TBO305 AiResearch Corp. turbocharger, a Turbo-Hydra-Matic transmission, a Trans Am front fender decal, a blacked-out grille, blacked-out taillights, a Trans Am grille panel decal, a Trans Am wraparound rear deck spoiler decal, a front center air dam, front and rear wheel opening air deflectors and a specific hood with an off-center power bulge designed to accommodate the turbocharger (with "Turbo 4.9 lettering on the left-hand side).

FIREBIRD TRANS AM TURBO 4.9 INDY PACE CAR - V-8 SERIES 2FW/LU8

The Trans Am Turbo 4.9 featured a 301-cid (4.9-liter) V-8 engine with a TBO305 AiResearch Corp. turbocharger mated to a Turbo-Hydra-Matic transmission. It had two-tone finish with gray upper body and white lower body, tri-color body accent stripes.

FIREBIRD TRANS AM TURBO 4.9 DAYTONA PACE CAR - V-8 SERIES 2FW/LU8

Trans Am Turbo 4.9 equipment included the 301-cid (4.9-liter) V-8 engine with a TBO305 AiResearch Corp. turbocharger, a Turbo-Hydra-Matic transmission, and optional Daytona 500 Pace Car door graphics.

HISTORICAL FOOTNOTES

The gas crunch put the crunch on the Firebird line in 1980. Total model-year production of Firebirds was only 107,340 units. Sales were even worse and stood at 81,592 for the calendar year. The Turbo Trans Am could do 0 to 60 mph in 8.2 seconds and cover the quarter mile in 16.7 seconds at 86 mph. Top speed was 116 mph.

THE 1981 TRANS AM HAD T-TOPS AND A FAMILIAR RACY LOOK.

1981

A shuffle of powertrains highlighted Pontiac Firebird changes for 1981. A new Trans Am option was a two-color hood decal in five combinations. Two-tone paint became optional on the Formula and several new cloth bucket seat options were made available, including a silver doeskin vinyl interior in place of the oyster vinyl offering.

Standard in Formulas was a Pontiac-made 4.3-liter V-8, also optional on Firebirds and Esprits. Trans Ams used a Pontiac-built 4.9-liter four-barrel V-8 with Electronic Spark Control. Trans Ams and Formulas offered a turbocharged 4.9-liter, which was now available in California. Base transmission for the Esprit was the automatic, while the standard Firebird stuck with a three-speed manual gearbox. A four-speed manual gearbox was again available in Formulas and Trans Ams with the four-barrel 5.0-liter V-8.

A famous publicity photo showed a 1967 Firebird convertible on the lower ramp of a transporter and a 1981 Trans Am coupe above it. They represented the first and last Firebirds assembled with Pontiac-built V-8s. Starting in 1982, the only V-8 would be a 5.0-liter made by Chevrolet or GM of Canada.

Among other 1981 improvements was a Computer Command Control engine-management system, a quick-take-up brake master cylinder, an early fuel-evaporation system and a new lightweight Delco Freedom battery with side terminals. The standard power brakes now included a low-drag front caliper.

Burt Reynolds's cult film *Smokey and the Bandit* had given national exposure to a Turbo Trans Am and Pontiac tried to capitalize on its popularity by featuring the actor, in his "Bandit" attire, in the centerfold of the 1981 Pontiac sales catalog. It did not do much to help the Firebird's sagging model-year production, which came in at 20,541 base Firebirds, 10,938 Esprits, 5,927 Formulas and 33,493 Trans Ams. The high price tag on the black-and-gold Special Edition may have been another thing driving sales down 34 percent.

The summer 1981 release of a sequel movie *Smokey and the Bandit II* prompted a New Jersey company to release a $30,000 Trans Am Bandit model that had its aftermarket upgrades, like a 380-hp 462-cid V-8, Doug Nash five-speed manual gearbox, Recaro seats, a Blaupunkt sound system and Goodyear Eagle GT tires. There was also a midyear, factory-issued $12,244 Daytona 500 Pace Car package built in a limited run of 2,000 copies. It is known to enthusiasts as the "NASCAR Turbo Pace Car" and was similar to the 1980 Indy Pace Car with black accents replacing the Indy car's charcoal accents.

FIREBIRD - V-6/V-8 - SERIES 2FS

Small external differences identified 1981 Firebirds. A white bird emblem was placed on the fuel filler door between the taillights. New up front was a black-finished grille with Argent Silver accents. There were new exterior colors. Engineering upgrades included low-drag front disc brakes, a quick-take-up brake master cylinder, early fuel evaporation system, new lightweight side terminal Delco Freedom battery and General Motors' Computer Command Control (CCC) system. Standard equipment for the base Firebird included a 3.8-liter (231-cid) two-barrel V-8 engine, three-speed manual transmission, floor shift, front console, power steering, and power front disc/rear drum brakes.

FIREBIRD ESPRIT - V-6/V-8 - SERIES 2FT

In addition to changes outlined for base Firebirds, the custom interiors used in the Esprit featured a new combination featuring Pimlico cloth bucket seats with Durand cloth bolsters in a new beige color choice. Standard equipment for the Esprit included the 3.8-liter (231-cid) two-barrel V-8 engine, Turbo-Hydra-Matic transmission, floor shift, a front console, body-color door handle inserts and body-color sport mirrors (left-hand remote controlled).

FORMULA FIREBIRD - V-8 - SERIES 2FV

The changes seen on the base Firebird were also characteristic of the 1981 Formula Firebird. Standard equipment for the Formula Firebird included a 4.3-liter (265-cid) two-barrel V-8 engine, Turbo-Hydra-Matic transmission, dual air scoop hood design, floor shift, front console, power steering, power front disc/rear drum brakes and a black-finished grille with Argent Silver accents.

FORMULA FIREBIRD TURBO 4.9 V-8 SERIES 2FW/LU8

The 1981 Turbo 4.9 Formula Firebird came with a 301-cid (4.9-liter) V-8 engine with a TBO305 AiResearch Corp. turbocharger, Turbo-Hydra-Matic transmission, a floor shift, a front console, power steering, power front disc/rear drum brakes, lower body accent color with striping and specific hood with an off-center power bulge designed to accommodate the turbocharger (with "Turbo 4.9" lettering on the left-hand side).

FIREBIRD TRANS AM - V-8 - SERIES 2FW

Pontiac had no big surprises in store for 1981 Trans Am buyers. The base engine was the 4.9-liter E/C V-8, also known as the Trans Am 4.9-liter. When the 5.0-liter V-8 was ordered, as a delete option, it came with dual resonators and pipes instead of chrome exhaust splitters. The Turbo 4.9-liter V-8 came with a special hood with an off-center power blister and a turbo-boost gauge. The styling changes seen on the base Firebird were also characteristic of the 1981 Trans Am.

THE '81 FORMULA CAME STANDARD WITH A 4.3-LITER V-8.

FIREBIRD TRANS AM BLACK SPECIAL EDITION - V-8 - SERIES 2FW/Y84

The Y84 Black Special Edition package returned with slightly gaudier gold graphics and accents. It was available for $735 without hatch roof panels or for $1,430 with the hatch roof. Standard Trans Am Black Special Edition equipment included a 4.9-liter E/C (301-cid) V-8 engine, Turbo-Hydra-Matic transmission, Trans Am front fender decal, a blacked-out grille, blacked-out taillights, a Trans Am grille panel decal, Trans Am wraparound rear deck spoiler decal, a front center air dam, front and rear wheel opening air deflectors, shaker hood scoop and air cleaner and "big bird" hood decal.

FIREBIRD TURBO TRANS AM BLACK SPECIAL EDITION - V-8 - SERIES 2FW/Y84

The Y84 Black Special Edition package could be combined with the turbocharged V-8. Standard features included the 301-cid (4.9-liter) V-8 engine with a TBO305 AiResearch Corp. turbocharger, Turbo-Hydra-Matic transmission, Trans Am front fender decal, , the WS6 Special Performance package, GR70-15 raised white letter steel-belted radial tires, Radial Tuned Suspension with larger front and rear

stabilizer bars, Starlight Black exterior body finish, gold body striping, gold interior and exterior accents and a removable hatch roof made by GM's Fisher Body Division.

FIREBIRD TRANS AM TURBO 4.9 - V-8 - SERIES 2FW/LU8

The Turbo Trans Am Turbo 4.9 again featured 301-cid (4.9-liter) V-8 engine with a TBO305 AiResearch Corp. turbocharger and a Turbo-Hydra-Matic transmission.

Y87 FIREBIRD TRANS AM TURBO 4.9 DAYTONA PACE CAR - V-8 - SERIES 2FW/LU8

Turbo 4.9 Daytona Pace Car equipment included all optional pace car graphics, Recaro front bucket seats with (black with red inserts) and, special interior trim with Firebirds embroidered into the door pads and the center of the rear seat and 15 x 8 white turbo cast-aluminum wheels.

HISTORICAL FOOTNOTES

Total model-year production of Firebirds was 70,899. Sales stood at 61,460 for the model year and 52,188 for the calendar year. The Turbo Trans Am could do 0 to 60 mph in 8.7 seconds and cover the quarter mile in 16 seconds at 86 mph.

THE 1982 TRANS AM SHOWED OFF THE F-CAR'S DRAMATICALLY DIFFERENT FRONT END.

1982

"The excitement began 15 years ago when those electrifying 'Birds' came rolling like thunder to capture the hearts of enthusiasts everywhere and a legend was born," said a 1982 Pontiac advertisement. "Now comes the road machine that will fire-up a new generation."

From its saber-like nose to its rakish tail, the new Firebird was a brilliant orchestration of aerodynamic function. All Firebirds rode on a 101-inch wheelbase and had a 189.8-in. overall length and a height of only 49.8 inches. The F-Car's .34 drag co-efficient was the best of any production car that GM had ever tested. The front tapered to a low nose with split grilles housed inside twin air slots below electrically powered hidden headlights. The windshield had a 62-degree slant. Taillights were in a full-width back panel. Reclining front bucket seats were standard.

The revised F-Cars came in base, luxury S/E and Trans Am models. Each one had its own suspension and tires. The base engine was a fuel-injected 151-cid (2.5-liter) four hooked to four-speed manual gearbox. S/Es carried a standard 173-cid (2.8-liter) two-barrel V-6, also with a four-speed.

The Trans Am had the 5.0-liter four-barrel V-8 with a four-speed. Trans Am buyers could also step up to a dual throttle-body (crossfire) fuel injection V-8 with fresh-air hood induction.

Standard Firebird equipment included a front air dam, power brakes and steering, front stabilizer bar and black-finished instrument panel. S/Es added full-width black taillights, body-color body side moldings, lower accent paint (with striping) and turbo cast-aluminum wheels. Trans Ams added hood and sail panel bird decals, front fender air extractors, front/rear wheel opening flares and a spoiler.

Despite a late, midyear release, the all-new Firebirds proved very popular and assemblies picked back up again, rising above 100,000 for the abbreviated model year. Pontiac's total output of the three Firebird models was: 41,683 base Firebirds, 21,719 Firebird S/Es and 52,960 Trans Ams.

FIREBIRD - (I-4/V-6/V-8) - SERIES 2FS

The all-new third-generation Firebird arrived in January 1982. The only body style was a wedge-shaped hatchback coupe available in "first-level" Firebird, Firebird S/E and Trans Am models. It was shorter, narrower and lower than the previous Firebird and more than 500 lbs. lighter in weight. The front tapered to an ultra-low nose with split grilles inside twin air slots. The parking lights were in slots above the grilles and below were electrically operated hidden headlamps with rectangular halogen bulbs. The windshield had a rakish 62-degree slant and the hatch consisted almost entirely of a piece of "frameless," contoured glass. The rear seats folded to provide 30.9 cu. ft. of cargo area with two-passenger seating. Standard equipment for the first-level Firebird included a 2.5-liter four-cylinder engine with electronic fuel injection, a four-speed manual transmission, dual black-finished grilles, a body-color one-piece resilient Endura front panel and front bumper, concealed rectangular quartz halogen headlights, electrically operated hide-away headlight housings, an Endura rear bumper, power steering, power front disc/rear drum brakes, dual outside mirrors (left-hand manual and right-hand manual convex), hidden headlights, a formula steering wheel, 195/75R14 glass-belted black sidewall tires, a compact spare tire, hubcaps, a wraparound glass hatch with strut supports, a black-finished instrument panel, reclining front bucket seats, side window defoggers, a GM Computer Command Control, rear wheel drive, a front stabilizer bar and a torque arm/track bar rear suspension.

FIREBIRD SPECIAL EDITION (S/E) - V-6/V-8 - SERIES 2FX

The new S/E was priced slightly lower than the Trans Am. It actually had more standard equipment upgrades than the Trans Am, but the S/E engine was a V-6 instead of the Trans Am's base V-8. When the V-8 was added, the price was higher than that for a base Trans Am. Standard equipment for the Firebird S/E included a 2.8-liter V-6 engine with two-barrel carburetor and a four-speed manual transmission.

FIREBIRD TRANS AM - V-8 - SERIES 2FW

Standard equipment for the first-level Trans Am included a 5.0-liter four-barrel V-8 engine with dual resonator exhaust and dual tailpipes, a four-speed manual transmission, dual black-finished grilles, a body-color one-piece resilient Endura front panel and front bumper, concealed rectangular quartz halogen headlights and Turbo cast-aluminum wheels with black-finished center caps. The Crossfire fuel-injected (EFI) V-8 was an $899 option for 1982 Trans Am without the UPC Y84 Recaro Trans Am option package.

FIREBIRD RECARO TRANS AM - V-8 - SERIES 2FW/Y84

The UPC Y84 Recaro Trans Am package was only available on Black Trans Am with gold accents. While it was basically an interior trim option, the Recaro package included styling and suspension upgrades and was available with either engine. If you ordered the Recaro package with the four-barrel V-8, the package was $2,486 and the base four-speed manual transmission was required. If you ordered the Recaro option with the EFI V-8, the engine was considered part of the package, but the price was $2,968 and automatic transmission was required at $72 additional cost. The Recaro Trans Am option included Recaro front bucket seats, a rear luxury seat, Parella cloth seat trim, luxury door trim panels, map pockets, custom seat belts, 215/65R15 steel-belted black sidewall tires, a special handling package, a limited-slip differential, a sport hood, four-wheel disc brakes, removable hatch roof panels and gold-finished Turbo cast-aluminum wheels.

HISTORICAL FOOTNOTES

Model-year production of Firebirds increased from just 70,899 in 1981 to 116,364 in 1982. The Firebird's share of the overall U.S. market rose from 1.06 percent the previous year to 2.26 percent in 1982.

THE 1983 TRANS AM CAME IN RECARO AND 25TH ANNIVERSARY LIMITED EDITIONS, BUT THE BASE TRANS AM WASN'T BAD, EITHER.

1983

The sleek, aerodynamic Firebird unveiled in 1982 featured upgraded power options for 1983. In addition to the base 2.5-liter fuel-injected four-cylinder engine, there was a 2.8-liter V-6 High Output engine and a 5.0-liter V-8 with a four-barrel carburetor. Then, on June 6, 1983, Pontiac announced the release of a 190-hp 5.0 H.O. V-8 for the Trans Am with high-performance hardware and cold-air-induction system. A limited Daytona edition Trans Am featured two-tone paint and pigskin Recaro bucket seats. Prices started at $10,810.

Base models featured a fuel-injected 2.5-liter four with four-speed manual shift. S/Es had new cloth seats and a split-folding back seat (also available with Custom trim). Lear Siegler articulated front bucket seats became optional. The Trans Am again had a standard 5.0-liter V-8, but with the five-speed and a 3.73:1 axle. Standard T/A equipment included power brakes and steering, reclining front bucket seats, a rear spoiler, wheel-opening flares and P195/75R14 glass-belted radial tires. The S/E added P205/70R14 SBR tires on turbo cast-aluminum wheels, a beefy suspension, a five-speed gearbox, sport mirrors, color-keyed body side moldings and lower accent paint with striping.

There were two special 1983 Firebirds. The 25th Anniversary Daytona 500 Limited Edition model commemorated Pontiac's 25th season as pace car for the Florida stock-car race. It had white upper and Midnight Sand Gray Metallic lower body finish. An aero package was included along with many options and special identification features. This model was priced around $18,000 and 2,500 production units were scheduled.

Another special model was the Special Edition Recaro Trans Am, which included a $3,200 package with black-and-gold finish, special gold trim, gold turbo-cast wheels, a gold sport hood appliqué, a hatch roof and Recaro seats.

THE 1983 PONTIAC FIREBIRD TRANS AM HATCHBACK.

Mecum Racing, then located in Spokane, Washington, also released a Motor Sports Edition or MSE Trans Am with suspension upgrades, special interior features and a killer Motorola sound system.

PMD was actively involved in motorsports following race driver Elliott Forbes-Robinson's successful 1982 season driving the yellow-and-blue No. 1 "STP Sun of a Gun" Trans Am built by Huffaker Engineering. The author attended several exciting Trans Am Territories at Elkhart Lake, Wisconsin, in this period and watched the down-sized Firebirds compete.

The base four-cylinder Firebird now had an $8,399 base price and model year production of 32,020. The S/E was about $2,000 pricier and 10,934 were built. Trans Am prices started at $10,396 and 31,930 were built.

FIREBIRD - (I-4) - SERIES 2FS

For 1983, Firebirds had some new engines and transmissions, suspension refinements, slight interior revisions and minor equipment changes including 13 new and five revised options. A 25th anniversary Daytona 500 Limited Edition Trans Am and Special Edition Recaro Trans Am were new, along with a midyear H.O. V-8 engine. The first-level Firebird had no changes in exterior appearance, but included a new wide-ratio four-speed manual transmission with an integral rail shifter. Also new was a set of redesigned Rally wheel rims with exposed black lug nuts. Another upgrade was an improved dual-retractor seat belt system. A front stabilizer bar was no longer included at base price. Standard equipment for the first-level Firebird included a 2.5-liter four-cylinder engine with electronic fuel injection and a four-speed manual transmission.

FIREBIRD SPECIAL EDITION (S/E) - V-6/V-8 - SERIES 2FX

The 1983 Firebird S/E had a few minor equipment deletions, including the rear hatch washer/wiper and custom pedal trim, but a split-folding seatback was new. A new option was a handling suspension that included 205/70R14 tires, 14 x 7-in. Turbo cast-aluminum wheels and rear stabilizer bars. Standard equipment for the Firebird S/E included a 2.8-liter H.O. V-6 with electronic fuel injection and a five-speed manual transmission.

FIREBIRD TRANS AM - V-8 - SERIES 2FW

The Trans Am also saw minor changes. The equipment list now specified Firebird decals, but no longer specified black mirrors or a black airfoil. A new standard transmission was also specified. Standard equipment for the first-level Trans Am included a 5.0-liter four-barrel V-8 engine with dual resonator exhaust and dual tailpipes and a five-speed manual transmission.

FIREBIRD SPECIAL EDITION RECARO TRANS AM - V-8 - SERIES 2FW/Y84

The UPC Y84 package was now called the Special Edition Recaro Trans Am option. It was only available on Black Trans Ams and included gold lower body accents, gold letter Recaro tape door handle inserts, cloisonné gold-and-black Firebird emblems on the sail panels, a gold hood appliqué and gold Turbo finned cast-aluminum wheels. Also featured in the package were leather-trimmed Recaro front luxury seats with adjustable thigh and lumbar supports, rear luxury seats, luxury doors, a split-folding rear seat, 215/65R15 black sidewall steel-belted tires, the Special Handling package, a limited-slip differential, a space saver spare tire (in place of a compact spare tire), an ETR AM/FM stereo radio (with cassette, seek/scan function, graphic equalizer and clock), four-wheel disc brakes and removable hatch roof panels. The price was $3,160 with the four-barrel V-8 and five-speed manual transmission or $3,610 with the Cross-fire-injected V-8 and automatic transmission.

FIREBIRD 25TH ANNIVERSARY DAYTONA 500 LIMITED EDITION TRANS AM - V-8 - SERIES 2FW

The Firebird 25th Anniversary Daytona 500 Limited Edition Trans Am was announced to the public on Nov. 1, 1982. The official press release said that production of 2,500 replicas was planned. This model-option was design specifically to mark Pontiac Motor Division's 25th season as pace car for the Daytona 500 stock car race. The car featured special mid-body two-tone paint with white upper finish and Midnight Sand Gray Metallic lower finish. It included a special aero package consisting of rocker panel extensions, an air dam, rocker fences, grille pads and special covers on its 15 x 7-in. Turbo-aero aluminum wheels. Also included was a sport hood appliqué, a locking fuel filler door, tinted glass all around, a power antenna and special Daytona 500 graphics. The interior sported Light Sand Gray Recaro front bucket seats with leather bolsters and headrests and Medium Sand Gray pigskin leather seat inserts. The sides and backs of the seats were upholstered in Pallex cloth and matching door panel inserts were Light Sand Gray with Pallex cloth inserts. In California, the 25th Anniversary Daytona 500 Limited Edition Trans Am came only with the 5.0-liter four-barrel V-8 attached to the automatic transmission. In other regions you could get it with the four-barrel V-8 and five-speed manual gearbox or with the Cross-fire-injected V-8 and automatic transmission.

HISTORICAL FOOTNOTES

Model-year production of Firebirds dropped back to 74,897 units in 1983. Of that total, 22 percent had four-wheel disc brakes, 80 percent had automatic transmission, 18.6 percent had a five-speed manual transmission, 80.2 percent had steel-belted radial tires, 56.4 percent had power windows, 36.1 percent had power door locks, 7.8 percent had a power seat, 0.3 percent had a stereo radio and cassette system, 25.3 percent had a limited-slip differential and 39.8 percent had removable roof hatches. The Firebird's share of the overall U.S. market was 1.32 percent in 1983. Mecum Racing of Arizona offered a Mecum Motor Sports Edition (MSE) Trans Am.

*FIREBIRDS AND TRANS AMS BOTH CAME WITH OPTIONAL
TWO-TONE PAINT SCHEMES FOR 1984.*

1984

A higher-output 5.0-liter engine replaced the Cross-Fire Injected engine as standard equipment in the 1984 Trans Am. Pontiac claimed 7.5-second 0 to 60-mph performance for the car with this power plant. A small hood bird emblem became standard on all Firebirds.

Other engines available in Firebirds included a 2.5-liter inline four-cylinder, a 2.8-liter V-6 and a more powerful 5.0-liter V-8. Prices started at $8,763. Trans Am buyers could add an optional Aero package with new front and rear fascias, a larger air dam, door and rocker panel extensions and wide lower body graphics. Also available: a Recaro package with gold strobe graphics and gold deep-dish turbo wheels.

Model-year production was 62,621 Firebirds, 10,309 S/Es and 55,374 Trans Ams. This was an 86 percent increase and base models were selling best.

FIREBIRD - (I-4/V-6/V-8) - SERIES 2FS

For 1984, there were no drastic styling changes for Firebirds. The base 2.5-liter four-

cylinder engine had new swirl-port cylinder heads and higher compression. New features found on the first-level Firebird included a black-finished mast-type radio antenna, fourth-generation all-weather radial tires and a tinted rear hatch glass. Dual horns were another new standard equipment item, along with an upshift indicator light when manual transmission was ordered. New options included two-tone paint and a rear deck lid spoiler. Standard equipment for the first-level Firebird included a Pontiac-built 2.5-liter, overhead-valve, four-cylinder engine with electronic fuel injection and a four-speed manual transmission.

FIREBIRD SPECIAL EDITION (S/E) - V-6/V-8 - SERIES 2FX

The 1984 Firebird S/E had a new steering wheel. It was a color-keyed version of the leather-wrapped Formula design. The headrests on the bucket seats were also redesigned and the base H.O. V-6 got 15 additional horsepower. Standard equipment for the Firebird S/E included the Chevrolet-built (this was actually specified on the sales sheet this year) 2.8-liter H.O. V-6 with electronic fuel injection hooked to the five-speed manual transmission.

FIREBIRD TRANS AM - V-8 - SERIES 2FW

The 1984 Trans Am also saw minor changes, but there were several option packages that could perk the interest of collectors. One was a slick-looking new Aero package consisting of front and rear fascia extensions, rocker panel extensions and fade-away lower body graphics. There was also a 15th Anniversary Trans Am package. Standard equipment for the Trans Am included a Chevrolet-built 5.0-liter four-barrel V-8 engine with dual resonator exhaust and dual tailpipes with a five-speed manual transmission.

FIREBIRD SPECIAL EDITION RECARO TRANS AM - V-8 - SERIES 2FW/Y84

The UPC Y84 package was again called the Special Edition Recaro Trans Am option. It now included the Aero package components with front and rear fascia extensions, rocker panel extensions and fade-away lower body graphics, plus a leather-wrapped formula steering wheel, a leather-wrapped shift knob, a leather-wrapped parking brake handle, a gold hood appliqué, gold 15 x 7-in. Turbo finned cast-aluminum wheels and leather-trimmed Recaro front luxury seats with adjustable thigh and lumbar supports. If that sounds like considerably less standard equipment than last year, it was. As a result the price of the Y84 package was only $1,621, about half as much as the previous year.

FIREBIRD 15TH ANNIVERSARY TRANS AM - V-8 - SERIES 2FW

The Firebird 15th Anniversary Trans Am was announced to the public early in the 1984 model year. This special model-option was finished in white with medium blue trim. The package included white aero skirting, white grille slot covers, 16-in. white aluminum high-tech wheels and a white rear deck lid spoiler. The interior had white Recaro bucket seats with blue inserts lettered with the Trans Am name. The Formula steering wheel was wrapped in white leather with a blue shield-shaped badge reading "Trans Am 15" in the center of its hub. The same special badge appeared on the sail panels and the Trans Am name, lettered in blue, adorned the lower body sides. A hatch roof with dark-colored glass panels set the roof off against the white body and multiple blue pinstripes traced around the perimeter of the body. On the hood was a blue "venetian blind" decal with a white outlined hood bird and 5.0-liter H.O. lettering. The 15th Anniversary model featured a 190-hp 5.0-liter V-8 under its hood. The engine came linked to the five-speed manual transmission. The package sold for $3,499 over the price of a base Trans Am. Pontiac said that it planned to build 1,500 of the $17,500-plus cars.

HISTORICAL FOOTNOTES

Model-year production of Firebirds climbed to 128,304 units in 1984. Of that total, 18.8 percent had a five-speed manual transmission, 1.5 percent had a four-speed manual transmission, 26.8 percent had four-wheel disc brakes, 58.2 percent had styled aluminum wheel, 88.4 percent had air conditioning, 100 percent had steel-belted radial tires, 57.1 percent had power windows, 38.8 percent had power door locks, 10.2 percent had power seats, 36 percent had an AM/FM stereo, 39.7 percent had a stereo cassette player, 15.2 percent had a graphic equalizer, 80.5 percent had a tilt steering wheel, 48.1 percent had cruise control, 5.1 percent had a rear window wiper and 41.2 percent had hatch roof panels. The Firebird's share of the overall U.S. market was 1.57 percent in 1984. Mecum Racing of Arizona again offered a Mecum Motor Sports Edition (MSE) Trans Am.

THE 1985 FIREBIRDS, INCLUDING THE SE, RECEIVED SOME NEW INTERIOR FEATURES AND A STANDARD RALLY TUNED SUSPENSION.

1985

The base Firebird and the Firebird LE model received new front and rear fascias for 1985, while the Trans Am's taillights, hood and striping graphics were revised. The high-performance model sported a new 5.0-liter V-8 with multiport fuel injection. An aero-wing rear deck lid spoiler was also available at extra cost. The Firebird's base four-cylinder engine was refined by adding roller lifters, a low-inertia clutch disc and improved engine control software. Prices started at $9,177.

A new exterior appearance package was available for base models. It included black door handles, sport mirrors, a spoiler and "bird" roof decals. Also available at extra cost were a two-tone paint treatment in 13 color combinations.

A refined Firebird S/E added details and features to improve its competitive position against the sophisticated and sporty imported cars. It had a new louvered hood, new taillights (shared with Trans Ams) and the same rear-end revisions as the base model. The Firebird's new optional overhead console was standard in the S/E, which also got the new optional electronic instrument panel as standard equipment. New diamond-spoke aluminum wheels were seen.

The Trans Am got a louvered hood with air extractors, new front and rear fascias and fend-er extractors. The integral aero package was revised to include a "whale-tail" spoiler. The Trans Am also had new integrated fog lamps and 16-inch aluminum wheels with 245/50R16 tires. A new heavy-duty, limited-slip axle was used with V-8s.

Although PMD was obviously trying to pump up sales of the hot-selling base Firebird, its model year production dropped to 46,644. PMD also assembled 5,208 S/Es and 44,028 T/As. Not only did production drop, but also the Trans Am nearly caught up to the base Firebird model in total popularity.

FIREBIRD - I-4/V-6/V-8 - SERIES 2FS

For 1985, the rally-tuned suspension became available on the base Firebird. In addition, the instrument panel and console were redesigned for a softer and more rounded look. The console was split into two parts and covered with a new soft vinyl material. A pod containing the radio was attached to the instrument panel. New standard features included Firebird decals on the hood and sail panel, black taillight bezels and black-finished front fascia pads. There was a new W51 exterior package available for the 1985 base Firebird. It included black door

THE TRANS AM RECEIVED A FEW EXTERIOR TWEAKS FOR 1985.

THE TRANS AM RECEIVED A FEW EXTERIOR TWEAKS FOR 1985.

THE SLEEK T/A HAD THREE AVAILABLE V-8 ENGINES FOR 1985.

handles, sport mirrors, a rear deck lid spoiler and Firebird decals on the sail panels. Also available at extra cost was a D84 two-tone paint treatment that was offered in 13 different color combinations. The standard equipment list for the first-level Firebird included a Pontiac-built 2.5-liter overhead-valve four-cylinder engine with electronic fuel injection. Buyers ordering the new UPC Y99 rally-tuned suspension got P215/65R15 steel-belted black sidewall tires on

15 x 7-in. wheels with a larger front stabilizer bar and an added rear stabilizer bar.

FIREBIRD SPECIAL EDITION (S/E) - V-6/V-8 - SERIES 2FX

Changes to the 1985 Firebird S/E were characterized by new front and rear fascia designs. Up front, black-finished bumper pads replaced the regular grille. They provided better aerodynamics and gave the S/E a more sophisticated look. The sail panel carried new Firebird decals and Firebird S/E lettering was on the lower front edge of the doors and new accent striping was seen.

FIREBIRD TRANS AM - V-8 - SERIES 2FW

The 1985 Trans Am came standard with an enhanced version of the 1984 Aero package. It was fully integrated into the front and rear fascias and new front fog lights were included. The new hood had louvers and engine air extractors. Also new was a better-integrated rear deck lid spoiler. The Trans Am served as the Daytona 500 Pace Car for the fifth year in a row. However, the factory did not issue a limited edition pace car package. Standard equipment for the Trans Am included a Chevrolet-built 5.0-liter four-barrel V-8 engine with dual resonator exhaust and dual tailpipes and a five-speed manual transmission (with upshift indicator lamp).

HISTORICAL FOOTNOTES

The 1985 Firebird line was introduced on Nov. 11, 1984, five weeks and two days later than the rest of the new Pontiacs. *Motor Trend* gave the new tune-port-injected EFI Trans Am a workout and wrote up the results in its October, 1984 issue. The magazine disliked the return of the "chicken" hood decal, but liked the WS6 suspension that was mandatory with the 205-hp V-8. The editors also liked the all-new digital electronic instrument panel. The test car moved from 0 to 60 mph in 7.79 seconds and did the quarter mile with an 84.5-mph terminal speed.

THE F-CARS CAME IN 12 DIFFERENT COLOR CHOICES FOR 1986.

1986

All 1986 Firebirds ordered with a V-6 or V-8 received performance suspensions and 15-inch wheels with P215/65R15 tires. Up front the stylists concocted a new center panel to facelift the new model and there were revisions to the taillights to add a more distinct look. The lower body was accented with contrasting paint colors and sports striping was standard. A restyled bird decal decorated the hood. All models featured a power pull-down hatch. A programmable inside rearview mirror that was adjustable for daytime or nighttime driving was optional. Prices started at $9,693.

Base and SE Firebirds with V-6s or V-8s now had the Rally Tuned Suspension. New lightweight pistons went into the base 2.5-liter "Tech IV" engine. S/Es included an MFI V-6. A 5.0-liter four-barrel V-8 was optional. Trans Ams had a standard 155-hp version of the 5.0-liter V-8. The 190-hp TPI version was an option. Five-speed manual shift was standard and a four-speed overdrive automatic transmission was required with the TPI engine.

The Trans Ams WS6 suspension included four-wheel disc brakes, a limited-slip axle, larger stabilizer bars and Gatorback tires. A new backlit instrument cluster used a 140-mph electric speedometer in Firebirds equipped with a TPI V-8. Pontiac made 59,334 Firebirds, 2,259 S/Es and 48,870 Trans Ams.

FIREBIRD - I-4/V-6/V-8 - SERIES 2FS

For 1986, the first-level Firebird featured an all-new taillight design that was distinctive from that of the other Firebird models. The standard equipment list was expanded to include RTS, Rally wheels, a spoiler, new mirrors, new tires and new paint treatments. Several new paint colors were offered. The seats were redesigned and a high-mounted stoplight was added. A rally-tuned modified MacPherson strut front suspension (RTS), a 2.5-liter inline four-cylinder Tech IV engine with throttle-body fuel injection and a five-speed manual transmission were standard.

FIREBIRD SPECIAL EDITION (S/E) - V-6/V-8 - SERIES 2FX

In addition to sharing some new features with the base Firebird, the 1986 Firebird S/E featured a new backlit instrument cluster as standard equipment, along with an electric remote-control deck lid release. The air conditioning condenser was redesigned to reduce vehicle weight and the base engine was now offered with a choice of two transmissions, the five-speed manual or a newly recalibrated four-speed automatic. The standard equipment list for the Firebird S/E included a rally-tuned modified MacPherson strut front suspension (RTS), a 2.8-liter V-6 engine with electronic multi-port fuel injection and a five-speed manual transmission.

FIREBIRD TRANS AM - SERIES 2FW - V-8

A revised hood bird decal, a backlit instrument panel, redesigned door map pockets and an improved rally-tuned suspension with 34-mm front and 23-mm rear stabilizer bars were among changes in the 1986 Trans Am. A 140-mph speedometer was added with optional engines and various option packages were upgraded. For example, the WS6 Special Performance package now featured 36-mm front and 24-mm rear stabilizer bars, Gatorback tires and four-wheel disc brakes. The standard equipment list for the Trans Am included an Aero body package, fog lamps integrated into the front fascia, front fender air extractors, concealed rectangular quartz halogen headlamps, hood air extractors, hood air louvers, an aero wing rear spoiler, body-color sport mirrors (left-hand remote control, right-hand manual), lower accent striping, neutral-density taillights, P215/65R15 steel-belted radial black sidewall tires, gold and silver 15 x 7-in. High-Tech turbo cast-aluminum wheels, cut-pile carpet, a full-length console integrated with the instrument panel, full gauge instrumentation with a tachometer and trip odometer, a Delco-GM monaural push-button radio, reclining front bucket seats, a folding rear seatback, a graphite-color three-spoke formula steering wheel, a Delco-GM Freedom II battery, power front disc/rear drum brakes, GM Computer Command Control engine management system, power steering, a Rally-Tuned modified MacPherson strut front suspension (RTS), a 5.0-liter four-barrel V-8 engine and a five-speed manual transmission.

HISTORICAL FOOTNOTES

On Sept. 12, 1985, Pontiac Motor Division General Manager J. Michael Losh held a press conference during Pontiac's national press preview at Waterford Hills Race Course. Losh stated that Pontiac expected to build 900,000 cars during model-year 1986 and set an all-time record for sales. Losh pointed out that "image" cars like the Firebird would lead the way towards increased sales in 1986. It was fitting that the conference was held at the Michigan racetrack, since Pontiac was emphasizing racing involvements in 1986. In fact, Pontiac's Motorsports Engineering Dept. turned out a *Performance Plus* book that gave enthusiasts information on Firebird drag racing vehicle construction with Super Duty parts. Among Super Duty items available were parts to turn the 2.5-liter four into a 3.0-liter 300-hp engine! A Super Duty V-8 block (part No. 10049804) and Super Duty aluminum heads for V-8s were also offered. A number of aftermarket companies were offering special Firebird conversion packages. Cars & Concepts, of Brighton, Michigan, offered a Skylite T-Roof treatment (kit no 4720051 AOO) for the 1986 Firebird. Chattanooga Custom Center, Inc., of Chattanooga, Tennessee, offered the Pontiac Pro/Am II Firebird. Coca-Cola gave away three 1986 Pontiac Trans Ams in a $50 million Gold Rush contest that ended on Oct. 4, 1986.

THE FORMULA FIREBIRD CAME WITH SIGNATURE GRAPHICS AND DECALS ALONG WITH COLOR-KEYED BODY SIDE MOLDINGS.

1987

A high-mounted stoplight set into a body-color spoiler was one of the biggest changes for the little-altered 1987 Firebird. Pontiac took the Firebird S/E off the model roster and added a Formula package to the options list. When Firebird buyers tested the new ripple cloth seats they found they could now adjust the headrest up or down. A 5.7-liter V-8 was available (with four-speed automatic transmission only) in the new-for-1987 GTA model. The base Firebird engine was the 2.8-liter V-6 and prices for V-6 models started at $10,773.

The Formula featured an aero-style spoiler, analog instruments, a domed hood, 16 x 8-inch Hi-Tech aluminum wheels and a performance suspension. Trans Ams added an aero body skirting package, hood and front fender air extractors, hood air louvers, fog lamps, soft ray tinted glass and a rally-tuned suspension. Trans Am buyers had a choice between the 5.0-liter four-barrel V-8 or the 5.0-liter MFI V-8. The injected version got a five-speed manual transmission option for the first time.

The new GTA version of the Trans Am added articulating front bucket seats, a limited-slip rear axle, a special aero package, a special performance suspension, a leather-wrapped steering wheel and lightweight 16 x 8-inch diamond-spoke gold wheels.

New options included body-color exterior moldings, molded door panel trim (except in GTAs) and a performance suspension for base models. A 5.7-liter MPI V-8 performance engine was optional in Formulas and standard in GTAs. Firebird production hit 42,558 Firebirds, 13,164 Formulas and 32,890 Trans Ams.

In August 1987, General Motors boarded up the F-Car plant in Norwood, Ohio, and all Firebirds (and Camaros) through 1991 were made in the Van Nuys, California, factory. Also ended was the GM80 program that had been launched to develop a plastic-bodied, front-wheel-drive replacement for F-cars.

THE 1987 PONTIAC FIREBIRD TRANS AM GTA RECEIVED A NEW TUNED PORT INJECTION (TPI) ENGINE THAT PROMISED AN INCREASE TO 210 HP.

FIREBIRD - V-6/V-8 - SERIES 2FS

Technically, the base Firebird was one of only two Firebird series that returned for 1987 — along with the Trans Am. However, a new Formula option package was offered, along with a new Trans Am GTA model-option. That gives collectors four 1987 Firebird "models" to chose from. Engine changes were the big news, as Pontiac prepared to go head to head in the sporty car sales battle with Ford's 5.0-liter Mustang. The slow-selling four-cylinder engine was discontinued. A multi-port fuel-injected 2.8-liter V-6 was standard in the first-level Firebird. The Firebird coupe also had a more integrated appearance that was achieved by relocating its center high-mounted stoplight in the body-color rear deck lid spoiler. Inside were new ripple cloth reclining bucket seats with separately adjusted headrests and custom door trim pads. Other new features included body-colored side moldings and a softer re-tuned suspension. A partial list of standard equipment in the base Firebird included the 2.8-liter V-6 with multi-port fuel-injection (MFI), a five-speed manual transmission, a center high-mounted stoplight, a full-length console with instrument panel, side window defoggers, a front air dam, the GM Computer Command Control engine management system, a hatch "pull-down" feature, concealed rectangular quartz halogen headlamps,

a MacPherson front suspension, power brakes, a U63 Delco AM radio, reclining front bucket seats with ripple cloth upholstery, a split-folding rear seat with ripple cloth upholstery, a formula three-spoke steering wheel, a lockable storage compartment, "wet-arm" windshield wipers, front disc/rear drum brakes and P215/65R15 black sidewall steel-belted radial tires.

FORMULA FIREBIRD - V-6/V-8 - SERIES 2FS

The Formula name returned to the Firebird line in 1987. The Formula option was available in two content levels. The W61 version retailed for $1,273. The W63 version included more power options and retailed for $1,842. Both cars had a "street machine" image and a V-8 was part of both packages. The standard equipment list for the Formula Firebird included, a WS6 Special Performance type modified MacPherson strut front suspension, a 5.0-liter four-barrel V-8 and a five-speed manual transmission.

FIREBIRD TRANS AM - V-8 - SERIES 2FW

The regular 1987 Trans Am was promoted as a "driving excitement" car. The standard equipment list for the Trans Am included an Aero body package, fog lamps integrated into the front fascia, front fender air extractors, concealed rectangular quartz halogen headlamps, hood air extractors, hood air louvers, a body-

THE FORMULA WAS BACK IN THE FIREBIRD LINE FOR 1987 AND CAME IN TWO EQUIPMENT LEVELS, BOTH WITH A BASE 5.0-LITER FOUR-BARREL V-8.

color aero rear deck spoiler, body-color sport mirrors (left-hand remote control, right-hand manual), lower accent striping, a Rally-Tuned modified MacPherson strut front suspension (RTS), a 5.0-liter four-barrel V-8 engine and a five-speed manual transmission.

FIREBIRD TRANS AM GTA - V-8 - SERIES 2FW

The first GTA was an option package for the regular Trans Am. It gave the hot Firebird a sleek, aerodynamic and powerful look. Pontiac described it as "the ultimate Trans Am." It was referred to as "210 hp of precision driving excitement ready to exert its influence over the road of your choice." Since the 5.7-liter TPI engine was available in limited quantities, the 1987 Pontiac sales catalog noted "limited availability — may be deleted."

HISTORICAL FOOTNOTES

A low-production, but historically significant, change this year was the release of a TPI V-8, similar to that used in the Corvette, as a Trans Am option. This 210-hp engine promised 6.5-second 0 to 60-mph times and enhanced the Trans Am's image among youthful new-car buyers. Nevertheless, model-year new-car sales by U.S. dealers came to 77,635 Firebirds in 1987, a decline from 96,208 in 1986. As a result, production of the Firebird and Camaro was chopped down to one factory in Van Nuys, California, and the facility in Norwood, Ohio, was permanently closed in August 1987. General Motors also canceled its GM80 program, which had the goal of developing a plastic-bodied, front-wheel-drive car to replace the Firebird/Camaro F-car series. Total model-year production of Firebirds (for all markets) stood at 88,623 cars compared to 110,483 in 1986. Based on an output of 80,439 Firebirds produced for the U.S. market only, 38.5 percent had the V-6, 30.3 percent had a carbureted V-8 and 31.2 percent had a fuel-injected V-8. Automatic transmission was used in 88.1 percent of those cars and 11.9 percent had the five-speed manual gearbox. Of the 80,439 cars, 14.8 percent had four-wheel disc brakes, 34.3 percent had a limited-slip differential, 20.8 percent had styled steel wheels, 72.6 percent aluminum wheels, 6.7 percent had automatic air conditioning and 91 percent had manual air conditioning, 67.3 percent had power windows, 56.2 percent had power door locks and 27.9 percent had an AM/FM stereo.

THE GTA RECEIVED FOUR-WHEEL DISC BRAKE, MORE POWER EQUIPMENT, AND 225-HP TPI ENGINE FOR 1998.

1988

For 1988, the Firebird was available in base, Formula, Trans Am and GTA iterations. A 2.8-liter V-6 teamed with a five-speed manual transmission was the base power train. The Formula and Trans Am came standard with a 5.0-liter V-8, while the 5.7-liter GTA V-8 was optional. Prices started at $11,413.

Seventeen major product changes were promoted. An improved TPI system for V-8s was even available on base models, which also gained serpentine drive belts, 15 x 7 in. deep-dish High-Tech Turbo or diamond-spoke aluminum wheels, a redesigned four-spoke steering wheel, an AM/FM stereo with seek-and-scan and clock, Pallex cloth interior trim, a new Camel-colored interior, monotone paint treatments and a choice of two new exterior hues, Silver Blue Metallic or Orange Metallic.

Formulas had new 16 x 8-inch High-Tech Turbo cast-aluminum wheels and a new 5.0-liter TPI V-8 that was also standard in Trans Ams. All 5.0- and 5.7-liter TPI V-8s now came with new analog full-gauge clusters and a 140-mph speedometer. New standard features for Trans Am GTAs included a remote deck-lid release, a power antenna, a right-hand visor vanity mirror, power windows and door locks, side moldings, air conditioning, tinted glass, lamps, a PASS-Key theft-deterrent system, controlled-cycle wipers, a rear window defogger, cruise control, tilt steering, AM/FM stereo with cassette and graphic equalizer, redundant radio controls, integral rear headrests and Metrix cloth trim.

Firebird model year production totaled 42,448 base Firebirds and 20,007 Trans Ams. The Formula and GTA models were considered option packages.

FIREBIRD - SERIES 2F - V-6/V-8

Base models shared an improved Tuned Port Induction (TPI) system on V-8 engines, which also had new serpentine accessory belt drives. Base models now came with standard 15 x 7 in. deep-dish High-Tech Turbo cast-aluminum or diamond-spoke aluminum wheels, a redesigned four-spoke steering wheel, a UM7 Delco ETR

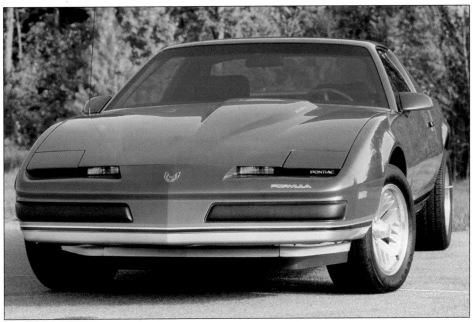

THE SPORTY FORMULA FIREBIRDS CAME WITH DOMED HOODS AND SOME DIFFERENT BODY GRAPHICS.

AM/FM stereo with seek/scan and clock, Pallex cloth interior trim, a new Camel colored interior, monotone paint treatments and a choice of two new exterior colors (Silver Blue Metallic or Orange Metallic). Base Firebirds also featured a 2.8-liter MFI V-6, a center high-mounted stop lamp, complete analog instrumentation, a full-length console with instrument panel, side window defoggers, a front air dam, the GM Computer Command Control system, a hatch "pull-down" feature, rectangular-shaped concealed quartz halogen headlights, cloth reclining front bucket seats, a folding rear seat, a lockable storage compartment, P215/65R15 BSW tires, a five-speed manual transmission, and "wet-arm" windshield wipers.

FORMULA FIREBIRD - SERIES F/S V-8

Formulas had new 16 x 8 in. High-Tech Turbo cast-aluminum wheels and a new 5.0-liter EFI/TBI V-8 engine that was also standard in the Trans Am. The high-output 5.0-liter EFI/

TPI V-8 was available at extra cost along with the 5.7-liter EFI/TPI V-8 and all cars with TPI engines now came with full-gauge analog clusters and a 140-mph speedometer.

FIREBIRD TRANS AM - SERIES F/W - V-8

Firebird Trans Ams featured a body Aero package, hood and front fender air extractors, hood air louvers, a body-color aero rear deck lid spoiler, fog lamps, Soft-Ray tinted glass, a 5.0-liter throttle-body-injection (EFI/TBI) V-8, and the Y99 Rally Tuned Suspension with P215/65R15 Goodyear Eagle GT black sidewall tires, a 32-mm front stabilizer bar a 23-mm rear stabilizer bar and 12.7:1 quick-ratio steering.

FIREBIRD TRANS AM GTA - SERIES F/W - V-8

To the standard Trans Am features GTAs also added four-wheel disc brakes, air conditioning, dual power mirrors, power articulating cloth front bucket seats, a power deck lid release,

THE 1988 FORMULA FIREBIRD RECEIVED NEW CAST-ALUMINUM WHEELS AND A NEW 5.0-LITER ENGINE.

power door locks, a Delco UT4 ETR "touch control" AM/FM stereo with cassette and anti-theft feature, a WS6 Special Performance package, a leather-wrapped steering wheel, P245/50VR16 Goodyear Eagle tires, a four-speed automatic transmission and 16 x 8-in. gold-colored lightweight diamond-spoke aluminum wheels. The 5.7-liter 225-hp Tune Port Injected (EFI/TPI) V-8 was standard with four-speed automatic transmission in the GTA. (It was also optional in Formula and Trans Am models).

HISTORICAL FOOTNOTES

Michael J. Losh continued as Pontiac Motor Division general manager in 1988, with E. M. Schlesinger heading up sales and service responsibilities. Bill O'Neill once again handled public relations. John Sawruk from Engineering was also the official Pontiac historian. All 1988 Firebirds were built in Van Nuys, California. Model-year production of Firebirds was 62,467 units. Model year U.S. dealer sales were 59,459 Firebirds. The fuel-injected V-6 was used in 35.3 percent of all Firebirds built and 64.7 percent were fitted with a fuel-injected V-

8. The four-speed automatic transmission was used in 85.2 percent of production, while 14.8 percent had the five-speed manual gearbox. All Firebirds had power steering and power brakes, 24.8 percent had four-wheel disc brakes, 100 percent had steel-belted radial tires and aluminum wheel rims, 12.3 percent had automatic air conditioning and 81.4 percent had manual air conditioning, 98.3 percent had Solar-Ray tinted glass, 70.9 percent had power windows, 62.5 percent had power door locks, 26.3 percent had power seats, 94.3 percent had an adjustable steering column, 67.6 percent had cruise control, 94.3 percent had windshield wipers with a delay feature, 98.9 percent had a digital clock, 72.4 percent had a rear window defogger, 100 percent had a remote-control left-hand rearview mirror and 29.7 percent had a similar right-hand rearview mirror. The hatch roof option was installed on 42.2 percent of all 1988 Firebirds, 12.2 percent had an AM/FM stereo, 56.5 percent had a stereo-cassette system, 30.2 percent had a premium sound system and 10.2 percent had premium radio speakers.

THE HOT 20TH ANNIVERSARY GTA BOASTED A TURBO V-6 POWER PLANT.

1989

To commemorate the first Trans Am, 1,500 copies of a special 20th Anniversary model were built in 1989. They had a 250-hp turbocharged V-6 was coupled to a four-speed automatic and limited-slip axle. All 20th Anniversary cars were white with a camel interior. The GTA nose emblem was changed to a cloisonné 20th Anniversary insignia with a similar emblem on the sail panels. Turbo Trans Am emblems were on the front fenders. This model featured a competition-type 18-gallon fuel tank, four-wheel power disc brakes, gold 16-in. diamond-spoke aluminum wheels, stainless steel exhaust splitters, analog gauges with a turbo boost gauge, contoured rear seats and Official Indy 500 Pace Car decals that could be installed by Pontiac dealers at the buyer's request.

All Firebirds had new basecoat/clearcoat paint for a glossy, long-lasting finish. A new color was Bright Blue Metallic. Door-glass seals were improved to allow less wind noise. The self-adjusting rear disc brakes were completely revised with a new caliper-and-rotor design. Standard equipment across the entire 1989 Firebird lineup included three-point lap and shoulder belts for rear-seat occupants. PASS-Key anti-theft protection, previously standard on GTAs,

was now standard on all models. An electronic resistor embedded in the ignition key activated a control module in the ignition lock to determine when the anti-theft system was activated. GM said that the system had reduced Corvette thefts by 40 percent and suggested that it should be helpful in reducing insurance costs.

The lowest-priced Firebird was the base model with a standard 2.8-liter V-6 and five-speed manual transmission. All V-6s now had the FE1 suspension package with 30mm front/18mm rear anti-roll bars. Added standard equipment for V-8 models included a Trans Am-style F41 suspension and air conditioning. Base Firebirds carried the same exterior striping package as Formulas.

The Formula was aimed at buyers interested in high-performance "street machines." It provided maximum "oomph" for a minimum price. This package's "Trans Am engine" had 10 additional horsepower thanks to a new dual catalytic converter low-back-pressure exhaust system. Pontiac claimed this equated to a two- to three-second cut in 0 to 60-mph times. Also standard was a WS6 suspension, air conditioning and revised exterior graphics with narrower stripes.

The Trans Am used a 5.0-liter TBI 170-hp V-

8, five-speed manual transmission, limited-slip differential, F41 suspension, Firestone Firehawk GTX tires, 15 x 7-in. cast-aluminum wheels and air conditioning.

Described as the "ultimate Firebird," the Trans Am GTA had a 5.7-liter 235-hp TPI V-8 borrowed from the Corvette and a long list of upgraded technical or upscale cosmetic features, including cross-laced aluminum wheels, cloth articulating bucket seats and redundant radio controls on the steering wheel hub. The GTA notchback also had 45/55 split folding rear seats with integral headrests. Special leather-upholstered bucket seats were optional.

Firebird model year production included 49,048 base Firebirds and 15,358 Trans Ams. Production of Formula and GTA model options was not broken out.

FIREBIRD - SERIES 2F - V-6/V-8

For 1989, Pontiac's premium performer continued its more-than-two-decades heritage of high-powered excitement. From performance machine enthusiasts to sporty car buyers looking for trademark styling, the Firebird offered a complete range of power and price. Again there were four regular models: Firebird, Formula, Trans Am and Trans Am GTA. There was also a special limited edition 25th Anniversary "Indy Pace Car" version of the GTA with a high-output V-6 pirated from the Buick GNX. All Firebirds came with V-8s and the base model also came with a V-6 for entry-level sports car buyers. Multi-tec fuel injectors were added to 1989 engines for more reliability and less susceptibility to fuel fouling. The self-adjusting rear disc brakes were completely revised with a new caliper and rotor design. PASS-Key anti-theft protection, previously standard only on the GTA, became standard on all Firebirds. An electronically coded resistor embedded in the ignition key activated a control module in the ignition lock, which determined when the anti-theft vehicle start-up system should be activated. GM noted that the system had been suc-

cessful in reducing Corvette thefts by 40 percent and said that it should be helpful in holding down Firebird owners' insurance premiums. Door glass seals were improved for better sealing and less wind noise. The entire Firebird line also got clearcoat paint over the base color for a long-lasting high-gloss finish. New in the color lineup was Bright Blue Metallic. Available options now offered across the F-car line included removable T-tops, a variety of radios and an all-new compact digital disc player with the Delco II theft deterrent system that rendered the unit inoperative if power was interrupted.

FORMULA FIREBIRD - SERIES 2F/S - V-6/V-8

For 1989, the Formula Firebird carried the same exterior striping package as the base model. The Formula Firebird was aimed at buyers interested in high-performance "street machines" and was designed to provide maximum "oomph" for a minimum price. This package provided the Trans Am engine, which had a 10-hp boost in power due to the use of a new dual catalytic converter low-back-pressure exhaust system. Pontiac claimed this equated to a .2 to .3-second cut in 0 to 60-mph acceleration times. Also standard on Formulas was the WS6 package and revised exterior graphics with narrower body side stripes. The Formula added a 5.0-liter EFI V-8, air conditioning, a body-color aero rear deck lid spoilers, a dome hood, "Formula" body graphics, two-tone paint and striping, High-Tech Turbo deep-dish cast-aluminum wheels and a special Level III performance suspension with P245/50ZR16 Goodyear Eagle steel-belted black sidewall tires.

FIREBIRD TRANS AM - SERIES 2F/W - V-8

The 1989 Trans Am had a standard 5.0-liter TBI V-8 engine, five-speed manual transmission and limited-slip differential. Also included were F41 underpinnings with 34-mm front and 23-mm rear anti-roll bars and recalibrated springs and shocks, Firestone Firehawk GTX tires, 15

THE 1989 TRANS AM GTA WAS EQUIPPED WITH A PERFORMANCE SUSPENSION AND THE BASE ENGINE WAS A TPI V-8 BORROWED FROM THE CORVETTE.

x 7-in. High-Tech Turbo cast-aluminum wheels and air conditioning. The Trans Am also added the 170-hp engine, an Aero body package, hood air louvers, a body-color Aero rear deck lid spoiler, integral fog lamps, a leather appointments group and a Level II suspension.

FIREBIRD TRANS AM GTA - SERIES F/W - V-8

The Trans Am GTA was described as the "ultimate Firebird" (even though the Indy Pace Car version really was the ultimate Firebird). The regular Trans Am GTA had a 5.7-liter TPI V-8 borrowed from the Corvette, plus four-speed automatic transmission, a limited-slip differential and the special level III WS6 performance suspension with Goodyear P245/50ZR16 steel-belted black sidewall tires.

FIREBIRD 20TH ANNIVERSARY TRANS AM GTA INDY PACE CAR - SERIES F/W – TURBOCHARGED V-6

To commemorate the 20th anniversary of the first Firebird Trans Am, a special series of 1,500 20th Anniversary Trans Ams was produced. These cars were above the level of the GTA model and were really the "ultimate" Trans Ams of this year. Power was provided by a 3.8-liter

V-6 with a Garrett T3 turbocharger and air-to-air intercooler that developed 250 hp. It was coupled to a four-speed automatic transmission and limited-slip rear axle. All 20th Anniversary Trans Ams were painted white and had camel-colored interiors. Externally, the GTA emblem on the nose was changed to a special "20th Anniversary" insignia. A similar cloisonné emblem could be found on the sail panels. "Turbo Trans Am" emblems on the front fenders replaced the standard GTA script in the same location. AEach of these cars came with a complete set of Official Indianapolis 500 Pace Car decals for the doors and windshield. These could be owner or dealer installed.

HISTORICAL FOOTNOTES

Firebird sales managed to stay about even with 1988, although Pontiac lost a bit of overall market share. Model-year production of Firebirds was 64,406 units. Of those cars, 2.4 percent had the turbocharged V-6, 38.8 percent had the regular V-6, 58.8 percent had a V-8, 85.9 percent had an automatic transmission and 14.1 percent had the five-speed manual transmission. *Road & Track* magazine road tested a Turbo Trans Am and recorded a 5.3-second 0-to-60 run. The car did the quarter mile in 13.91 seconds at about 90 mph.

PONTIAC PRODUCED ONLY 1,054 REGULAR TRANS AMS FOR MODEL YEAR 1990.

1990

Vital to Pontiac's future plans in 1990 was GM's decision to replace the aging F-Car platform. Once again, there were rumors floating around the auto industry that perhaps no replacement at all would be forthcoming. But the corporation would soon snuff out the scuttlebutt by announcing a major decision to source both Firebirds and Camaros from a factory in Canada. As a result, a build out of the current model was scheduled for mid-December 1989 at the Van Nuys, California, factory where F-Cars were manufactured.

Firebirds grew larger in 1990 and were upgraded to a new 3.1-liter base V-6 engine. All TPI V-8s (standard in Trans Ams) had a speed-density-metering system. All Firebirds also got driver and passenger airbags, a new self-adjusting parking brake, dual body-color sport mirrors and new instrument panel switches for the rear defogger, rear hatch release and fog lamps. Brilliant Red Metallic was a new color for the year.

Base Firebirds had new seat and armrest trim, plus a different rear spoiler design. Standard features included a five-speed manual gearbox, FE1 suspension, P215/65R15 tires,

front disc/rear drum brakes and AM/FM stereo with clock. The 15 x 7-in. High-Tech aluminum wheels were standard.

Formulas got more of a performance image with a new aero-style rear deck lid spoiler. Also standard were air conditioning, tinted glass, a WS6 sport suspension, P245/50ZR16 tires and a TBI V-8 engine. The Formula's 6-in. deep-dish, High-Tech wheels had machine-finished faces and silver metallic ports.

The Trans Am switched from the TBI V-8 to a hotter TPI V-8. It also had an F41 handling suspension, limited-slip differential, P215/65R15 Firehawk GTX tires and 15-in. deep-dish, High-Tech, turbo cast-aluminum wheels with machined faces and charcoal metallic ports, plus a leather appointment group. The luxury version of the Trans Am was the fully loaded GTA with its 5.7-liter TPI V-8, dual catalytic converter exhaust system, four-speed automatic transmission, four-wheel disc brakes, P245/50ZR-16 Goodyear performance tires and 16 x 8-in. gold crosslace aluminum wheels. Also standard were a leather-wrapped steering wheel, articulating custom bucket seats with inflatable lumbar and

THE 1990 GTA WAS LOADED INSIDE AND OUT AND USUALLY FEATURED A 5.7-LITER H.O V-8.

lateral supports, a rear defogger, a cargo screen, a full-featured Delco ETR AM/FM stereo cassette with equalizer, a power antenna, power side view mirrors, power windows and power door locks.

Model-year production was 18,046 base Firebirds and 2,570 Trans Ams. That was a 68 percent reduction from 1989, caused by a recession that severely impacted automobile sales across the entire market spectrum.

FIREBIRD - SERIES 2F/S - V-6/V-8

For 1990, Firebirds had a larger and more powerful base V-6. All TPI V-8s (standard in Trans Ams) had a speed- density metering system. All Firebirds also had an inflatable airbag restraint system, a new self-adjusting parking brake, dual body-color sport mirrors and new instrument panel switches for the rear defogger, rear hatch release and fog lamps. Brilliant Red Metallic was a new color replacing Flame Red. Base Firebirds had new seat and armrest trim, plus a different rear spoiler design. Standard features included a 3.1-liter V-6 with MFI, the GM Computer Command Control engine management system, a hatch pull-down feature, concealed rectangular quartz halogen head-

lamps, a monochromatic paint theme, a PASS-Key theft-deterrent system, a five-speed manual transmission and High-Tech Turbo cast-aluminum wheels with locks.

FORMULA FIREBIRD - SERIES F/S - V-8

The Formula package was actually an option for the base Firebird, but it was merchandised almost as if it was a separate model. For 1990, the Formula Firebird had more of a performance image. Its equipment list added an aero-style rear deck lid spoiler, air conditioning, tinted glass, the WS6 suspension and a TBI V-8 engine. The Formula's 6-in. deep-dish High-Tech wheels had machined-finished faces and silver metallic ports. Standard features included a 5.0-liter V-8 engine with EFI, air conditioning, a body-color aero rear deck lid spoiler, a dome hood, Formula graphics, a special Level III performance suspension, P245/50ZR16 speed-rated Goodyear Eagle steel-belted black sidewall tires, two-tone paint and striping and deep-dish High-Tech Turbo cast-aluminum wheels with locks.

TRANS AM - SERIES F/W - V-8

For 1990, the Trans Am had a more powerful

engine, an F41 handling suspension, a limited-slip differential and 15-in. deep-dish High-Tech Turbo cast-aluminum wheels with machined faces and charcoal metallic ports. The Trans Am added a 5.0-liter TPI V-8, an aero body package, hood air louvers and air extractors, a body-color aero rear deck lid spoiler, fender air extractors, fog lamps, a leather appointment group, a Level II suspension and P215/65R15 steel-belted black sidewall Firestone Firehawk GTX radial tires

TRANS AM GTA - SERIES F/W - V-8

The GTA package was actually an option for the Trans Am, but it was merchandised almost as if it was a separate model. The GTA had a 5.7-liter H.O. V-8 with TPI, an aero package, hood air louvers, hood air extractors, a limited-slip axle, a body-color aero rear deck lid spoiler, four-wheel power disc brakes, cruise control, fog lamps, a leather appointment group, dual power Sport outside rearview mirrors, power articulating front bucket seats, a power rear deck lid release, power door locks, power windows, a Delco ETR "touch control" AM/FM stereo with cassette and graphic equalizer and Delco-Lock anti-theft system, a special Level III performance suspension, a leather-wrapped steering wheel with supplemental restraint system and redundant radio controls, P245/50ZR16 Goodyear "Gatorback" steel-belted black sidewall radial tires, a four-speed automatic transmission and diamond-spoke aluminum wheels.

HISTORICAL FOOTNOTES

Pontiac's model-year production was 49,657 Firebirds. That represented a mere .79 percent of all cars built in the U.S. The four-speed automatic transmission was used in 93.6 percent of the cars. The rest had the five-speed manual gearbox. Of the 46,760 cars made for sale in the U.S. (the balance were built here but sold in another nation), 21 percent had a limited-slip differential, 10.5 percent had four-wheel disc brakes, 9.3 percent had manual air conditioning, 79.1 percent had power door locks and windows, 64.6 percent had cruise control, 40.4 percent had dual power rearview mirrors, 57.2 percent had hatch roofs, 52.3 percent had an AM/FM stereo with cassette, 43.6 percent had a premium sound system and 1.8 percent had a CD player. Model-year sales of Firebirds hit just 39,781 cars.

THE GTA WAS FAST, BUT IT WASN'T THE HOTTEST FIREBIRD AROUND IN 1991. PONTIAC HAD SOME EVEN FASTER BIRDS RACING IN THE SCCA TRANS-AM SERIES AFTER A SEVEN-YEAR HIATUS.

1991

Although they seemed minor on the surface, 14 major changes were made on the 1991 Firebirds that bowed, early in 1990, as 1991 models. By the spring of 1990, these cars were hitting Pontiac dealerships. PMD called them "perpetual emotion machines." They had 14 major changes led by new styling that was backed up by a hot Street Legal Performance (SLP) option. A new Firebird convertible was a running addition to the model lineup.

The most visible change was a new exterior appearance. All models had restyled front and rear fascias. The front fascias — made of body-color resilient "Endura" thermoplastic — incorporated low-profile turn signals and integral air dams. At the rear, the GTA, Trans Am and Formula got a redesigned spoiler. New fascias on GTA and Trans Am models incorporated restyled taillights.

The base Firebird's Sport Appearance package included fog lights in the fascia and carried the aero look to the sides with distinctive lateral skirting. The headlights were more compact, with no sacrifice of light output. Available from dealers for all 5.0- and 5.7-liter TPI V-8s was the SLP kit, which boosted engine performance without engine modifications. It could be dealer installed or owner installed.

On all models the standard radio was upgraded to an AM/FM cassette stereo. The GTA included a cassette with five-band graphic equalizer. Acoustics were improved. New colors included Dark Green Metallic and Bright White.

Models and options were unchanged and equipment offerings were about the same. Pontiac's new general manager John G. Middlebrook announced, "Convertibles will be built on Firebird's fun-to-drive image" and a new ragtop — the first since 1969 — debuted. The Firebird version was $19,159 and the Trans Am convertible was $22,980. Both had a standard Sport Appearance package.

PMD teamed up with PAS — the firm that helped it make the 1989 20th Anniversary model's Turbo V-6 — to create a Firefox GTA with a 5.7-liter TPI V-8 in 1991. It was promoted as the prototype of a future production option. It produced 330 hp and had a ZF six-speed transmission. It could do 0-to-60 mph in 5.6 seconds and cover the quarter mile in 13.38 seconds at 103.5 mph.

Firebird model year output for 1991 went up a bit: 23,977 base models and 6,343 Trans Ams. Convertible production came to 2,000 units.

FIREBIRD - SERIES 2F/S - V-6/V-8

The new 1991 Firebirds were actually introduced in the spring of 1990. Their most visible change was a new exterior appearance. All models benefited from restyled front and rear fascias. The front fascia was made of body-color resilient "Endura" thermoplastic and incorporated low-profile turn signals and integral air dams. Pontiac General Manager John C. Middlebrook announced convertible versions of the base Firebird and the Trans Am on Jan. 3, 1990. All Firebirds had a driver's side airbag. All 1991 Firebirds were also protected by a PASS-Key theft deterrent system. The standard radio was upgraded to an AM/FM cassette stereo and the GTA included a cassette with five-band graphic equalizer. Acoustics were improved in all models. The Sport Appearance package on the base Firebird included fog lights in the fascia and carried the aero look to the sides with distinctive lateral skirting. The headlights were more compact, without sacrificing light output. Standard features included a 3.1-liter V-6 with MFI, power brakes, a center high-mounted stoplight, the FE1 suspension, P215/65R15 steel-belted black sidewall tires, a four-speed automatic transmission and 15 x 7-in. High-Tech cast-aluminum wheels with locks.

FORMULA FIREBIRD - SERIES 2F/S - V-8

The new 1991 Formula was fitted with a redesigned rear deck lid spoiler. New fascias on GTA and Trans Am models incorporated restyled taillights. The Formula added a 5.0-liter TBI V-8, a five-speed manual gearbox, the WS6 Sport Suspension, P245/50ZR16 tires, 16 x 8-in. deep-dish High-Tech Turbo cast-aluminum wheels, a limited-slip differential and air conditioning.

FIREBIRD TRANS AM - SERIES 2F/W - V-8

The new Trans Am also had a redesigned rear deck lid spoiler that included restyled taillights. The Trans Am added or substituted a 5.0-liter TPI V-8, the F41 Rally Tuned Suspension, 16 x 8-in. diamond spoke wheels, an aero package with special side treatment, a leather appointment group (including leather-wrapped steering wheel) and a four-way manual driver's seat adjuster.

FIREBIRD TRANS AM GTA - SERIES F/W - V-8

At the rear, the 1991 GTA was fitted with a redesigned rear deck lid spoiler incorporating restyled taillights. The GTA featured the 5.7-liter TPI V-8, a four-speed automatic transmission, the WS6 Sport suspension, P245/50ZR16 tires, 16 x 8-in. diamond spoke wheels, a limited-slip differential, disc/drum brakes and a Performance Enhancement group (with engine oil cooler, dual converters and performance axle).

HISTORICAL FOOTNOTES

Pontiac's model-year production in the United States included 50,247 Firebirds. That represented 0.87 percent of total U.S. auto production. The model year sales total was recorded as 24,601 Firebirds. Of the 30,323 cars made as 1991 models during the 1991 model year (some '91s were built in the 1990 model year and counted as 1990s), 92.9 percent had power door locks and windows, 60.7 percent had cruise control, 60.5 percent had a rear window defogger, 72.1 percent had dual power rearview mirrors, 54.6 percent had hatch roofs, 44 percent had an AM/FM stereo with cassette, 52.1 percent had a premium sound system and 3.9 percent had a CD player. Available in 1991 for Firebirds with 5.0- and 5.7-liter TPI V-8s was a new "Street Legal Performance" (SLP) package of GM high-performance hardware. The SLP kit, created by SLP Engineering, was available from GM dealers. It boosted engine performance without modifications to the power plants.

THE HATCHBACK GTA CAME WITH AN $18,105 PRICE TAG.

1992

Pontiac made the base Firebird a little more affordable in 1992. The range of prices started at $12,995, as opposed to $13,159 the year before. However, at the upper end of the spectrum the pricier models ran to $26,370 as opposed to a high of $24,999 for the '91 models. There were few alterations, though Pontiac promoted "structural enhancements" and new asbestos-free brake pads. New colors for the year included Yellow, Dark Jade Gray Metallic and Dark Aqua Metallic. The AM/FM cassette radio had revised graphics and a Beige interior was introduced. Strangely, there was no special package to celebrate the nameplate's 25th anniversary.

Engines for the Firebird, Firebird Formula, Trans Am and Trans Am GTA were carried over from 1991, except for the power plant used in a new Formula Firehawk model. This wasn't a factory-built car — it was a special creation that stemmed from a partnership between PMD and SLP Engineering, an aftermarket modifier. Firehawks were based on Formulas with the 5.0-liter TPI V-8 and came in "street" and "competition" versions. The $39,995 street version produced 350 hp. The competition kit cost nearly $10,000 and provided even higher output.

SLP kits were available through GM Service Parts Organization's 1992 high-performance catalog. SLP Engineering installed only 25 kits. They went on 24 coupes and one convertible. Interestingly, these cars carried serial numbers between 1 and 27 because cars no. 18 and no. 25 were never built.

With the country in a recession, the Firebird series, with a production total of only 25,180 cars, was getting the same "evil eye" it had felt 10 years earlier. General manager John Middlebrook admitted to *Automotive News* that Firebird sales were down by 6 percent. A month later, GM announced huge layoffs and multiple plant closings. Industry observers then predicted doomsday for the F-Cars. However, an all-new Firebird due in the fall and released late in 1993 would turn things around and secure the future of the marque a second time.

FIREBIRD -
SERIES F/S - V-6/V-8

Pontiac announced the first Firebird convertible in 21 years in 1991 and only 2,000 were built. The open model was continued in 1992. The full line consisted of Firebird, Firebird Formula, Trans Am and Trans Am GTA models. The convertible was available as a base Firebird or as a Trans Am. Other changes for 1992 included structural enhancements and non-asbestos brake pads. New Yellow, Dark Jade Gray Metallic and Dark Aqua Metallic exterior paint colors were also added. The interiors had revised AM/FM cassette radio graphics and new knobs and rings, plus a revised beige interior. Standard features of the base Firebird included a front air dam, a 3.1-liter V-6 engine with multi-port fuel injection and a five-speed manual transmission.

FORMULA FIREBIRD -
SERIES F/S - V-8

The Firebird Formula added or substituted a 5.0-liter EFI V-8, the WS6 Sport suspension, P245/50ZR16 tires, 15 x 7-in. deep-dish High-Tech aluminum wheels, air conditioning and a leather appointment group with leather-wrapped steering wheel.

TRANS AM - SERIES F/V - V-8

Standard Firebird Trans Am features included an aero body package (with aerodynamic front and rear fascias, rocker panel extensions and quarter panel extensions), a 5.0-liter H.O. TPI V-8 and a five-speed manual transmission. The Trans Am convertible also came with a choice of black or beige cloth tops that stowed away neatly under a tonneau cover and leather-clad articulated bucket seats.

TRANS AM GTA -
SERIES F/V - V-8

The GTA added or substituted the following over the Trans Am: 5.7-liter TPI V-8, a four-speed automatic transmission, the WS6 Sport suspension, P245/50ZR16 tires, dual catalytic converters, a performance axle, a Delco ETR AM/FM stereo with CD and five-band equalizer, a power antenna, the leather appointment group, a four-way manual driver's seat adjuster, power windows and door locks, cruise control, a remote deck lid release, a rear window defogger and power outside mirrors.

HISTORICAL FOOTNOTES

John Middlebrook was Pontiac Motor Division's general manager in 1992. E.M. Schlesinger was in charge of general sales and service. E.S. Lechtzin was the company's director of public relations. Lynn C. Myers was the director of marketing and production planning. B. L. Warner was chief engineer. Total production in U.S. and Canada was 27,567 Firebirds. That represented 0.49 percent of total U.S. auto production. The model-year sales total was recorded as 23,401 Firebirds. Calendar year sales were 21,501 Firebirds. Of 25,180 cars built for the domestic market in model year 1992, 89.1 percent had the four-speed automatic transmission, 7 percent had a five-speed manual gearbox, 99.7 percent had a manual air conditioner, 93 percent had power door locks and windows, 67.9 percent had cruise control, 63.3 percent had a rear window defogger, 84.4 percent had dual power rearview mirrors, 53.4 percent had hatch roofs, 41.6 percent had an AM/FM stereo with cassette, 54.4 percent had a premium sound system and 4.0 percent had a CD player. SLP Engineering of Tom's River, New Jersey, offered a Formula Firehawk conversion this year, as well as a "Street Legal Performance" kit that was made available through the GM Service Parts Organization.

*THE 1993 TRANS AM WAS AGAIN PLENTY SPORTY WITH FOG LAMPS,
TINTED WINDOWS, T-TOPS AND A REAR SPOILER.*

1993

Firebirds had all-new sheet metal for 1993, when the brand's fourth-generation Firebird arrived. The radically new F-car was 90 percent different than its predecessor. Firebird, Formula and Trans Am coupes were offered in the model line up. Driver and passenger-side front airbags was a standard safety feature.

All Firebirds had a 68-degree windshield, new aluminum wheels and tires, composite body panels that were resistant to minor impacts and rust, new instruments, new suspensions and a standard new 3.4-liter V-6. A new 5.7-liter V-8 was standard in Formula and Trans Am models, which also got a six-speed manual transmission. Advanced four-wheel anti-lock brakes were standard on all Firebird models with four-wheel disc brakes standard on Formulas and Trans Ams.

Standard on all Firebirds was a front air dam, tinted glass, sport mirrors, aero rear-deck spoiler, side-window defogger, four-spoke steering wheel with adjustable steering column, P215/60R16 steel-belted touring tires, rack-and-pinion steering and a five-speed manual transmission. The high-performance Formula added body-color sport mirrors, smoothly contoured taillights with neutral-density lenses and 16-inch aluminum wheels. Trans Am buyers also got specific front and rear fascia panels and a specific deck-lid spoiler, plus fog lamps, rocker-panel extensions and Goodyear Eagle GS-C performance tires.

Back and more popular was SLP Engineering's Formula Firehawk, described as, "The most aggressive profile this side of Madonna." With 300 hp, it went from 0 to 60 in 4.9 seconds and did the quarter mile in 13.53 seconds at 103.5 mph. The price came down to $24,244 and sales went up to 250 units.

Only 14,112 Firebirds were built in model year 1993, but that was mostly due to the late introduction. Production of the cars in a factory in Ste. Therese, Quebec, Canada, did not start until November 1992. They were first due out early in calendar 1993 and didn't appear in showrooms until even later than that.

FIREBIRD - SERIES F/S - V-6/V-8

Pontiac's fourth-generation Firebird arrived in 1993 with 90 percent new content. This radical revision found most every component of the Firebird completely new or extensively updated. The full line consisted of Firebird, Formula Firebird and Trans Am three-door hatchback coupes. Included among the many changes for 1993 were a 68-degree windshield angle, new aluminum wheels and tires, composite body panels that were resistant to minor impacts and rust, new instrumentation, a locking glove box and new front and rear suspensions. A new 3.4-liter V-6 was standard in the Firebird and a LT1 5.7-liter V-8 was standard in Formula and Trans Am models. A new six-speed manual transmission was also standard in Formulas and Trans Ams. Other new features included advanced four-wheel antilock brakes (standard on Firebirds with four-wheel disc brakes including all Formulas and Trans Ams) and dual front airbags. A keyless entry system was now available on all Firebirds and standard on Trans Ams. Standard equipment on the base Firebird included power front disc/rear drum brakes with antilock braking system (ABS), a 3.4-liter V-6 with sequential-port fuel injection, a Ride & Handling package and a five-speed manual transmission.

FORMULA FIREBIRD - SERIES 2F - V-6/V-8

The 1993 Formula Firebird was promoted as "Pontiac's new and improved Formula for performance." The 275-hp LT1 5.7-liter V-8 was standard and linked to the new six-speed manual transmission. A more rigid body structure, an Opti-Spark ignition system, a gear-driven water pump, de Carbon monotube shock absorbers and Goodyear Eagle GT touring tires contributed to the Formula Firebird's high-performance image.

TRANS AM - SERIES F/V - V-8

The 1993 Trans Am was promoted as "legendary excitement reborn." Standard equipment on the Trans Am included the 5.7-liter LT1 V-8 with sequential-port fuel injection, a low oil level monitor and warning, a performance rear axle with 3.23:1 axle ratio, an engine oil cooler, a Performance Ride & Handling suspension and a six-speed manual transmission.

HISTORICAL FOOTNOTES

John Middlebrook was Pontiac Motor Division's general manager in 1992. Total production in U.S. and Canada included 15,475 Firebirds. The model-year sales total was recorded as 19,068 Firebirds. Of 14,112 Firebird cars built for the domestic market in model year 1993, 90 percent had the four-speed automatic transmission, 4 percent had a five-speed manual gearbox, 6 percent had the new six-speed manual transmission, 99.9 percent had a manual air conditioner, 95.9 percent had power door locks and 96.3 percent had power windows, 5.8 percent had power seats, 96.3 percent had cruise control, 87 percent had a rear window defogger, 96.3 percent had dual power rearview mirrors, 10.8 percent had hatch roofs, 34.3 percent had an AM/FM stereo with cassette, 43 percent had a premium sound system and 22.7 percent had a CD player. SLP Engineering of Tom's River, N.J. offered a Formula Firehawk conversion this year, as well as a "Street Legal Performance" kit that was made available through the GM Service Parts Organization. The fourth-generation Firebirds came out later than other 1993 Pontiacs. Production began in November 1992 at a General Motors assembly plant in Ste. Therese, Quebec, Canada. The first cars were scheduled to arrive in dealer showrooms early in calendar year 1993, but actually appeared even later in the year. SLP also produced a potent 300-hp "Firehawk" version of the 1993 Trans Am, of which 201 examples were made.

THE FIREBIRD FAMILY (CLOCKWISE FROM LEFT):
TRANS AM, BASE COUPE, FORMULA AND TRANS AM GT.

1994

The big news in Firebird country for 1994 was the release of a new drop-top model. This could be had as a base Firebird or a Trans Am and buyers could add the Formula or GT option to the more expensive version. Traction control was made available on Firebirds with a V-8 engine and automatic transmission. Prices for the year ranged from $14,589 to $21,999.

Additional new Firebird features included a Dark Aqua Metallic color, flood-lit interior door switches, visor straps, a Delco 2001 Series radio, a compact disc player without equalizer, a 5.7-liter sequentially fuel-injected (SFI) V-8, a Mass Air Flow Control System, a four-speed electronically controlled automatic transmission, driver-selectable automatic transmission controls, a 1-4-gear-skip feature on six-speed-

manual-transmission models and two-part basecoat/clearcoat finish.

The new Trans Am GT package included body-colored side moldings, an air-foil-styled spoiler, an electric rear-window defogger, a Remote-Keyless Entry system, rear carpet mats, a Delco 2001 sound system, a four-way manual driver's seat and leather-wrapped steering wheel, shift knob and brake handle.

On January 27, 1994, Pontiac announced a special model to honor the silver anniversary of the Trans Am. This 25th Anniversary Edition Trans Am included Bright White exterior finish, a Bright Blue center-line stripe, anniversary logos and door badges, lightweight 16-inch aluminum wheels painted Bright White and white Prado leather seats with blue 25th Anniversary embroidery. Buyers received a special 25th Anniversary portfolio when they picked up a car.

As a special nod to Trans Am history, PMD headquarters announced that it would build a very limited number of 25th Anniversary Trans Am GT convertibles to honor the eight famous T/A ragtops made when the sports-performance model was first released in mid-1969.

SLP Engineering again made Formula Firehawks and 500 were assembled. Model year production was 45,922 Firebirds. Model year sales more than doubled from 19,068 in 1993 to 46,499 in 1984.

FIREBIRD - SERIES 2F - V-6/V-8

Pontiac's theme for its Firebird 1994 lineup could have been the "return of the ragtop." Each of its series — Firebird, Formula and Trans Am — had its 1993 coupe-only offering bolstered with the addition of a convertible. The Trans Am convertible was part of its GT series, while the coupe version was offered both as a Trans Am and a GT. New features for the overall Firebird line included a new Dark Aqua Metallic exterior color, flood-lit interior door switches, visor straps, a Delco 2001 Series radio, a compact disc player (without graphic equalizer), a 5.7-liter SFI V-8, a Mass Air Flow Control System, a four-speed electronically controlled automatic transmission, driver-selectable automatic transmission controls, a six-speed manual transmission with a 1-4 gear skip shift feature, a 3.42:1 axle ratio, a traction-control system (V-8 automatic only) and two-component clearcoat paint. Additional standard equipment on the base Firebird included 16 x 7 1/2-in. cast-aluminum wheels, power front disc/rear drum brakes with antilock braking system (ABS), a brake/transmission shift interlock feature with automatic transmission, a 3.4-liter V-6 with sequential port fuel injection, a stainless steel exhaust system, extensive anti-corrosion protection, a Ride & Handling suspension package and a five-speed manual transmission. Firebird convertibles also featured a power-operated top

with a fully trimmed headliner, a glass rear window with electric defogger, front and rear floor mats, dual power sport mirrors and a three-piece tonneau cover.

FORMULA FIREBIRD - SERIES F/S - V-8

The Formula series also gained a convertible in the middle of the 1994 model year. The Formula was promoted as a safe and high-performance sports car. It included a hot V-8, disc brakes at all corners, a standard six-speed manual gearbox (or optional four-speed automatic with "normal" and "performance" driver-selectable shift calibrations) and suspension and steering upgrades. The rigid body featured two-sided galvanized steel panels, rustproof composite panels (used for the fenders, doors, hood and hatch) and front fenders that could even spring back from minor impacts.

TRANS AM - SERIES F/V - V-8

The 1994 Trans Am could be spotted by its unique front end, which had no grille and two round fog lamps. Traction Control became available on Trans Ams after midyear. There was no convertible in the first-level Trans Am model line up. Standard equipment for the Trans Am included a black fixed mast antenna, air conditioning, the PASS-Key II theft-deterrent system, a Delco Freedom II battery, power four-wheel disc brakes with an antilock braking system (ABS), a brake/transmission shift interlock feature with automatic transmission and the 5.7-liter V-8 with sequential port fuel injection and a stainless steel exhaust system.

TRANS AM GT - SERIES F/V - V-8

The Trans Am GT had styling features that set it apart from the first-level Trans Am. The main difference was the design of the rear deck lid spoiler. It also had different tires, an upgraded sound system and other perks for buyers who wanted a top-of-the-line Firebird.

THE TRANS AM GT HAD SEVERAL STYLING DIFFERENCES FROM THE OTHER F-CARS, INCLUDING THE SHAPE OF THE SPOILER.

25TH ANNIVERSARY TRANS AM GT -SERIES F/V - V-8

The 25th Anniversary Trans Am was introduced on Jan. 27, 1994. As a special nod to Trans Am history, Pontiac also announced that it would build a very limited number of 25th Anniversary convertibles to honor the eight Trans Am convertibles made in 1969. The 25th Anniversary model also included the GT-type rear deck lid spoiler, the UT6 upgraded 10-speaker sound system, a leather-wrapped steering wheel with radio controls and a Tilt-Wheel adjustable steering column, Bright White exterior finish, a Bright Blue centerline stripe, Anniversary logos and door badges, Bright White 16-in. lightweight aluminum wheels, White Prado leather seating surfaces with blue embroidery and a special 25th Anniversary portfolio for owners, a 3.23:1 performance ratio rear axle, an engine oil cooler, rear-wheel drive, power rack-and-pinion steering, a short/long arm front suspension, a torque arm/track bar rear suspension and a Performance Ride & Handling suspension package.

HISTORICAL FOOTNOTES

Total production in Canada included 51,523 Firebirds. The model year sales total was recorded as 46,499 Firebirds for a 0.5 percent share of the total U.S. market. Of 45,922 Firebirds built for the domestic market in the model year, 80.4 percent had the four-speed automatic transmission, 11 percent had a five-speed manual gearbox, 8.6 percent had the six-speed manual transmission, 0.1 percent had traction control (introduced at midyear), 43.7 percent had a limited-slip differential, 99.7 percent had a manual air conditioner, 90 percent had power windows, 90.5 percent had power door locks, 9.5 percent had power seats, 88.9 percent had cruise control, 72.1 percent had a rear window defogger, 77.9 percent had dual power rearview mirrors, 42.3 percent had hatch roofs, 26 percent had an AM/FM stereo with cassette, 52.3 percent had a premium sound system and 21.7 percent had a CD player. The 25th Anniversary Trans Am did the quarter mile in 14.2 seconds at 99 mph, which compared to 14.6 seconds at 99 mph for the original 1969 1/2 Trans Am. It had an estimated top speed of 152 mph, compared to 135 mph for the first Trans Am. SLP Engineering also built 501 Formula Firehawks and 12 Firehawk T/As.

THE FORMULA FIREBIRD AGAIN SHARED A FORMIDABLE 5.7-LITER
ENGINE WITH THE TRANS AM.

1995

Pontiac's lone rear-wheel-drive car, the Firebird, continued being built in a Canadian factory. For 1995 it was offered in Firebird, Formula and Trans Am models. Each came as a coupe or a convertible.

By 1995, even the base Firebird was a heavily contented car. It featured soft fascia-type bumpers and composite body panels on the doors, front fenders, roof, rear deck lid and rear spoiler. Electrically operated concealed quartz-halogen headlamps were standard, along with one-piece multi-color-lens taillamps and a center high-mounted stop lamp. Body-color body-side moldings were on convertibles. Dual power remote-control Sport mirrors with blue glass were fitted.

The cars were finished with a waterborne base coat and two-component clearcoat system. A black, fixed-mast antenna was mounted at the right rear of the body. Solar-Ray tinted glass was standard. Also new were 16-inch,

five-spoke aluminum wheels, speed-rated tires, a power antenna, a four-spoke Sport steering wheel and a remote CD changer.

Features that were standard exclusively to convertibles included: cruise control; electric rear window defogger; power automatic door locks; remote keyless entry; four-way manual front driver seat/two-way manual front passenger seat; and power windows with "express-down" feature. All 1995 Firebirds also had new maintenance-free ball joints and lubed-for-life front-end components.

The Formula Firehawk was merchandised in 300- and 315-hp models and got new optional chrome rims and a Hurst six-speed shifter. The price of the kit was up about $500 to $6,495, but Firehawk sales rose to 750 units. After a 143 percent rise in 1994, the Firebird enjoyed an additional 13 percent increase in production during 1995. Total model year output was 50,986 cars.

FIREBIRD - SERIES F/S - V-6/V-8

Pontiac's lone rear-wheel drive vehicle was offered in 1995 in coupe and convertible versions in three series: Firebird, Formula and Trans Am. The Canadian-produced muscle machines had several changes. First, a Traction Control system was available for V-8-powered cars with either manual or automatic transmission. Blue Green Chameleon, Medium Dark Purple Metallic and Bright Silver Metallic were new exterior colors. New Bright Red (all) and Bright White (convertible only) leather interiors were seen. Also new were 16-in. five-spoke aluminum wheels on V-8-powered Firebirds, all-weather speed-rated P245/50Z16 tires, a power antenna, a four-spoke Sport steering wheel and a remote compact disc changer (as a dealer-installed option). Standard equipment on the base Firebird included a 3.4-liter V-6 with sequential port fuel injection, a stainless steel exhaust system, extensive anti-corrosion protection, the GM Computer Command Control engine management system, a low oil level monitor and warning, rear-wheel drive, power rack-and-pinion steering, a short/long arm front suspension, a torque arm/track bar rear suspension with de Carbon gas-charged monotube shock absorbers, a Ride & Handling suspension package, a five-speed manual transmission, a three-year/36,000-mile no-deductible warranty program and 24-hour Roadside Assistance program providing lockout assistance, dead battery assistance, out-of-fuel assistance, flat-tire assistance and courtesy transportation. Firebird convertibles also featured a power-operated top with a fully trimmed headliner.

FORMULA FIREBIRD - SERIES F/V - V-8

"Now you're playing with fire," said the 1995 Pontiac sales catalog about the new Formula Firebird. Its standard equipment included a power four-wheel disc brakes with antilock braking system (ABS), a brake/transmission shift interlock feature with automatic transmission, a 5.7-liter V-8 with sequential port fuel injection and a stainless steel exhaust system.

TRANS AM - SERIES F/V - V-8

Buyers could also choose between coupe and convertible versions in the Trans Am series. The Trans Am's standard equipment included a high-performance 10-speaker sound system, HSS speakers and tweeters in doors, 6 1/2-in. subwoofers in sail panels, a subwoofer amplifier in rear quarters and 4-in. speakers and tweeters in rear quarters), a brake/transmission shift interlock feature with automatic transmission, a 5.7-liter V-8 with sequential port fuel injection and a stainless steel exhaust system.

HISTORICAL FOOTNOTES

Total production in Canada included 56,723 Firebirds. The model year sales total was recorded as 41,947 Firebirds for a 0.5 percent share of the total U.S. market. Of 50,986 Firebirds built for the domestic market in the model year, 75.3 percent had the four-speed automatic transmission, 10.9 percent had a five-speed manual gearbox, 13.8 percent had the six-speed manual transmission, 6.3 percent had traction control, 42.8 percent had a limited-slip differential, 99.8 percent had a manual air conditioner, 85.7 percent had power windows, 86.6 percent had power door locks, 10.6 percent had power seats, 87.8 percent had cruise control, 76.7 percent had a rear window defogger, 85.7 percent had dual power rearview mirrors, 52.1 percent had hatch roofs, 24.3 percent had an AM/FM stereo with cassette, 44.8 percent had a premium sound system, 30.9 percent had a CD player and 69 percent had keyless remote entry system. SLP Engineering's Formula Firehawk was merchandised in 300- and 315-hp models and sales rose to some 671 units, all of which were Formula Firehawks. Also produced were two Comp T/A coupes and 70 Comp T/A T-tops.

*A 1996 FORMULA FIREBIRD WITH THE RAM AIR V-8 AND T-TOPS
WAS AN APPEALING COMBINATION.*

1996

The Pontiac Firebird roared into 1996 with more excitement and more powerful engines. There were several new high-performance packages for V-8 models. Trans Am coupes had a new WS6 Pontiac Ram Air performance-and-handling option that was instantly desirable and appealed to late-model muscle car collectors. The Ram Air-equipped Trans Ams were promoted almost as if they were separate models. Prices ranged from $16,119 to $27,869.

A 3800 Series II 200-hp V-6 was the new standard engine for 1996 Firebird coupes and convertibles. It was available with a 3800 Performance Package featuring four-wheel disc brakes, a limited-slip differential, an up-level steering wheel, dual exhausts and five-spoke aluminum wheels.

The optional WS6 Ram Air Performance & Handling Package was available on Formula and Trans Am coupes with the 5.7-liter V-8. It included a Ram Air induction system, functional air scoops, 17-inch five-spoke aluminum wheels, P275/40ZR17 speed-rated tires and dual exhausts.

Model-year production was 30,937 Firebirds of all types.

FIREBIRD – CARLINE/SERIES F/S - V-6/V-8

The 1996 Firebirds were members of a dwindling breed: rear-wheel-drive American muscle cars. Standard equipment on the base Firebird included a rear deck spoiler, Solar-Ray tinted glass, concealed quartz-halogen headlights, P215/60R16 steel-belted radial black sidewall touring tires, bright silver 16 x 8-in. Sport cast-aluminum wheels, a short-and-long arm suspension with front and rear stabilizer bars and the F41 Ride & Handling package, the PASS-Key II theft-deterrent system, a 3.8-liter V-6 and a five-speed manual transmission.

FORMULA FIREBIRD – CARLINE/SERIES F/V – V-8

The Formula Firebird was again the street performance model. Standard equipment included a 5.7-liter V-8 and a five-speed manual transmission. A new option available for the

THIS FORMULA FIREBIRD WAS ONE OF ONLY 524 WITH THE RAM AIR ENGINE OPTION.

1996 Trans Am coupe was the WS6 Ram Air Performance and Handling package that included a Ram Air induction system, specific 17-in. five-spoke aluminum wheels, P275/40ZR17 tires, specific dual outlet exhaust and a tuned suspension. The sales catalog said, "For 1996, Trans Am gives you a new perspective on performance, especially when outfitted with the WS6 Ram Air package. Like that fitted to the original 1969 1/2 Trans Am, the available package increases the Tran Am's V-8 horsepower from 285 to 305, while it enhances handling with special chassis components (shocks, bushings, springs and massive, speed-rated 17-in. tires)."

HISTORICAL FOOTNOTES

Total production in Canada included 32,799 Firebirds. The calendar year sales total was recorded as 32,622 Firebirds, which represented 6.2 percent of total Pontiac calendar year sales. Of 30,937 Firebirds built for the domestic market in the model year, 72.2 percent had the four-speed automatic transmission, 12.9 percent had a five-speed manual gearbox, 14.9 percent had the six-speed manual transmission, 8.5 percent had traction control, 55.5 percent had a limited-slip differential, 99.8 percent had a manual air

conditioner, 80.7 percent had power windows, 81.9 percent had power door locks, 9.2 percent had power seats, 30.7 percent had leather seats, 86.8 percent had cruise control, 79.2 percent had a rear window defogger, 80.7 percent had dual power rearview mirrors, 54.9 percent had hatch roofs, 0.6 percent had an AM/FM stereo with cassette, 56.4 percent had a premium sound system, 43 percent had a CD player, 68.2 percent had the keyless remote entry system and 24.6 percent had an alarm system. A special Firebird model offered in 1996 was called the Harley-Davidson Edition Trans Am. The Milwaukee, Wisconsin, motorcycle maker took a black Trans Am equipped with the WS6 Ram Air package (without the factory upholstery) and added leather-and-fabric seats with the Harley-Davidson logo embroidered on them. The Harley-Davidson Edition Trans Am also had Harley decals on the front quarter panels just behind the tires. Only 40 such cars are believed to have been produced. Most of them were sold in Southern California. Also produced in 1996 were 10 Comp T/A hardtops and 35 Comp T/A T-tops — all had the WS6 Ram Air package.

Jerry Heasley photo

THE 1997 TRANS AM WITH THE RAM AIR V-8 PRODUCED 305 HP.

1997

In 1997, you could get a Firebird in a variety of flavors, from affordable to expensive, from economical to guzzler, and from sports car to muscle car — but you couldn't get a Firebird that would please everyone.

The typical buyer of a V-6 Firebird coupe was a 36-year-old person making $55,000 a year. Just over half were married and just below half were male college graduates working in a professional field. At the other end of the Firebird spectrum, Trans Am buyer demographics indicated a median age of 40, average household income of $75,000 and that slightly over 50 percent of buyers were married males with a college degree and professional occupation.

Models and engine carried over from 1996, but new performance and appearance options were added. A Ram Air Performance and Handling Package was offered for convertibles. Ram Air ragtops featured a 5.7-liter V-8, twin scoops with Ram Air logos on each "nostril," high-polished dual exhaust tips and 17-in. aluminum rims. A new package, introduced in mid-1996, was a Sport and Appearance package for V-6 Firebirds with ground effects, fog lamps and dual exhausts with cast-aluminum extensions. New Firebird interior features included a console with an auxiliary power outlet for electronic devices, a pull-out cup holder and revised storage. Air conditioning became standard and all-leather power seats were now available. A four-way seat adjuster and daytime running lamps were added standard equipment. New options included a 500-watt Monsoon sound system. Pontiac built 30,754 Firebirds in the model year.

FIREBIRD – SERIES F/S – V-6/V-8

"Either you get it or you don't!" That's what a perceptive copywriter said about '97 Firebirds. "The first rule of success is to equip yourself with the proper tools. This axiom not only applies to business, but to automobiles as well. Firebird provides drivers with what's needed for command of the road." Standard equipment included dual front airbags, air conditioning, power front disc/rear drum four-wheel antilock brakes, side window defoggers, a UPC L36 3800 Series II 200-hp SFI V-6 engine, Solar-Ray tinted glass, full instrumentation with a tachometer and trip odometer, sport exterior mirrors (left-hand remote controlled), a rear deck lid spoiler, the PASS-Key II theft-deterrent system, an AM/FM stereo ETR radio

THE 1997
TRANS AM
WITH THE
RAM AIR V-8
PRODUCED
305 HP.

Jerry Heasley photo

and cassette P215/60R16 touring tires with a high-pressure compact spare, a UPC MM5 five-speed manual transmission and bright silver 16 x 8-in. cast-aluminum wheels. Convertibles also included (in addition to or in place of the respective coupe features) cruise control, a rear window defogger, power door locks, remote keyless entry, dual blue-tinted power mirrors, a six-speaker sound system and power windows with express-down feature.

FORMULA FIREBIRD –
SERIES F/V – V-8

The Formula Firebird also came in hatchback coupe and convertible models. The Formula came standard with a 5.7-liter 285-hp SFI V-8. A Ram Air Performance and Handling Package was offered for the Formula Firebird coupe. Ram Air Formulas featured twin scoops with Ram Air logos on each "nostril," a 305-hp rating, high-polished dual exhaust tips, 17-in. five-spoke aluminum rims, P275/40ZR17 tires, specific dual outlet exhaust and a tuned suspension.

TRANS AM –
SERIES F/V – V-8

The Trans Am was again the ultimate Firebird in 1997. It also came as a hatchback coupe or a convertible. A Ram Air Performance and Handling Package was offered for the Trans Am coupe. Ram Air cars featured twin scoops with Ram Air logos on each "nostril," a 305-hp rat-

ing, high-polished dual exhaust tips, 17-in. five-spoke aluminum rims, P275/40ZR17 tires, specific dual outlet exhaust and a tuned suspension. Standard equipment on the Trans Am coupe included the 5.7-liter V-8 with sequential-port fuel injection. The convertible also had the Firebird/ Formula type rear deck lid spoiler, rather than the uplevel style used on the Trans Am coupe.

HISTORICAL FOOTNOTES

Total production in Canada included 32,692 Firebirds. The calendar year sales total was recorded as 32,524 Firebirds, which represented 5.8 percent of total Pontiac calendar year sales. Of 30,754 Firebirds built for the domestic market in the model year, 77.4 percent had the four-speed automatic transmission, 8.7 percent had a five-speed manual gearbox, 13.9 percent had the six-speed manual transmission, 7.0 percent had traction control, 58.1 percent had a limited-slip differential, 90.1 percent had power windows, 91.3 percent had power door locks, 12.4 percent had power seats, 32.9 percent had leather seats, 23.4 percent had memory seats, 92.8 percent had cruise control, 19.2 percent had chrome styled wheels, 81.8 percent had aluminum wheels, 83 percent had a rear window defogger, 90.1 percent had dual power rearview mirrors, 65 percent had hatch roofs, 23.3 percent had a premium sound system, 76.7 percent had a CD player, 68.3 percent had the keyless remote entry system and 35.3 percent had an anti-theft device.

THE "TWIN-NOSTRIL" HOOD WAS AGAIN A CALLING CARD OF THE WS6 RAM AIR PACKAGE, SEEN HERE ON A BRIGHT RED FORMULA.

1998

For 1998, Pontiac Motor Division's stable of aggressively styled cars included a bold new Firebird with a new appearance guaranteed to up its legendary status among sports car enthusiasts. The base Firebird model now shared its front fascia design with the Formula model. The front end design incorporated twin center ports below the hood and restyled, round, outboard-mounted fog lamps.

Two new paint colors, Navy Metallic and Sport Gold Metallic, were available. The Formula Firebird also had new rear-end styling. Inside were gauges with clear white characters on black analog faces to help keep drivers informed of what was going on with their cars.

The hot, rear-drive 2+2 Firebird offered five model choices in 1998, since the Formula convertible was dropped. Previously, base, Formula and Trans Am convertibles were offered, but production failed to top 3,000 units in 1996-1997. Production numbers for 1998 were close to 2,100 ragtops out of 32,157 total cars. Coupes were again featured in base, Formula and Trans Am trim levels.

Formulas and Trans Ams got a new, all-aluminum 5.7-liter 305-hp V-8 with a six-speed manual transmission. A Ram Air package provided 320 hp.

Styling was freshened with a front fascia that incorporated a new headlamp design. There were updated taillights, too. Suspension tuning was revised and base models received a one-piece drive shaft. Firebird V-8s with four-speed automatic transmissions had a larger torque converter. All Firebirds got standard four-wheel disc brakes. A midyear Formula option was an AutoCross package with a beefed-up suspension. A $1,125-delete option that turned the Formula into a stripped-down street performance car was also new.

FIREBIRD – SERIES F/S – V-6/V-8

A hatchback coupe and a convertible were featured in the base Firebird series. Firebird V-8s with four-speed automatic transmissions had

THE FIREBIRD
RECEIVED A FEW
UPDATES FOR
1998, INCLUDING
NEW HEADLIGHT
AND TAILLIGHT
ASSEMBLIES.

a larger torque converter. All Firebirds got standard four-wheel disc brakes. Standard equipment on the base Firebird coupe included extensive acoustical insulation, dual front airbags, air conditioning, a black fixed-mast antenna at right rear, a brake/transmission shift interlock safety feature with automatic transmission, power four-wheel disc brakes with four-wheel ABS, the UPC L36 3800 Series II 200-hp SFI V-6 engine, cruise control, the UPC MM5 five-speed manual transmission and bright silver 16-inch five-spoke cast-aluminum wheels.

FORMULA FIREBIRD – SERUES F – V-6/V-8

The Formula Firebird convertible was gone. Previously base, Formula and Trans Am convertibles had been offered, but ragtop production failed to top 3,000 units in 1996-1997. Production numbers for 1998 were close to 2,100 ragtops. Formulas got a new, all-aluminum LS1 5.7-liter 305-hp V-8 with a six-speed manual transmission. The WS6 Ram Air package provided 320 hp. A midyear Formula option was an AutoCross package with a beefed-up suspension. A $1,125-delete option that turned the Formula into a stripped-down street performance car was also new.

TRANS AM – SERIES F/V – V-8

The 1998 Trans Am came as a coupe or a convertible. Like Formulas, Trans Ams got a new, all-aluminum LS1 5.7-liter 305-hp V-8 with a six-speed manual transmission. The WS6 Ram Air package provided 320 hp. Styling was freshened by the new front fascia that incorporated a new headlamp design and the updated taillights. Trans Ams with four-speed automatic transmissions had a larger torque converter. Standard equipment on the Trans Am coupe included extensive acoustical insulation, dual front airbags, air conditioning, a power antenna, a brake/transmission shift interlock safety feature with automatic transmission, power four-wheel disc brakes with four-wheel ABS, UPC LS1 5.7-liter SFI V-8 engine, high-performance 10-speaker sound system in coupe or six-speaker sound system in convertible, remote keyless entry and a six-way power front driver's seat.

HISTORICAL FOOTNOTES

Total production in Canada included 33,299 Firebirds. The model-year sales total was 33,578 Firebirds, which represented 0.4 percent of total U.S. new car sales. Of 32,157 Firebirds built for the domestic market in the model year, 80.1 percent had the four-speed automatic transmission, 8.0 percent had a five-speed manual gearbox, 11.9 percent had the six-speed manual transmission, 17.3 percent had traction control, 60.4 percent had a limited-slip differential, 87.3 percent had power windows, 87.3 percent had power door locks, 71.4 percent had power seats, 48.3 percent had leather seats, 27.6 percent had memory seats, 30.6 percent had chrome styled wheels, 69.4 percent had aluminum wheels, 83 percent had a rear window defogger, 93.8 percent had dual power rearview mirrors, 76.8 percent had hatch roofs, 10.7 percent had a premium sound system, 89.3 percent had a CD player and 70 percent had the keyless entry.

THE 30TH ANNIVERSARY TRANS AM WAS A LOADED MODEL DECKED OUT IN A STRIKING WHITE PAINT SCHEME AND TRIMMED WITH A SPECIAL INTERIOR.

1999

A new 30th Anniversary Limited Edition Trans Am added a little distinction to the 1999 Firebird offerings. Otherwise, there were only minor changes. Formulas and Trans Ams now had a four-speed automatic transmission as standard equipment. Buyers could choose from it or a six-speed manual, which had a Hurst shifter. Traction control was available on V-6 Firebirds. Specific V-6 Firebirds also got a Torsen II slip-reduction rear axle as standard equipment. An Electronic Brake Force Distribution system and solenoid-based Bosch anti-lock brake system enhanced stopping capabilities. Also new was an upgraded sensing and diagnostic module to improve the passenger-protection system.

Part of the reason for little change was that "end-of-the-Firebird-line" rumors were floating around again. GM eventually said that the marque would be continued at least for a few more years with special-edition packages offered.

The 30th Anniversary Trans Am package was conceived as something very special. Each one of the cars was individually numbered to enhance its collectibility. The package also featured 30th Anniversary cloisonné door badges, striping and console emblems, floor mats with a metallic 30th Anniversary logo, specific blue-tinted, high-polished, 17-inch aluminum wheels, white leather seating surfaces and the buyer's choice of either a full ragtop or a T-top coupe. The anniversary edition Trans Ams were powered by the 5.7-liter Ram Air V-8.

Model year production reflected a substantial 28 percent increase to 41,226 units. Sales held fairly consistent at 32,899 cars versus 33,578 in 1998, 30,459 in 1997 and 36,546 in 1996. The Firebird registered a 0.4 percent share of total U.S. auto sales for the fourth year in a row.

FIREBIRD – SERIES F/S – (V-6)

The availability of GM's Traction Control

system was extended to V-6-powered Firebirds this year. All Firebirds with a V-8 and some with a V-6 had a Zexel Torsen II slip-reduction rear axle. An Electronic Brakeforce Distribution (EBD) system replaced the old hydraulic proportioning valve for improved brake performance. Also new was a solenoid-based Bosch antilock braking system. An enhanced Sensing and Diagnostic Module (SDM) recorded vehicle speed, engine rpm, throttle position and brake use in the last five seconds prior to airbag deployment. Standard equipment for the Firebird coupe included extensive acoustical insulation, dual front airbags, air conditioning, a black fixed-mast antenna at right rear, a brake/transmission shift interlock safety feature (with automatic transmission), power four-wheel disc brakes with four-wheel ABS, UPC L36 3800 Series II 200-hp SFI V-6 engine and the UPC MM5 five-speed manual transmission.

FORMULA FIREBIRD – SERIES F/V – V-8

Pontiac's 1999 sales catalog described the Formula as a car that "sports a functionally aggressive nose, a rumbling exhaust and tires wide enough to double as steamrollers." Standard equipment for the Formula Firebird coupe included the UPC LS1 5.7-liter SFI V-8 engine Formulas with the WS6 Ram Air Performance and Handling package included a Ram Air induction system, functional air scoops, five-spoke 17-in. high-polish aluminum wheels, P275/40ZR17 speed-rated tires, a specific low-restriction dual outlet exhaust system and a specific tuned suspension. This year the WS6 cars had to have Artic White, Pewter Metallic, Navy Blue Metallic, Black or Bright Red finish and the optional UPC GU5 rear axle was required in cars with the four-speed automatic transmission. The price of the package was $3,150.

TRANS AM – SERIES F/V – V-8

The 1999 Pontiac sales catalog pictured a Navy Blue Metallic Trans Am convertible with the standard 300-plus-horsepower LS1 aluminum 5.7-liter V-8 and a black Trans Am coupe with the 320-hp WS6-equipped Ram Air LS1 V-8. It described the latter engine (also offered as a Formula option) as "the heart of the modern muscle car." Trans Ams with the WS6 Ram Air Performance and Handling package included a Ram Air induction system, functional air scoops, five-spoke 17-in. high-polished aluminum wheels, P275/40ZR17 speed-rated tires, a specific low-restriction dual outlet exhaust system and a specific tuned suspension. This year the WS6 cars had to have Artic White, Pewter Metallic, Navy Blue Metallic, Black or Bright Red finish and the optional UPC GU5 rear axle was required in cars with the four-speed automatic transmission. The price of the package was $3,150.

30TH ANNIVERSARY TRANS AM – SERIES F/V – V-8

In March 1969 the first Trans Am made its debut at the Chicago Auto Show, so in February 1999, a special 30th Anniversary Trans Am was on display at the same event. The anniversary car was actually a joint effort of Pontiac Motor Division and the American Sunroof Corp. (ASC) and the cars were constructed in both firm's factories in St. Therese, Quebec, Canada. All 30th Anniversary models carried special features and included the WS6 Ram Air package. A limited run of 1,600 cars was made, of which 1,065 were coupes and 535 were convertibles. The United States market got 1,000 coupes and 500 ragtops and the balance were sold in Canada. A 30th Anniversary Trans Am also served as pace car for the Daytona 500 stock car race. The basis for the package was an Artic White WS6 Trans Am coupe or convertible carrying all standard Trans Am coupe or convertible equipment. The anniversary package included high-polished 17-in. aluminum wheels with a medium blue color tint, dual two-tone blue racing stripes, white Prado leather seats with blue stitching, specially embroidered smooth headrests, white perforated vinyl door inserts with

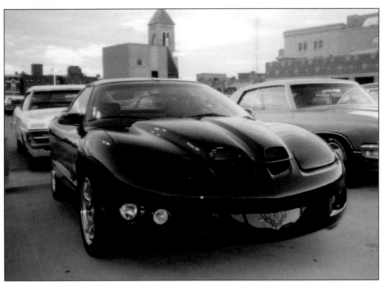

ONLY ABOUT 1,600 FORMULA FIREBIRDS LEFT THE LOT FOR MODEL YEAR 1999. THIS WS6 VERSION IS EVEN RARER.

blue stitching, specific 30th Anniversary front floor mats, a specially embroidered cargo area mat, cloisonné blue 30th Anniversary emblems with a white Firebird logo, a white Firebird logo on the black rear taillight panel, unique blue WS6 emblems and a sequentially numbered instrument panel plaque below the radio. 30th Anniversary Trans Am convertibles also had a dark blue convertible top. The only options for the fully loaded cars were traction control, a Hurst shifter for the six-speed manual transmission and a 12-disc CD player.

HISTORICAL FOOTNOTES

Total production in Canada included 36,219 Firebirds. The model-year sales total was 32,899 Firebirds, which represented 0.4 percent of total U.S. new car sales. Of 31,226 Firebirds built for the domestic market in the model year, 72.1 percent had the four-speed automatic transmission, 6.2 percent had a five-speed manual gearbox, 21.7 percent had the six-speed manual transmission, 41.9 percent had traction control, 33.6 percent had a limited-slip differential, 89 percent had power windows, 89 percent had power door locks, 78 percent had power seats, 49.9 percent had leather seats, 28 percent had memory seats, 23.9 percent had chrome styled wheels, 76.1 percent had aluminum wheels, 89.7 percent had a rear window defogger, 94.8 percent had dual power rearview mirrors, 78 percent had hatch roofs, 18.7 percent had a name brand CD changer, 81.3 percent had another CD player, 71.2 percent had the keyless remote entry system and 71.2 percent had an anti-theft device.

GM photo

THE TRANS AM WAS ONE OF THREE F-CAR MODELS THAT ACCOUNTED FOR A SALES TOTAL OF 31,826 FOR THE 2000 MODEL YEAR. THIS ONE HAS THE WS6 OPTION.

2000

The 2000 Firebird entered the new millennium with all the horsepower and performance it had been famous for. Both Formula and Trans Am models were available with new 17-in. wheels as part of a Ram Air package.

Also new was a Maple Red Metallic exterior color and ebony colored interior. On V-8s, the throttle linkage was revised to give cars with a manual transmission a more progressive "launch response." Child seat tethers were added to all models and all 2000 Firebirds complied with California low-emissions-vehicle (LEV) rules.

FIREBIRD – SERIES F/S – V-6/V-8

Two rear child seat tether anchors were added on all models. The throttle linkage on all V-8-powered Firebirds was revised. Standard Firebird coupe equipment included extensive

acoustical insulation, dual front airbags, air conditioning, a black fixed-mast antenna, the brake/transmission shift interlock safety feature (with automatic transmission), power four-wheel disc brakes with four-wheel ABS, the UPC L36 3800 Series II 200-hp SFI V-6 engine, P215/60R16 touring tires with a high-pressure compact spare, the UPC MM5 five-speed manual transmission, and bright silver 16-in. five-spoke cast aluminum wheels.

FORMULA FIREBIRD – SERIES F/V – V-8

Once again in 2,000 the Formula series offered only the two-door hatchback coupe. Although the basic body design had not changed since last year, the engine had new cast-iron exhaust manifolds, a better starter design, and an improved canister for the onboard refuel-

GM photo

**THE TRANS AM HATCHBACK LISTED FOR ABOUT $27,400 IN 2000.
THE PRICE GREW WITH THE OPTION LIST, WHICH INCLUDED A RAM AIR V-8.**

ing vapor recovery system. Formula Firebirds equipped with the WS6 Ram Air option package sported new 17-in. alloy wheel rims.

TRANS AM – SERIES F/V – V-8

Standard Trans Am equipment included power four-wheel disc brakes with four-wheel ABS, the UPC LS1 5.7-liter 305-hp aluminum V-8 engine, high-performance 10-speaker sound system in coupes, HSS speakers and tweeters in doors, 6.5-in. subwoofers in sail panels, subwoofer amp, and four speakers and tweeters in rear quarter panels), reclining front bucket seats, a six-way power front driver's seat, and P245/50ZR16 speed-rated all-weather tires.

HISTORICAL FOOTNOTES

Total production in Canada was 31,826 Firebirds. Revel model company made a scale model of Al Hofmann's 2000 Firebird funny car. An option returning to the Firebird offerings in 2000 was the Firehawk package. It was now merchandised as a regular production option, although SLP Engineering produced the final vehicle. The 2000 Formula Firehawk included a unique hood, a 327-hp engine, an upgraded suspension and special wheels and tires.

THE TRANS AM CONVERTIBLE, LIKE THE COUPE, CAME STANDARD WITH THE LSI V-8.

2001

"Firebird: The muscle car lives," said Pontiac in 2001. The new F-Car took performance to new levels. The model lineup started with the Firebird coupe and convertible. Standard features included a hidden headlamp design, integrated fog lamps, fender-mounted air extractors and a sleek, aerodynamic body.

Pontiac celebrated its 75th anniversary in 2001. It released a hardcover book called *75 Years of Pontiac: The Official History* and transported a collection of historic vehicles and concept cars to events such as the Detroit Auto Show, Chicago Auto Show, New York Auto Show, Iola Old Car Show, Pontiac Oakland Club International Convention and Woodward Dream Cruise. At the latter event, held in the Detroit area in August, a "once-in-75-years" collection of 35 rare and unique Pontiacs was seen.

On Sept. 25, 2001, General Motors Corp. announced plans to drop the Pontiac Firebird and Chevrolet Camaro after 2002 and close the Canadian plant where they were made. GM termed the halt in production a "hiatus," rather than a final termination and said that the decision to drop the two cars was due to a drop in demand in the sporty car segment, which experienced a 53 percent decline in sales in the past decade.

FIREBIRD – SERIES F/S – V-6/V-8

The F-Car remained true to its heritage while taking performance to new levels, although enthusiasts of the nameplate would be shocked by the announcement, in the fall of 2001, that General Motors would be stopping all Firebird (and Camaro) production after model year 2002. For more than three decades, the rear-wheel-drive Firebird had defined high-powered driving excitement. The 2001 lineup started with Firebird coupe and convertible. Firebird hood and rear quarter panels were made of two-sided galvanized steel, while the doors, hatch, roof, fenders and fascias were formed from composite materials that were lightweight and impervious to rust or corrosion. Base Firebird features included a hidden headlamp design, integrated

THE 2001 RAM AIR TRANS AM.

fog lamps, fender-mounted air extractors and a sleek, aerodynamically shaped body. Standard equipment included air conditioning, cruise control, a fold-down rear seat and a center console with an auxiliary power outlet and dual cup holders. Standard for the base Firebird coupe and convertible was a 3800 V-6 that delivered 200 hp. It came hooked to a five-speed manual or available four-speed automatic transmission. A slick-shifting six-speed manual transmission was also available at no extra charge. An optional Hurst shifter was available on models equipped with the six-speed transmission. The Firebird's high-performance attitude was not limited to its engine compartment – it was also found in the wide selection of audio systems available. Base equipment for the Firebird coupe was a Delco 2001 Series electronically tuned radio with AM/FM stereo, a CD player, a seven-band graphic equalizer, four speakers, a clock and touch controls for seek, search and replay. All convertibles featured a standard Monsoon radio

and eight speakers. A Sports Appearance package offered for the base Firebird hatchback and base Firebird convertible included dual exhaust outlets, a distinctive chin spoiler, rocker panel extensions and a deeper rear valance. Base Firebirds with the optional V-8 engine had 5 more horsepower and 5 more ft. lbs. of torque than the 2000 base V-8. New exterior and interior colors were also available.

FORMULA FIREBIRD – SERIES F/V – V-8

The 2001 lineup included the Formula Firebird coupe. It had all of the Trans Ams performance features combined with much of the cleaner look of the base Firebird coupe. It no longer came with the WS6 Ram Air Formula option. Those who wanted a WS6 Firebird had to move up to the Trans Am series. Standard Formula Firebird equipment included the 5.7-liter 16-valve 310-hp LS1 V-8, four-speed automatic transmission.

PONTIAC USED THE TRANS AM COLLECTOR EDITION AS A SEND-OFF FOR THE F-CARS. PRODUCTION OF THE FIREBIRD LINE WAS SCHEDULED TO HALT AFTER THE 2002 MODEL YEAR.

2002

Changes in the 2002 Firebirds were very modest. A power antenna was made standard on all models, along with power remote mirrors, power automatic door locks and power windows with "express-down" driver's side window controls. A power steering cooler also became standard equipment on all cars with V-8 engines. A 3.8-liter V-6 and five-speed manual transmission were standard on the Firebird coupe. The Firebird convertible combined the same engine with a 4L60-E four-speed automatic transmission. The base Firebirds featured hidden headlamps, integrated fog lamps, fender-mounted air extractors and a sleek, aerodynamic body.

Pontiac introduced the yellow 2002 Firebird Trans Am "Collector Edition" model option in the fall of 2001. Available for both the coupe and the convertible, it featured a "screaming chicken" decal that put a contemporary spin on the eye-catching hood designs of the past, plus black painted WS6 wheels, black anodized front and rear brake calipers, black painted axles, Goodyear Eagle F1 performance tires and exclusive interior trim appointments. A specially issued Collector Edition owner's portfolio provided a crowning touch.

FIREBIRD – SERIES F/S – V-6/V-8

Changes in the 2002 Firebirds were very modest. A Standard equipment included the 3.8-liter 200-hp V-6, a five-speed manual transmission, rear-wheel drive, 16 x 8-in. alloy rims and P215/60R16 all-season tires.

FORMULA FIREBIRD – SERIES F/V – V-8

The Formula Firebird hatchback coupe got four new standard features, including a removable hatch roof with sunshades, remote keyless entry, a six-way power driver's seat and an audible theft deterrent system. Formula coupe appointments included low-profile Z-speed-rated tires, silver 16-in. five-spoke sport wheels, a performance-oriented suspension and a 10-speaker version of the Monsoon CD audio system.

TRANS AM – SERIES F/V – V-8

Trans Am models used the same standard drive train as the Formula coupe. The Trans Am came in coupe and convertible editions with standard removable roof panels with sunshades, leather seating surfaces and an uplevel rear spoiler for the coupe. Trans Am drivers got 310

THE 2002 COLLECTOR EDITION T/A CAME AS EITHER A COUPE OR CONVERTIBLE.

hp and Trans Am drivers opting for Ram Air got 325 hp. Available transmissions for the LS1 V-8 included a six-speed manual transmission. Standard Trans Am equipment included the 5.7-liter 310-hp V-6 and a four-speed automatic transmissionThe Trans Am convertible added a convertible top with glass window, front reading lights and a trunk light. Trans Am coupe and convertible models with the WS6 Ram Air Performance and Handling package benefited from functional air scoops, Ram Air induction, low-restriction dual-outlet exhaust and a suspension specifically tuned for maximum handling performance. The WS6 package also sported P275/40ZR17 performance radial tires mounted on 9 x 17-in. highly polished alloy wheels featuring a five-spoke spoke design.

COLLECTOR YELLOW EDITION TRANS AM – SERIES F/V – V-8

To celebrate 35 years of Firebird, Pontiac introduced the 2002 Firebird Trans Am "Collector Edition" model option in the fall of 2001. Elements unique to the Collector Edition included a special Collector Yellow paint scheme, detailed interior appointments, special edition emblems and the WS6 Performance and Handling package. The package was available for both the coupe and the convertible. In addition to its paint scheme, the Collector Edition featured a special "screaming chicken" graphic package that put a contemporary spin on the eye-catching hood designs of classic '70s and '80s Firebird and

Trans Am models. Two black "racing stripe" designs adorned the hood and wrapped themselves around the car's doors and rear quarter panels. The rear fascia also got special attention with a two-tone yellow and black treatment, while both Collector Edition and Trans Am nameplates accented the lower doors. Staying true to the tradition of the WS6 performance and handling package's exterior appointments, the Collector Edition included black-painted WS6 wheels with a machined face surface, black anodized front and rear brake calipers and black painted axles. Goodyear Eagle F1 performance tires were standard. Inside were exclusive interior trim appointments that highlighted the design cues of Firebird and Trans Am through the years. The seats were wrapped in ebony leather with the headrests featuring embroidered Collector Edition logos. Also sporting the Collector Edition logo were the front floor mats and a trophy shelf mat. A specially issued Collector Edition owner's portfolio provided the finishing touch to the vehicle's interior. The standard Ram Air WS6 package featured the LS1 5.7-liter V-8 that churned out 325 hp and 350 lbs.-ft. of torque (with WS6 package refinements).

HISTORICAL FOOTNOTES

On Sept. 25, 2001, GM announced that the 2002 Firebird would be the last of the breed. However, the automaker left the gate open to use the Firebird name on a new type of car in the future.